NAS Monograph Series No. 3

Series editor Gerald Grainge

Nautical Archaeology Society

I0085726

The Hulks of Forton Lake, Gosport

The Forton Lake Archaeology Project 2006–2009

Mark Beattie-Edwards and Julie Satchell

with contributions by

Paul Donohue, Mary Harvey, Alison James, Colin McKewan,
Jane Maddocks, Daniel Pascoe, Philip Simons
and Julian Whitewright

BAR British Series 536
2011

Published in 2016 by
BAR Publishing, Oxford

BAR British Series 536

Nautical Archaeology Society Monograph Series (NAS) 3

The Hulks of Forton Lake Gosport

ISBN 978 1 4073 0813 5

BAR Publishing is the trading name of British Archaeological Reports (Oxford) Ltd.
British Archaeological Reports was first incorporated in 1974 to publish the BAR
Series, International and British. In 1992 Hadrian Books Ltd became part of the BAR
group. This volume was originally published by Archaeopress in conjunction with
British Archaeological Reports (Oxford) Ltd / Hadrian Books Ltd, the Series principal
publisher, in 2011. This present volume is published by BAR Publishing, 2016.

Printed in England

BAR
PUBLISHING

BAR titles are available from:

BAR Publishing
122 Banbury Rd, Oxford, OX2 7BP, UK
EMAIL   info@barpublishing.com
PHONE   +44 (0)1865 310431
FAX   +44 (0)1865 316916
www.barpublishing.com

Nautical
Archaeology
Society

The Forton Lake Archaeology Project was a community archaeology project jointly led and managed over the years 2006–2009 by the Nautical Archaeology Society and the Hampshire and Wight Trust for Maritime Archaeology.

Contents

List of Colour Plates, Figures and Tables
Colour Plates

Figures

*Now available to download in A3 format from: http://www.barpublishing.com/additional-downloads.html

Tables

Abbreviations

ALC	Assault Landing Craft	MTL	Mean Tide Level
AHBR	Archaeology and Historic Buildings Record	MU	Maintenance Unit
		NAS	Nautical Archaeology Society
ASD	Admiralty Sailing Dinghy	NGR	Ordnance Survey National Grid Reference
BP	Before Present[1]		
CBA	Council for British Archaeology	NGRE	National Grid Reference Easting
C&N	Camper & Nicholsons	NGRN	National Grid Reference Northing
DGV	Degaussing Vessel	NHB	Naval Historical Branch
DNC	Director of Navy Contracts	NMR	National Monuments Record
FC	Fleet Craft	NRHS	National Register of Historic Ships
FPB	Fast Patrol Boat	NSB	Naval Servicing Boat
GAFIRS	Gosport and Fareham Inland Rescue Service	OD	Ordnance Datum
		RCAHMS	Royal Commission on the Ancient and Historical Monuments of Scotland
GPS	Global Positioning System		
HER	Historic Environment Record	RCT	Royal Corp of Transport
HL(D)	Diesel Harbour Launch	RCTV	Royal Corps of Transport Vessel
HL(S)	Steam Harbour Launch	RMLI	Royal Marines Light Infantry
HSTTL	High Speed Target Towing Launch	RNPS	Royal Naval Patrol Service
HWTMA	Hampshire and Wight Trust for Maritime Archaeology	RNVR	Royal Naval Volunteer Reserve
		SCOPAC	Standing Conference on Problems Associated with the Coastline
LCA	Landing Craft Assault		
LCI (S)	Landing Craft Infantry (Small)	SMR	Sites and Monuments Record – Now termed Historic Environment Record (HER)
LCM	Landing Craft Mechanized		
LST	Landing Ship Tank		
MFV	Motorized Fishing Vessel	SPA	Special Protection Area
MGB	Motor Gun Boat	SSSI	Site of Special Scientific Interest
ML	Motor Launch	TRSB	Torpedo Recovery Service Boat
MMS	Motor Minesweeper	TRSV	Torpedo Recovery Service Vessel
MTL	Mean Tidal Level	UID	Unique Identifier
MTB	Motor Torpedo Boat	WSS	World Ship Society

---

1   Used for radio-carbon dating; 'present' is taken as 1950 (Renfrew and Bahn, 1991, 123).

Acknowledgements

The authors must firstly thank the many individuals who participated in the three years of fieldwork undertaken as part of the Forton Lake Archaeology Project. Without their efforts this book could not have been written. These hardy folk included: Eric Walker, George Akhurst, Paul Donohue, Ian Barefoot, Colin McKewan, Dr Julian Whitewright, Emily Loughman, Roger Forster, Rebecca Causer, Julian Jansen van Rensburg, Michael Carroll, Charlotte Pham, Chris Jones, Laura Frost, Robert Briggs, Ken Pavitt, Francesco Caputo, Steve Kemp, Mark Littlewood, Susie Hammond, Carol Miller, Diana Forster, John Chittenden, Nicky Richens, Fiona Richie, Pam Hughes, Phil Such, Malcolm Holden, Mary Harvey, Daniel Pascoe, Stephanie Goffin, Tim Parker, Viv Hamilton, Kat Holt, Will Tabner, David Wood, Jackie Karmy, Sue Oakes, Daniel Karmy, Danny Garnham, Graham Linington and Julie Stonehouse.

A great deal of assistance has been provided in the preparation of this monograph. Particular mention must be made of David Fricker, Philip Simons, Danny Lovell, Tony Holtham, Terry Holtham, Colin Poole, Michael Wright, Colin Baxter, Donald Smith, Bill Puddle, Gordon Leith (Royal Air Force Museum), Tim Parker, John Harbidge-Rose, Mark Dunkley and Peter Murphy (English Heritage), Philip Robertson (Historic Scotland) and Bob Mowat (Royal Commission on Ancient and Historical Monuments of Scotland).

The project is especially grateful to Jane Maddocks, formerly of St Vincent College, Gosport, for all her hard work and determination to make the project a local success and to Morrisons Supermarket (Gosport) for their promotion of the project. Thanks must also go to Ted Sutton who originally inspired the investigations in a muddy lake in Gosport and to Gerald Grainge for his editorial skills. The authors also wish to express their appreciation to all who have given permission for the reproduction in this monograph of copyright material, including English Heritage, Fox Photos/Getty Images, the Trustees of the Royal Air Force Museum, the *Hampshire Magazine*, the Jack Smale collection, Colin Baxter, Ian Boyle (www.simplonpc.co.uk/), Tony Dixon, Roger Forster, David Fricker, Terry Holtham, Gustav Milne and colleagues, Tim Parker, Ken Pavitt and Philip Simons.

If we have missed anyone from the list please accept our apologies.

In support of the project both the Nautical Archaeology Society (NAS) and the Hampshire and Wight Trust for Maritime Archaeology (HWTMA) have invested additional time in project development and management and to ensure completion of various aspects of fieldwork and reporting. In particular the HWTMA would like to acknowledge the support of a number of sponsors, including Hampshire County Council, the Aiken Foundation, the Charlotte Bonham Carter Charitable Trust, the George Cadbury Trust, the Gosling Foundation, the John Coates Charitable Trust, the Robert Kiln Charitable Trust, the Roger Brooke Charitable Trust and the Rowan Bentall Charity Trust.

Finally, we must acknowledge the organizations that have provided grant support to the project over five years – the Local Heritage Initiative (Heritage Lottery Fund), the Nationwide Building Society, The Crown Estate, the Robert Kiln Charitable Trust and Gosport Borough Council. The creation of this monograph has only been possible with the substantial support of The Crown Estate's Marine Communities Fund. The aim of the Marine Communities Fund is to provide support to initiatives and programmes which contribute to the development of best practice and make a significant contribution to the good management and stewardship of the marine estate.

THE CROWN ESTATE

Heritage LOTTERY FUNDED

grant aided by **GOSPORT** BOROUGH COUNCIL

Nationwide

St Vincent COLLEGE

Chapter 1: Introduction to the Forton Lake Archaeology Project
by Mark Beattie-Edwards

Introduction

This monograph is the result of four years' work investigating the archaeology of Forton Lake in Gosport, Hampshire, England. This chapter provides an introduction to the Forton Lake Archaeology Project and to the location of the lake. Chapter 2 details the archaeology and history of the area around Forton Lake. Chapter 3 concentrates on the implementation of the project, the archaeological methodologies employed and the ways in which skills training and public engagement opportunities were maximized. Chapter 4 catalogues the results of the surveys and excavations under the headings of transportation, ferries and lifeboats, fishing, military and unclassified remains. Finally Chapter 5 discusses the project in the context of the development of intertidal hulk recording methods and management strategies for intertidal archaeological remains and makes recommendations for further study.

Project Background

In 2005 the NAS was approached by Ted Sutton (an NAS and HWTMA Member) about a collection of abandoned vessels lying in Forton Lake, one of Portsmouth Harbour's tidal creeks. He had visited the lake in 1997 and had undertaken a visual inspection and a photographic survey and had made some sketches of the hulks. His interest had led to discussions with the HWTMA and the University of Portsmouth, which had resulted in the Portsmouth Harbour Project, undertaken in the late 1990s and early 2000s (Sparks *et al.*, 2001). This included the development of an online resource,[1] which made available basic information on some of the Forton Lake hulks, and the deposition of copies of Mr Sutton's recording forms and photographs with the Hampshire County Archaeology and Historic Buildings Record (AHBR). This work had developed a basic record of the hulks, but it had been recognized that they would benefit from more detailed survey and research. Against this background the HWTMA were pleased to work with the NAS to develop a community archaeology project that would seek to record the maritime archaeology of Forton Lake.

Following the 2005 meeting, in March 2006 a £24,294 grant application was made to the Local Heritage Initiative (Heritage Lottery Fund) for support towards a two-year (2006–2007) community-based initiative that would allow the inhabitants of Gosport to research, record and display their heritage. At the same time an application for £3500 was also submitted to the Nationwide Building Society Community Awards. This application focused on organizing and delivering a series of activity days to be held within the local Gosport community to enhance the value of the main Local

Heritage Initiative application. The activity days would use hands-on activities to engage and enthuse the local community with the wealth of maritime heritage that surrounds them. Sessions would be held specifically to target different groups, including young children. Both of these grant applications were successful and the Forton Lake Archaeology Project was born.

Project Aims

From the outset the aims of the project were threefold:

1   To investigate the archaeology of Forton Lake

The project aimed to enhance knowledge and understanding of the development of Forton Lake, including all aspects of the human past from prehistory to the modern day. Ted Sutton's preliminary work had highlighted the research potential of the area. There had, however, not been a systematic appraisal of the archaeological resource. This would be addressed through a combination of desk-based research and on-site recording. Desk-based aspects of the project would consider available maritime and terrestrial archives, local knowledge and current archaeological interpretation. This would provide the context for field recording, with preliminary fieldwork providing baseline data on the visible archaeological remains. This data would then be assessed in combination with results of the desk-based investigation to identify a number of sites for more detailed levels of recording. The outcome would be the interpretation of the history and development of Forton Lake.

2   To raise awareness of the archaeology of Forton Lake

An important aspect of the project would be raising awareness of the history and archaeology of Forton Lake. Outreach to local residents and visitors to the area would be achieved through community involvement in fieldwork, public lectures, open days and displays. Additionally specialist and academic audiences would be targeted to ensure the dissemination of the results of the research. This would include the publication of the project results through annual reports, presentations and the internet.

3   To involve the local community in investigating their heritage

It was recognized that the support of local groups and organizations would be vital for the project. St Vincent College, backing on to the south-west end of Forton Lake, was to be involved in the project through their archaeology teacher, Jane Maddocks. This provided the opportunity for the direct involvement of students and staff. The active involvement of local people in all aspects of the project was to be encouraged, with hands-on help being sought with recording and research. It was hoped that increasing local awareness through

---

1   http://www.envf.port.ac.uk/geo/research/portsmouth/background.htm.

Introduction

participation would foster a sense of ownership of the heritage and ultimately have a positive effect on the long-term conservation of Forton Lake and of its maritime historic environment.

Further Project Funding

Towards the end of 2007 the project had already undertaken two years of fieldwork and had disseminated the results through interim reports, project web pages and through the local press. However, all the parties agreed that the work was not yet complete. The NAS and HWTMA wished to undertake another year of fieldwork and to spend a final twelve months presenting the results of the research using a variety of media.

In October 2007 the NAS applied to The Crown Estate's Marine Communities Fund for two years' financial support. In early 2008 the project was awarded a £27,000 grant spread over the two years to deliver the final phase of the project. This was to include a third year of fieldwork, schools events, updated web pages, a local history booklet, a museum exhibition, a permanent display panel situated on the banks of Forton Lake, as well as bringing together all the work in this monograph publication.

Gosport Borough Council also contributed financially to the project. Two awards, each of £1,000 were made in 2009 to support the printing of the local history booklet, completed in October 2009, and the production of the museum exhibition, put on at the Gosport Local Studies Centre in January 2010. In October 2009 the Robert Kiln Charitable Trust also provided a grant of £1,000 which has been used to increase the number of colour images used in this monograph.

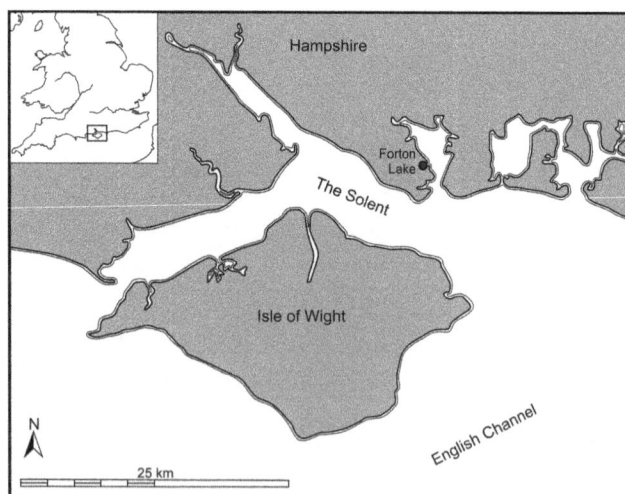

Fig. 1.1 Location of Forton Lake

Forton Lake, Gosport, Hampshire, England

Forton Lake is located in the town of Gosport in Hampshire (Figs 1.1 and 1.2). This tidal lake lies approximately 1.8 km north-west of the entrance to Portsmouth Harbour (within Ordnance Survey National Grid Reference (NGR): SU 6100). It is approximately 1 km in length on a south-west/north-east axis and varies in width from approximately 100 m to approximately 200 m. Being tidal the creek naturally varies in depth and is recorded on the chart number SC5600.11B designed for small craft sailors (part of Admiralty Folio - SC5600 Solent & Approaches). The lake is almost entirely owned by The Crown Estate.

For centuries Portsmouth Harbour has been the site of extensive naval and commercial port facilities, as well as urban development, and as a result much of the present shoreline is defined by walls and other structures that have been built to provide docking and other shore facilities. Former low lying wetlands have been drained and protected from flooding and erosion, while some former intertidal areas have been used as landfill sites. Historic maps show that Forton Lake has changed its shape as a result of such land reclamation since at least the late 19th century. The changing archaeological and historic landscape of the area around Forton is dealt with in more detail in the next chapter.

The northern half of the harbour, including the Forton Lake foreshore forms part of the Portsmouth Harbour Site of Special Scientific Interest (SSSI) and is also a Special Protection Area (SPA)[2] and Ramsar site. Ramsar sites are wetlands of international importance designated under the Ramsar Convention, signed in Ramsar, Iran, in 1971. Portsmouth Harbour was designated as a Ramsar site in February 1985 for its range of intertidal, brackish and terrestrial habitats and for important wintering populations of waterfowl. In 2008 Forton Lake was included within the area of Portsmouth Harbour that is seeking UNESCO World Heritage Site status.[3]

Today the land surrounding Forton Lake is used by a variety of different organizations for different functions. Starting on the south-eastern bank the lake is overlooked by modern housing regeneration on the site of the Royal Clarence Yard (NGR: SU 6100) (Fig. 1.2.). To the west of this development is the extensive Royal Navy Oil Fuel Depot whose boundary wall forms a 400-m length of the southern side of the lake. Next to the fuel depot is another area of residential housing before reaching The Maritime Workshop complex with their slipway and moorings. This is on the site of a boatyard formerly owned by Frederick Watts, who was in business in the late 1930s, 1940s and 1950s, and is probably the reason why so many hulks now lie in the lake. Next to The Maritime Workshop at the western end of the lake is St Vincent College, formally HMS St Vincent, a Royal Navy training establishment, which closed in 1967.

North of St Vincent College on the north-west side of the lake is an area of grassland. This is believed to have been used as a military cemetery in the 18th and 19th centuries (Fig. 2.3). Situated at the western end of the grassland

---

2   SPAs are areas which have been identified as being of international importance for the breeding, feeding, wintering or the migration of rare and vulnerable species of birds found within European Union countries (http://www.naturalengland.org.uk/ourwork/conservation/designatedareas/spa/default.aspx).

3   http://www.rad.clara.net/heritage/index.html.

Entrance to Portsmouth Harbour and the Millennium Footbridge

Royal Clarence Yard

Royal Navy Fuel Depot

Ferrol Road, Parham Road residential area and The Maritime Workshop

Priddy's Hard

Mud Cottage Lake

St Vincent College

N

0   50   100   200   300   400   500
Metres

Fig. 1.2   Aerial survey of Forton Lake at low spring tide undertaken in 2006

Introduction

are the remains of an outdoor tidal swimming pool built as part of the HMS St Vincent. The shoreline of the lake then turns to the north to form a small bay. Historically this bay, which appears in La Fabvolliere's map of 1630, Fullerton's map of 1830 and the 1925 Ordnance Survey map[4] and was known as 'Mud-Cottage Lake' since at least 1858, would have been much larger, stretching further north, but it was subject to extensive reclamation in the early and middle of the 20th century. Next, to the east along the foreshore of Forton Lake is the site of Priddy's Hard (NGR: SU 6101). Formerly the site of the Royal Navy Ordnance Yard, this now consists mainly of residential housing and extends along the northern bank to the opening with Portsmouth Harbour. The entrance to

Forton Lake is approximately 170 m wide and is crossed by the Forton Lake Opening Bridge. This bridge was opened in 2000 as part of the Landmark Millennium scheme known as the Renaissance of Portsmouth Harbour, part funded by the Millennium Commission.

Finally, the entrance to Forton Lake is partly protected by a 300-m long spit or causeway and an island. This island, called Burrow Island (NGR: SU 6200), alternatively Rat Island (AHRB Unique Identifier (UID) 19264), is known to have existed since at least the 17th century when it appears on La Fabvolliere's map of the harbour in 1630. There remains some uncertainty whether the shingle bank is a natural phenomenon or whether it may have been built to provide access to Burrow Island.

---

4   Digitized versions of these maps can be found at
     http://www.envf.port.ac.uk/geo/research/portsmouth/port4.htm.

Chapter 2: The History and Archaeology of Forton, Gosport, Hampshire

by Jane Maddocks

An understanding of the archaeological and historical development of the Forton Lake area is essential to provide material for a realistic appraisal of the archaeological potential of the area, now or in the future. The lake, as a tidal creek, takes water from Portsmouth Harbour and what happened in Portsmouth and the harbour would have directly affected human activity in the environs of Forton Lake. The landscape has changed over time, especially from the post-medieval period onwards, largely as a result of land reclamation and of the use of the lake for military purposes (Fig. 2.1).

Geology

The underlying geology of Portsmouth Harbour comprises easily eroded tertiary strata, except for the north of the harbour where there is more resistant upper chalk. Since it is an intertidal creek, the surface deposits of the Forton Lake area are comprised of alluvium and the low lying shore areas contain some river terrace deposits. Although there are no published studies of the geology of Forton Lake, it is likely that, as the buried channel under the entrance to Portsmouth Harbour is quite deep, it would be expected that the Pleistocene floor of the lake would be fairly steep in an easterly direction and at the eastern end might lie under the alluvium at a depth of perhaps 10 m to 15 m below Ordnance Datum (OD).

Our knowledge of archaeological and palaeo-environmental sites of Portsmouth Harbour and its margins is currently weak. The evidence for coastal evolution and relative sea level change along southern England was examined by Dix (2001: 6–14) and by Waller and Long (2003: 351–9). In Waller and Long's paper the mean tidal levels (MTLs) for the Solent region, including the Isle of Wight and the adjacent areas to the west of Forton Lake, were published and are summarized below (Table 2.1).

Age (cal. Year BP)	Age (BC/AD)	Mean Tidal Level (metres OD)	Geological/Archaeological period
7400	5450 BC	-9 m	Early–Mid Holocene/Mesolithic
6000	4050 BC	-6 m	Mid Holocene/Mesolithic
5000	3050 BC	-4 m	Mid Holocene/Late Mesolithic – Early Neolithic
4000	2050 BC	-3 m	Mid Holocene/Late Mesolithic – Early Neolithic
2500	550 BC	-2 m	Late Holocene/Early Iron Age
1900	50 AD	-1 m	Late Holocene/Iron Age

Table 2.1   Summary of changes in mean tidal level in the Solent (from Waller and Long 2003: 356)

With a sea level around 9 m below Ordnance Datum (OD) it is likely that for most of the Mesolithic period

Fig 2.1 Montage of aerial photographs of Forton Lake taken in February 1949 (courtesy of English Heritage)

Fig. 2.2   Forton Tide Mill: painting c. 1820 by Robert Strickland Thomas

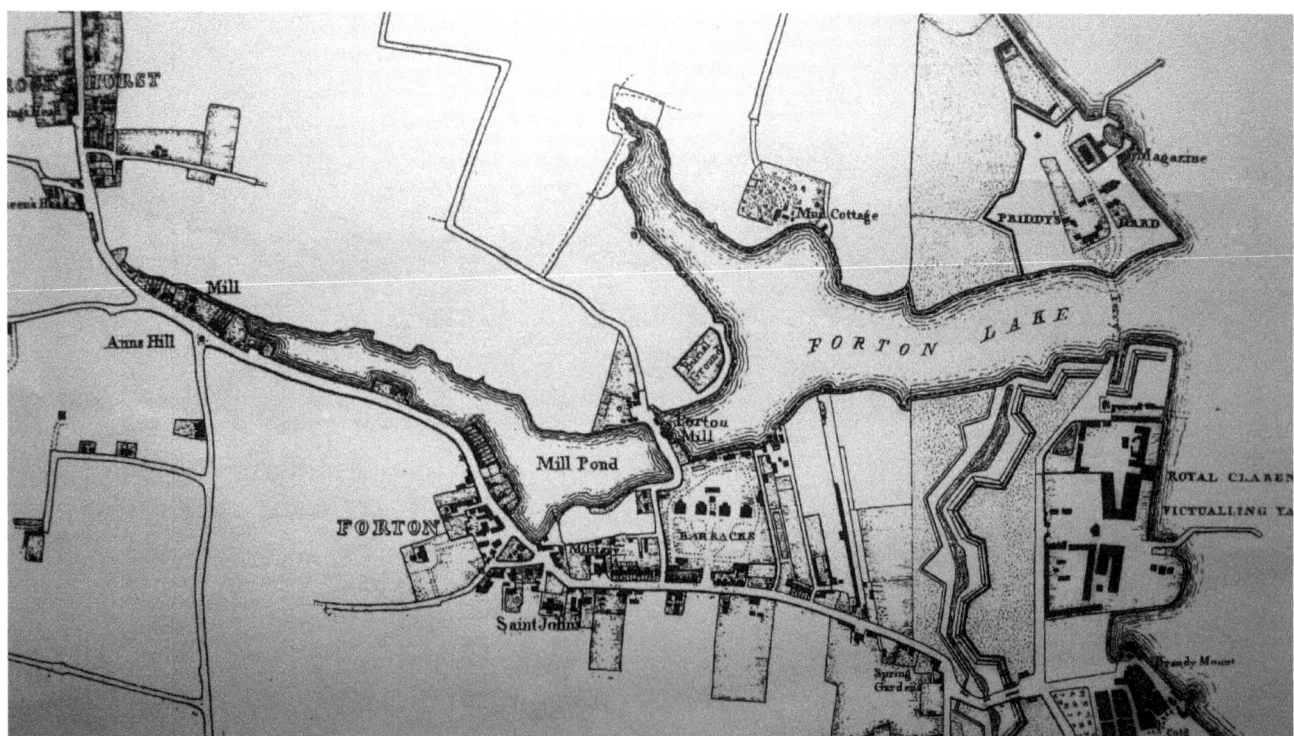

Fig. 2.3   Forton Lake: map by I.T. Lewis c. 1832, showing the tide mill and the cemetery mentioned in Chapter 1 (page 2)

Portsmouth Harbour was a smaller tributary feeding into the Solent River and that, as sea levels rose, waterborne sediments were deposited on the newly drowned landscapes (Bates, 2001: 27–45). The report of submerged peat deposits discovered near Weevil Lake (off Royal Clarence Yard) in 1943 at a depth of 59 ft (17 m to 18 m) below OD (Godwin, 1945: 152) would indicate that this area would have been above mean high water during the Mesolithic period, since peat does not form in salt water.

These sealed peat horizons found just outside the entrance to Forton Lake indicate the potential for finding similar horizons in the lake itself (Dr Ian West, pers. comm.). Therefore during the 2006 and 2008 field work auger surveys were carried out. In 2006 the very westerly part of the lake was subjected to an auger survey. A 20-m baseline was set up across the narrow creek at low tide (A–B in Fig. 4.1) with samples collected every 5 m along the baseline. Unfortunately these samples were unsuccessful and it was planned to repeat the exercise at an alternative location during subsequent fieldwork. Thus a second auger survey was undertaken in 2008 in a small creek on the north-west shore near to hulks FL3 and FL4, in the area known as Mud Cottage Lake. This area was chosen as it was most likely to be undisturbed by modern activity. A 20-m baseline (C–D in Fig. 4.1) was set up on either side of the creek with auger samples collected every 5 m along the baseline. Ten samples were taken in total, five on each side, and although different sediments were identified, including different types of clay, the auger samples did not go below 5.5m depth and further work is needed to shed more light on the geology of the lake.[1]

Prehistory

Research at the Hampshire Archaeology and Historic Buildings Record (AHBR) and the National Monuments Record (NMR) has shown a number of find spots of material from the Palaeolithic, Mesolithic and Neolithic period in the Gosport area, but these are not directly associated with Forton Lake. The earliest material to be found associated with Forton Lake consists of scrapers dated to the Late Bronze Age, recovered during a watching brief at Royal Clarence Yard (AHBR UID 57096: 2009). At that time the area of what is now the lake would still have been dry land beside the Portsmouth Harbour River, at the beginning of the process of inundation which would create Forton Lake.

It is probable that the area around Forton Lake was occupied during the Iron Age, but there is no direct evidence to confirm this. Any material from that period is likely to have been removed or covered during the extensive land reclamation and building that took place from the 18th century onwards.

---

1 http://www.nauticalarchaeologysociety.org/projects/forton%20lake/Forton_Lake_Project_YR3_Report_Final.pdf: 63–4, 73–4.

Romans (AD 43–AD 410)

No structural Roman remains have been found around Forton Lake. This is unsurprising because the amount of land reclamation and the construction of military buildings at Royal Clarence Yard and Priddy's Hard may well have obscured fragmentary remains. However, Roman pottery vessels were discovered at a depth of 4.87 m (AHBR UID 19158) on the eastern edge of Burrow Island during dredging operations to discover the rate of silting of Burrow Bank. The recovery of pottery, combined with the proximity of Forton Lake to Portchester Castle, built in the late 3rd century AD, suggests that the military command would have known of the existence of the creek and may have used it without leaving tangible evidence of that use.

Saxo-Norman period (AD 500–AD 1200)

The same lack of direct archaeological evidence for occupation or use of Forton Lake occurs during the Saxo-Norman period, although there were at least two small Saxon villages in the vicinity at Rowner and Alverstoke (White, 1989: 6–10). A Norman motte and bailey castle was constructed at the crossing point of the River Alver, before it emptied into Stokes Bay. These villages and the later motte and bailey were all within a radius of two miles of Forton.

Later medieval period (1200-1500)

The earliest mention of a settlement at Forton, on the westernmost part of the Lake, is in 1283, when a charter was drawn up by Prior Andrew of St Swithun's Priory, freeing the men of Forton from serfdom. The first borough reeve to be appointed was Thomas de Forton (White, 1989: 13).

At that time there was a tide mill on Forton Lake, situated in the centre of fertile farming land that the Prior of St Swithun's had recognized as being of good quality and justifying higher rents (White, 1989: 13). In 1268 the existence of the Forton tide mill was confirmed when ownership of Forton and the tide mill was transferred to the Bishop of Winchester, who continued to own the mill until 1858, when it was bought by the Board of Ordnance (a predecessor of the Ministry of Defence) and ceased to function (Figs 2.2 and 2.3). The archaeological potential for the existence of substantial buried remains on the site of the mill is high. The tide mill required the construction of a causeway and the maintenance of its banks to ensure the water flow was directed through the mill. The causeway is extant, although the western side is now part of the land reclaimed by the Board of Ordnance from 1858 onwards (Merritt, 1977: 7).

It is likely that grain and flour would have been transported to and from the mill by boat, as well as by cart. The possibility of the remains of medieval boats existing in the sediments of the old creek bed and banks, especially in the reclaimed areas of the old mill pond, should be borne in mind during any redevelopment of the area.

The history and archaeology of Forton

Some medieval pottery vessels were found in the eastern part of the creek, an area encompassing Burrow Bank and Burrow Island, when the bank was dredged in 1955 to discover the rate of silting on the bank (AHBR UID 19159). As the material was recovered during dredging and was not confined to medieval material, but included Roman and post-medieval material, the context of its deposition cannot be established with any degree of confidence.

Post-medieval period (1500–1945)

A major factor in the development of the use of Forton Lake would have been the extensive development of Portsmouth Harbour as a naval base begun by Samuel Pepys in 1665, following the Restoration of King Charles II in 1660. The expansion of the dockyard and the Royal Navy was partly a response to the second Anglo-Dutch war in February 1665 (Palmer and Palmer, 1996: 189). Because of its proximity to Portsmouth Harbour entrance, Sir Bernard de Gomme was instructed to build fortifications around Gosport, beginning in 1677/8. This development included the construction of two forts, one closer to the entrance of Portsmouth Harbour, Fort Charles (AHRB UID 19013) on Gosport Hard, the other, Fort James (AHRB UID 19264), on Burrow Island. Both forts were completed c. 1678/9, but by 1707 Fort James was in poor condition (Williams, 1974: 34). It was partially demolished in 1827. The gravel spit leads out from Priddy's Hard and has narrow gauge railway lines going halfway across to Burrow Island. A puzzle bottle (AHBR UID 19157) dating to c. 1680–1710 found on Burrow spit is un-provenanced and cannot be directly related to the construction of Fort James or to any specific activity relating to Forton Lake.

The Gosport entry in *Kelly's Directory* (1894: 452) says 'about a mile to the north is Forton Lake, a large basin or creek of the harbour that accepts vessels of considerable burthen. On Priddy's Hard north of this lake and connected with the harbour by a small cut through the sand is the strongly arched bomb-proof magazine for powder' (Fig. 2.3).

An expanding Royal Navy would have needed a good supply of gunpowder. Originally this was stored in the Square Tower in Portsmouth. However, as a result of concern in Portsmouth about the dangers of major explosions, land was bought at Priddy's Hard (Burton and Musselwhite, 2004: 41). In 1771 Priddy's Hard Gunpowder Magazine was completed; its function was to provide ammunition for warships, as well as to defend the harbour. A camber dock[2] was constructed on the harbour side of the hard and boats would be loaded there to go out to Spithead to the warships anchored there. During the second half of the 19th century the range of armaments expanded and Priddy's Hard responded. By 1904 it covered 100 acres (40 hectares). In the run-up to D Day

in June 1944 it employed over 3000 people. After the war production wound down and the site closed in the early 1970s. The site is now modern housing and the site of Explosion! Museum of Naval Firepower (Burton and Musselwhite, 2004: 42).

Opposite Priddy's Hard, Royal Clarence Yard was established in 1828 (AHRB UID 17568). It used to be a fleet watering point; the land had been privately owned and contained malt houses, brew houses and a cooperage, but was bought by the Admiralty in 1749. Eventually all the Portsmouth victualling activities were transferred to this site, which later became known as Royal Clarence Yard. It became renowned for the mass-baking of biscuits, a huge slaughterhouse and cooperage and the issue of a wide range of other food, rum, beer and clothing (Burton and Musselwhite, 2004: 47–52). As at Priddy's Hard, many of the ships and crews involved in the D Day landings were provisioned from Royal Clarence Yard. A small wharf was found during a watching brief, perhaps large enough for a small barge to come alongside to lighter material out to other vessels for distribution (Pete Higgins, pers. comm.). By the 1990s Royal Clarence Yard had closed and has been redeveloped for private housing. Both Priddy's Hard and Royal Clarence Yard were the subject of archaeological watching briefs before their redevelopment.[3]

Further up the lake there was a boatbuilding yard, with a slip, boat builders' cottages and a ropewalk along what is now Parham Road. In 1894 this slip was called White's Slip (*Kelly's Directory*, 1894: 512). There is a locally held belief that the boatyard dated from the late 16th century, but further research is needed to substantiate this, since current evidence indicates a 19th century date as being more likely. The boat builders' cottages on Parham Road date from the mid-19th century (AHRB UID 11031189, 235, 6358; Merritt, 1977: 8).

In 1800 the building of Forton Barracks began. In 1848 this became the base of the Royal Marines Light Infantry (RMLI) (Burton and Musselwhite, 2004: 59). The barracks were large, and the parade ground was thought to be one of the largest in the country. The RMLI left Forton Barracks in 1923. In 1927 the name of the site was changed to HMS St Vincent; it became a naval training establishment initially for boy entrants and continued as a naval base until 1968. In 1975 the site re-opened as St Vincent School, which became St Vincent Sixth Form College in 1987.

The tide mill was still working in the 1850s and repairs were being carried out on the causeway, with stone facings on the seaward side and brick on the northern edge. A tentative dating of the brickwork by the author would suggest an early 19th-century date. Both sides of the causeway showed greenheart timber posts, similar to those at Royal Clarence Yard, to protect the causeway from damage by boats coming alongside. The mill itself, the causeway and the stone facings with the greenheart piles are evident in two paintings, one by Robert

---

2   Not to be confused with Camber Dock, Portsmouth. The *OED* (*s.v.* camber) includes among the definitions of 'camber': 'The part of a dockyard where cambering is performed, and timber kept. Also, a small dock in the royal yards, for the convenience of loading and discharging timber' (Smyth, 1867: *Sailor's Word-bk.*).

3   http://www.tvas.co.uk/reports/pdf/PHG04-20wb.pdf.

Strickland Thomas *c.* 1820 (Fig. 2.2) and one by Martin Snape (1853–1930). At this stage it is likely that the causeway would have been in use during the building of Forton Barracks, if not during the building of the Forton Prison at Lees Lane in 1716 or of the military hospital indicated on a map of 1799 (Burton and Musselwhite, 2004: 59).

With the closure of Forton Mill and its acquisition in 1858 by the Board of Ordnance, the process of land reclamation was begun. Two main areas were reclaimed, one the western arm of the lake stretching from the causeway to the area of Gosport known as Camden Town, the other, Mud Cottage Lake reclaimed up to the Grove Road area. The shape of the western reaching lake is still visible in the landscape, evidenced by changes in house building styles.

The area around the small boatyard at the bottom of Ferrol Road was exceptionally busy (Fig. 2.4). It has

been suggested that in the early to middle of the 20th century there were three different boatyards in the area of Ferrol Road and Parham Road. Two of these companies were involved in building small launches and motorized fishing vessels (MFVs) at 45 feet (14 m) and 60 feet long (18 m) (Colin Poole, pers. comm.). These were the Gosport and Portsea Steam Launch Company, known as White's, located at 31 Ferrol Road (*Kelly's Directory*, 1938–39: 46) and John Morris and Co (Gosport) Ltd on Parham Road, who also had a boat yard in Fareham (*Kelly's Directory*, 1938–39: 100). At the end of World War II Forton Lake was used to beach or keep vessels for sale or repair. One of the boatyards using the lake for this purpose was owned by Frederick Watts; it was listed in the local *Kelly's Directory* from 1938 until 1954 and would have played an important role in the movement of vessels to Forton Lake. The concentration of vessels now lying in Forton Lake, which have been the focus of research for this monograph, almost certainly owes its presence to these boatyards.

Fig 2.4   RAF aerial photograph from April 1950 showing the vessels moored at the F.J. Watts Boatyard (courtesy of English Heritage)

Chapter 3: Forton Lake Archaeology Project 2006–2009

Archaeological Methodology

(Mark Beattie-Edwards)

Fieldwork preparation

Very little was known about the range of archaeological material present in Forton Lake prior to the project. The initial photographic survey of the vessels undertaken by Ted Sutton in 1997 proved to be an invaluable resource; along with Jane Maddocks' local knowledge, this meant that initial visits to the site in 2005 could begin to determine which features could be easily accessed and which would prove more problematic or impossible. At this early stage, other than for the better known vessels, further investigation was required to establish the archaeological or historical significance of the remains. Some of these vessels are actively decaying; this could be seen when comparing photographs taken in 1997 with the remains in 2005. The lessons learnt during the hulk recording project undertaken at Whitewall Creek, Kent, in the early 1990s (Milne *et al.,* 1998) and the experience of the HWTMA on the Hamble and Itchen Rivers suggested that the principal aims of the survey of the vessels should be:

> first that it should be achievable within the constraints of time and safety

> that it should be capable of being undertaken by a team of trained volunteers

> that it should provide a baseline of the state of the remains at the time of recording and finally

> that it should be detailed enough to provide clues to each vessel's age and type

This programme would be complemented by contact with local residents and by research in archives and libraries to establish, where possible, the identity of individual vessels and to gather other relevant information about them.

Before venturing out into the intertidal zone at Forton a site visit was undertaken to review the environmental conditions. An assessment was made, in particular, of access and exit routes of individual sites and the areas around them, sediment depths and the speed of the changing tidal cycle. A summary of safety issues to consider when working on the foreshore can be found in *Nautical Archaeology on the Foreshore* (Milne *et al.,* 1998: 77). Risk assessments were undertaken for individual sites and mitigation plans were put in place to ensure all the appropriate health and safety measures were taken, including appropriate vaccinations for supervisors and volunteers, possible use of mud boards, suitable clothing and footwear, as well as cleaning and storage facilities. St Vincent College kindly allowed the project the use of a building to serve as a base for each season's work.

Numbering system

When Ted Sutton undertook his photographic survey of eleven of the vessels at Forton Lake, he allocated unique identifiers (UIDs) to each vessel with an 'FL' prefix (FL1–FL11). The project retained this identification system and incrementally increased the numbered sequence as more vessels came to light. To distinguish between the features originally surveyed and those recorded during the 2006 survey a break of three numbers was placed in the FL sequence. Subsequently, the newly recorded features can be identified as FL15–FL31.

As a result of previous work by Ted Sutton and the HWTMA, data on a number of the vessels within Forton Lake had already been submitted to the Hampshire AHBR. Wherever this was the case the appropriate Hampshire County Council (AHBR) UID was added to the remains. It is worth noting here that due to the lack of detail in one of the Hampshire AHBR entries (AHBR 53072) it was not possible to identify which site in the lake it referred to.

2006 fieldwork season

The 2006 fieldwork took place between 10 and 16 July and began with the project volunteers being given an NAS Introduction to Foreshore and Underwater Archaeology course; this involved classroom instruction on basic archaeological principles, survey techniques and recording methodology. After instruction in the classroom they were given further guidance, health and safety briefings and supervision in the field by supervisors Paul Donohue and Colin McKewan. Volunteers received the same preliminary training in 2007 and 2008. The volunteers were then divided into groups to begin the recording of the accessible vessel remains and intertidal structures. Twenty one features with UIDs FL1 to FL27 were recorded in 2006 (HWTMA/NAS, 2006).[1]

2007 fieldwork season

The 2007 fieldwork took place between 7 and 13 July. The project volunteers were divided between the two major tasks to be carried out as part of the 2007 session – vessel survey and excavation. Throughout the week they were rotated between tasks, to give each as much experience as possible. The vessel survey was supervised by Colin McKewan and the excavation by Paul Donohue. Five vessels with the UIDs FL1, FL3, FL5, FL15 and FL29 were recorded (or re-recorded in more detail) in 2007 (HWTMA/NAS, 2007).[2]

2008 fieldwork season

The 2008 fieldwork session took place between 24 June and 2 July. As in 2007 the volunteers were divided

---

1   http://www.nauticalarchaeologysociety.org/projects/forton%20lake/Forton%20Lake%20Project%20YR1%20Final%20Report.pdf

2   http://www.nauticalarchaeologysociety.org/projects/forton%20lake/Forton_Lake_Project_YR2_Report_Final.pdf

between vessel survey and excavation and were rotated between tasks during the week. The vessel survey was supervised by Dr. Julian Whitewright and the excavation by Dan Pascoe. Eight vessels with the UIDs FL1, FL2, FL5, FL9, FL17, FL23, FL29 and FL30 were recorded in 2008 or re-recorded in greater detail (HWTMA/NAS, 2008).[3]

2009 fieldwork

Following analysis of the survey results undertaken for this publication it was necessary to return to Forton Lake in December 2009 to undertake a survey of an additional vessel not recorded in previous years. This vessel was numbered FL31 and was recorded by Roger Forster and Dr. Julian Whitewright.

Vessel survey strategy

The vessel remains at Forton Lake lie at various locations, although a large proportion are located in an area on the southern shore near to the old F.J. Watts Boatyard and others on Ferrol Road and Parham Road (Fig 4.1). As part of the project each vessel was surveyed individually. The survey methodology employed by the project included:

A photographic record of overall vessel and detailed features if accessible

Collection of GPS co-ordinates of the vessel at opposite ends

Sketch drawings where possible

The completion of a 'Hulk Recording' proforma (see Fig. 3.1)

Collection of basic measurements of length and breadth where possible

Detailed plans and elevations where possible and required

The hulk recording form used was one that had changed little since its creation for recording a collection of hulks at Whitewall Creek on the Medway in Kent in the early 1990s (Milne *et al.*, 1998: 55). The recording form (Fig. 3.1) is broken into two main parts, the upper section to be completed during an assessment survey (as carried out in 2006) and the lower part to be completed during any subsequent detailed survey or excavation (as carried out on selected vessels in 2007 and 2008). Detailed guidance for completing the hulk recording proforma has been provided in Appendix C.

The photographic survey compiled for each vessel was undertaken in both digital and 35-mm colour and black and white film formats. The detailed plans were undertaken using standard offset method (Plate 3.1; Fig. 3.2). Baselines were laid using 30-m or 50-m tapes; from these the location of items of detail was established using open reel tapes or 3-m hand tapes to measure horizontal offset and plumb bobs to measure vertical offset. One-metre square planning frames were also used where

detailed structural elements were to be recorded. The survey plans were drawn to a scale of 1:20 with the exception of FL9, an MFV, which was drawn to a scale 1:100.

Excavation strategy

For the hulks that were substantially buried in the foreshore it was not possible to determine what type of vessel they represented and how much was still intact below the sediments; excavation was needed to reveal more. As excavation is a destructive process, it was undertaken in a controlled fashion to ensure all parts of the vessel, its components and any artefacts that might be within the hull were uncovered gradually and were numbered and recorded. In fact no artefacts were recovered during the course of the excavations at Forton Lake. Further details of the specific excavations undertaken on each site are included in Chapter 4.

Over the three years of fieldwork only three sites were excavated (FL5, FL15 and FL29). These were all wooden vessels and were potentially amongst the oldest vessels within Forton Lake. At each site a number of trenches were excavated, running across the hull from side to side, to show the depth at which the remains were buried, the variety of component hull parts and features in that area and the dimensions of the vessel. When survey and excavation work was completed the records gained in the field were developed into a series of scale drawings.

The duration of daily excavation periods depended on the tidal windows, as work could only be conducted when the water was low enough for the features to be exposed. Tide tables were consulted before excavation work to maximize time on site. The trenches were dug using hand excavation tools and techniques. Primary tools used were trowels, mattocks and spades. The soil deposits located within the hull were removed and the structural elements of the vessels were uncovered. As the deposits were removed, they were placed upon tarpaulin sheets and on completion the material was returned to the trenches. Each evening the excavated areas were cordoned off with road irons and hazard warning tape and would have to be bailed out the following day.

Archaeological Skills Training

(Mary Harvey)

The provision of archaeological skills training for those taking part was seen as an integral part of the work and, from the outset, funding was set aside to provide it. The volunteers came from a range of different backgrounds with a range of archaeological experience. They could be broadly split into four groups; local residents with an interest in their heritage, but little or no training in archaeological techniques, archaeology students from St Vincent College with theoretical knowledge, but limited practical experience, members of the HWTMA and the NAS with some experience and knowledge of the NAS training programme and several work experience volunteers. Training would enable all participants to make meaningful contributions to the project, with a level of supervision appropriate to their experience.

---

3   http://www.nauticalarchaeologysociety.org/projects/forton%20lak
     e/Forton_Lake_Project_YR3_Report_Final.pdf

Nautical Archaeology Society

Recording Form Series
Hulk Recording

PERSONAL DETAILS	SITE DETIALS
Name:	Site Name:
Contact details:	Location/position:
	Orientation:
Tel No.:	Archaeological references:

From Milne, G. et. al. 1998. *Nautical Archaeology on the Foreshore*. RCHME.

1:10000 sheet no.		NMR		SMR		Vessel no.	
Survey Zone						Site Code	
County		District		Parish		Status	
100 km sq		NGRE		NGRN		Qualifier	

Visible remains	Visible dimensions	(m) L x B x D
		X X
	Size class	
	Type	
	Hull construction:	clinker carvel dugout
	Other -	
	Material	

Propulsion:	Engine sail rig manpower towed
Site conditions:	

Comments/Identification marks:

Period		Date & name		CHECKED			
Surveying elements		End visible	Bow	Stern	Scantling:	depth x width (mm)	
Keel		Keelson					
Flat bottom planking		Floors					
Futtocks							
Ordinary external planking							
Internal planking							
Wales/stringers:	Internal			External			
Metal knee							
Timber knee:	Grown			Cut			
Other							
Bulkhead		Deck		Frame spacing centre to centre			
Engine remains		Rudder		Deck structures			
				Mast & spars		Mooring gear	
Fastenings:	Treenail		Iron	Non-ferrous		other	
Seam waterproofing							
Toolmarks							
Surface treatment							
Contents							
Drawing nos:	Plan		Section	Elevation		Profile	Photo nos
Timber sample nos				Find/Sample nos			
Continuation sheet		YES / NO		CHECKED			

Fig. 3.1 Hulk-recording proforma

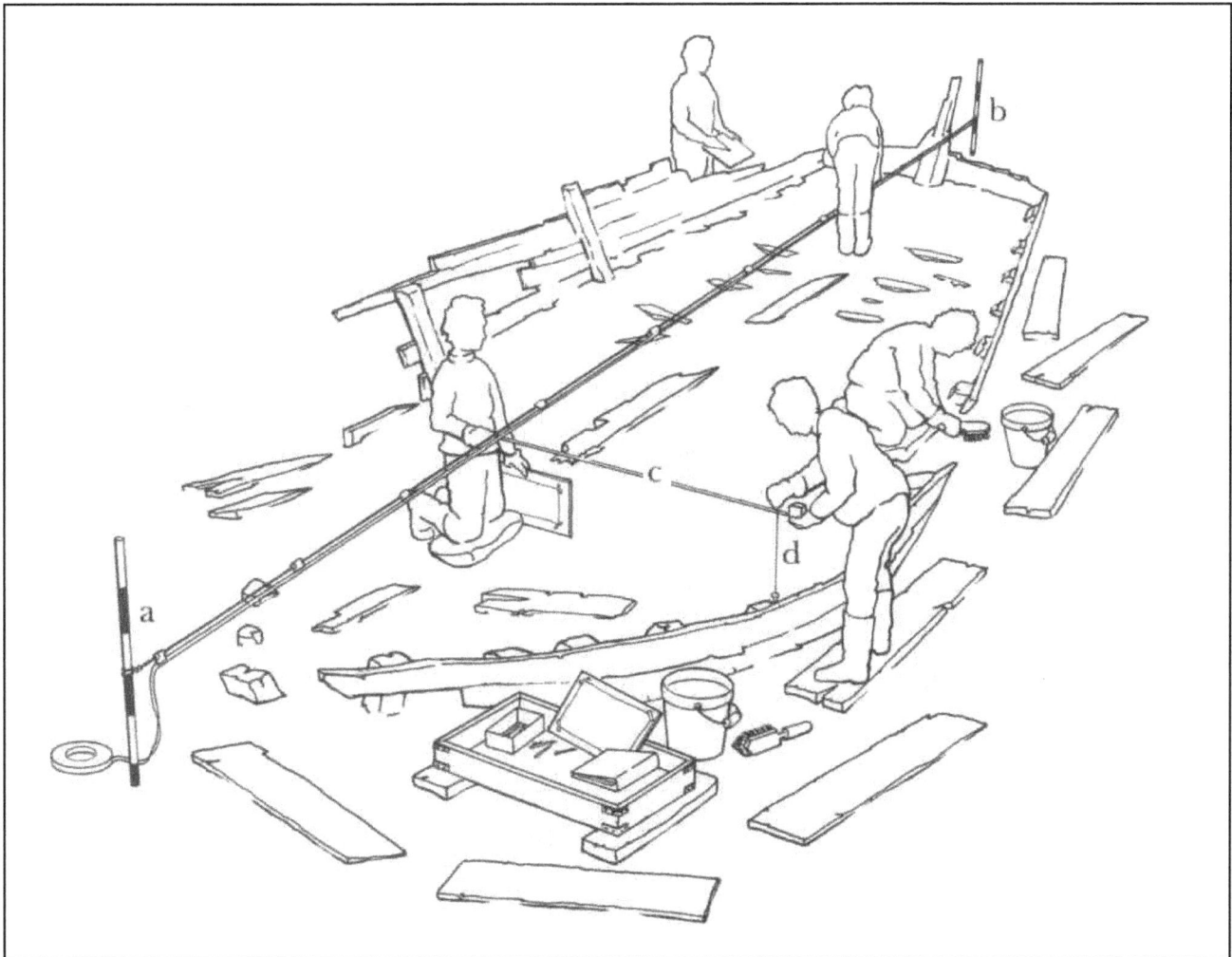

Fig. 3.2 Surveying method: a–b is the base line, c is the horizontal offset and d the vertical offset. Artwork by Ben Ferrari, reproduced with permission from Milne et al. (1998)

It was considered that the best approach, in order to offer the maximum benefit both to participants and to the project, would be to offer the NAS course 'An Introduction to Foreshore and Underwater Archaeology' at the beginning of each season before the active fieldwork began; it was felt that this would bear greater fruit than trying to develop skills during the active phase of the project. The course was open to all who had not previously attended and was tailored to cover information pertinent to working at Forton Lake and to the historic environment of Gosport, not included in the standard syllabus. The standard underwater practical session, during which participants practise two-dimensional survey skills in a swimming pool or in a confined open water environment, was replaced by additional time spent covering the methods which would be used on the foreshore during the project and by a chance to practice them on site. The course sessions looking at archaeological processes, different site types, dating methods and information on heritage legislation and protection enabled participants to place Forton Lake and their local maritime history within a wider context and help them to understand better the work being undertaken. The course also provided a solid platform for those who might at some time wish to continue with maritime archaeology.

Over the three years of active fieldwork a total of eleven volunteers took the Introduction course and all stated that they benefited hugely from the initial training and from the opportunities to put this into practice. For those volunteers who were A-level archaeology students, the training and subsequent fieldwork brought the textbooks and concepts learnt in the classroom to life. The results achieved by the volunteers on the project also demonstrate the benefits of providing individuals with initial training backed up by continuing guidance and supervision during the active fieldwork phase of the project.

For those who had already completed an NAS training course the project aimed to provide opportunities to build on their experience and to develop their practical fieldwork skills. Although there was no formal instruction during the active fieldwork of the project, the foreshore environment created excellent opportunities for continuing education. Participants were able to focus on learning and improving archaeological skills without having to consider the additional skills and knowledge associated with scuba diving and working in an underwater environment. In particular, this enabled questions to be asked and explanations to be given on site and in context, allowing issues to be addressed as they arose.

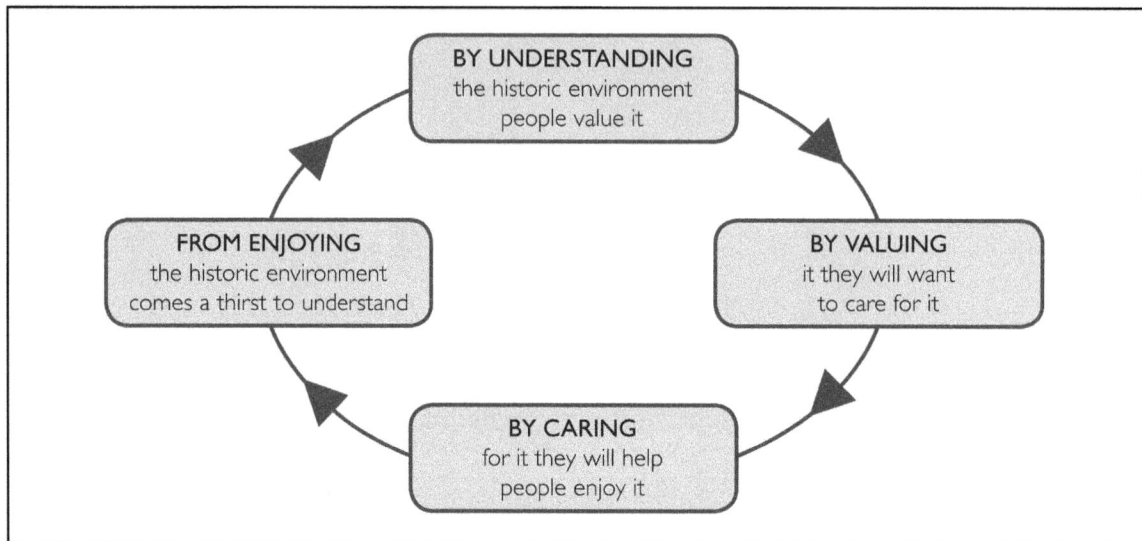

Fig. 3.3 The Heritage Cycle (courtesy of English Heritage)

During the three years of fieldwork the volunteers helped to undertake pre-excavation surveys, detailed vessel recording, excavation, as well as developing skills in drawing and photography. There were opportunities for them to develop the technical skills required to use specialist surveying equipment.

The project allowed volunteers to work towards their NAS Part II Intermediate Certificate in Foreshore and Underwater Archaeology. An element of this requires participants to undertake a short research project and to present the results in the form of a short report. Volunteers working for Part II were able to tackle a small aspect of the Forton Lake project; they selected a particular hulk to survey and followed this up with research to attempt to identify the vessel and its place in the history of the lake. With the advice and guidance of more experienced volunteers and professionals five high-quality Part II reports were submitted, which have become a part of the project archive held by the HWTMA and the Hampshire AHBR.

In this way the archaeological skills training offered during the project made use of the existing NAS training programme from the Introduction course through to continuing education and guidance for the Part II Certificate. Providing individuals with basic training prior to the active project work gave them the theoretical background to underpin the practical work that would be undertaken and was able to start volunteers on the first step of a structured programme that would enable them to build their skills and experience in the future. The experience was further enhanced by the advice and guidance available to volunteers during the active phase of the project, whether they were new to archaeology or wished to build on previous knowledge and experience. The benefits of using a real site for training were clearly demonstrated during the project by the attitude of participants, who gained satisfaction from contributing to a real archaeological investigation rather than carrying out exercises purely for training purposes. Furthermore the success is highlighted by several of the volunteers who returned to the project year after year and progressed

from having little practical archaeological experience, needing supervision during the first season, to being able to work independently to a high standard during the final season of fieldwork.

Outreach

(Alison James and Mark Beattie-Edwards)

From the conception of the project active outreach was seen as integral to its success. Both the HWTMA and the NAS have established backgrounds in providing high-quality outreach and the HWTMA was one of the first organizations in the UK to employ two full-time education and outreach officers. The project drew on this experience in developing its outreach programme.

Outreach has long been recognized as key to ensuring the future of maritime archaeology and over recent years has become an increasingly important part of any archaeological project. English Heritage's 'Heritage Cycle' (Fig. 3.2) illustrates how encouraging people to appreciate their historic environment helps to create a cycle that will ultimately ensure the long term survival and appreciation of cultural heritage.

It is only by interesting communities in their local heritage that they will recognize its value and its long-term preservation can be secured. Local people often know little about what lies on their shores. The hulks in Forton Lake are an easily recognizable part of the landscape, yet before the project the local people did not know much about the heritage on their own doorstep. Anecdotal evidence heard during the project suggested that at least the last two generations of teenagers have used the hulks as a good place to congregate in the evenings!

The project's three-year outreach programme involved all aspects of the local community and included family open days, hands-on participation, workshops for schools and a local history booklet. It was believed that creating in this way a sense of the value of the local heritage would both promote the survival of the physical remains, such as the hulks, and foster a sense of ownership of the site and of the vessels in all generations.

Open days

It was important to make the local community feel welcome on the site and part of the archaeological investigations. To this end, team members readily talked to passers-by about the project and their work; it was an unwritten policy to be as approachable and friendly as possible. During the first season an open day to launch the project was held and in the following years the outreach activities culminated in an open day for local residents. This gave the public an opportunity to come onto the site, meet the archaeologists, learn about the archaeology in general and the results of the season's work in particular and find out about how they could become involved. These events included displays of archaeological work from both the NAS and HWTMA. Other groups with a local or marine element, such as Gosport.info, Gosport and Fareham Inland Rescue Service (GAFIRS) and the Council for British Archaeology (CBA) Wessex, took part with displays and activities.

Members of the public were invited to join a guided tour of the archaeology of Forton Lake. The open days resulted in more stories and old photographs of the lake coming to light from people attending. The HWTMA and the NAS provided a number of activities, such as drawing with a planning frame and the 'feely box challenge', designed to recreate the experience of archaeologists working under water in low visibility. Badge making and face painting with a maritime theme were also popular. In 2007, to encourage more families to attend, a pirate-themed fancy dress competition was organized and judged by the Mayor of Gosport (Plate 3.2).

The grant awarded by the Nationwide Building Society in 2006 funded a number of off-site activity days during the project. Sessions especially for young children and families were held at a number of different venues, so as to reach as many people as possible, including:

National Archaeology Weekend, Fort Cumberland
Hurst Castle Maritime Archaeology Extravaganza
Southsea Show
Underwater Archaeology Centre, Isle of Wight
Eastleigh Museum

Throughout the fieldwork seasons evening lectures open to the public were given at St Vincent College on the current archaeological work, giving details of the ongoing investigations into many of the hulks. Many of the audience had memories that were used to support the project. The lectures gave a face to the archaeologists investigating the local landscape and allowed the community a way to become part of the process.

School Visits

The pupils of the local schools are the next generation of local residents who may be encouraged to value their local heritage, potentially local councillors who can promote it in their community and even possibly archaeologists who will come back investigate it again in the future. As such they were viewed as key to the future survival of the site.

As archaeology is seldom taught in schools as a separate discipline, the project had to raise its profile through a number of indirect approaches. At a basic level, simply providing children with an appreciation of this under-studied aspect of their cultural heritage imparts knowledge that stays with them throughout their life; at a more advanced level it may inspire them to take their interest in maritime archaeology further, perhaps into higher education.

Before the project, both the NAS and HWTMA had delivered workshops in schools. However, children had frequently asked to go out with the archaeologists and gain direct hands-on experience. Over the course of the project children from all the local schools, primary and secondary, were invited to accompany archaeologists onto the foreshore to give them a direct and tangible experience of maritime archaeology (Plate 3.3). In all some three hundred children from four local schools accepted the invitation. During these workshops pupils were treated as 'Maritime Archaeologists for an Hour' (Plate 3.4). This started with a brief tour of Forton Lake and an introduction to the concept of archaeology. The children were then given the task of creating a sketch plan of a hulk, doing some basic measurements and interpretative work, trying out archaeological survey techniques, including using planning frames and drawing sections and plans. These tasks enabled them to apply many subjects learned at school and to use their maths skills in a very different context, encouraging cross-curricular learning. Worksheets were developed that were used with Key Stages 2 and 3 (7–14 years – Appendix B).

Local History Booklet and Exhibition

Grants from The Crown Estate's Marine Communities Fund and the Gosport Borough Council included funding for a local history booklet and for a museum exhibition; the Marine Communities Fund also funded a permanent display panel on the banks of Forton Lake to be installed by the end of 2010.

The booklet, *Forton's Forgotten Fleet* with 28 pages printed in full colour (Plate 3.5), was written with local residents in mind. It covered the background to the area from prehistory to present day and presented some of the more interesting results for the main hulks, such as the ferries and the military craft. The final section of the booklet concentrated on the future of Forton Lake and advised how people could get involved in nautical archaeology, with contact details of the principal organizations involved. The project was fortunate to receive the support of the Mayor of Gosport, Councillor Mrs Diane Searle , who kindly supplied the summary for the back cover of the booklet; in it she challenged the local community to 'shed more light on the unsolved mysteries of Forton's Forgotten Fleet'.

An exhibition was put on at the Local Studies Centre in the Gosport High Street to complement the booklet (Plate 3.6). This used the text and the illustrations from the booklet to present the project's findings to the public. The exhibition ran from 4 January to 29 January 2010.

Chapter 4: The Results

4.1: Hulk catalogue

Introduction

As with many creeks that have been filled with abandoned vessels over a long period, Forton Lake has a collection of craft of different types and ages. Site survey and subsequent research has allowed the identity of some of the vessels to be discovered and it has been possible to determine the main function of others. Despite the work undertaken, it was not possible to identify the type or identity of all the craft in the lake. This chapter presents the catalogue of the hulks located in Forton Lake between 2006 and 2009, classified by function or theme: transportation, ferries, fishing industry, military and unclassified vessels. The location of each of the craft investigated is shown in Fig. 4.1 and summary details are given in Table 4.1.

Transportation

(Julie Satchell)

The economic development of Britain, as an island nation, has relied on the success of the transport of goods, people and ideas by sea. Despite the advent of air travel, maritime trade still predominates with up to 95% of Britain's overseas trade by volume being seaborne (British Ports Association).[1] The Romans understood that the transport of goods via sea was faster and cheaper than using roads and had established trade routes around Britain and the continent. These routes further expanded with the development of ship technology and exploration, with the establishment of world-wide connections and infrastructure that are utilized today.

Vessels engaged in trading activities vary in their function and hence their design has been developed to be appropriate to fulfilling a particular role. This could mean a vessel designed for the transportation of a limited type of cargo on a regular route or more multi-purpose trading vessels. The trading vessels represented within Forton Lake include wooden and metal barges dating from the past 150 years. These craft may have been engaged in trade and transport locally, nationally or internationally. Although it has not been possible specifically to identify any of these craft by name, assessment of their form has allowed interpretation of their potential role and scope of use.

Wooden Barges

The remains of three wooden barges are located within Forton Lake. From their construction it is believed that these represent some of the older vessels that have been recorded as part of the project. Excavation was undertaken on all three sites (FL5, FL15 and FL29) to allow their size, form and construction to be determined.

---

1   http://www.britishports.org.uk/public/uk_ports_industry

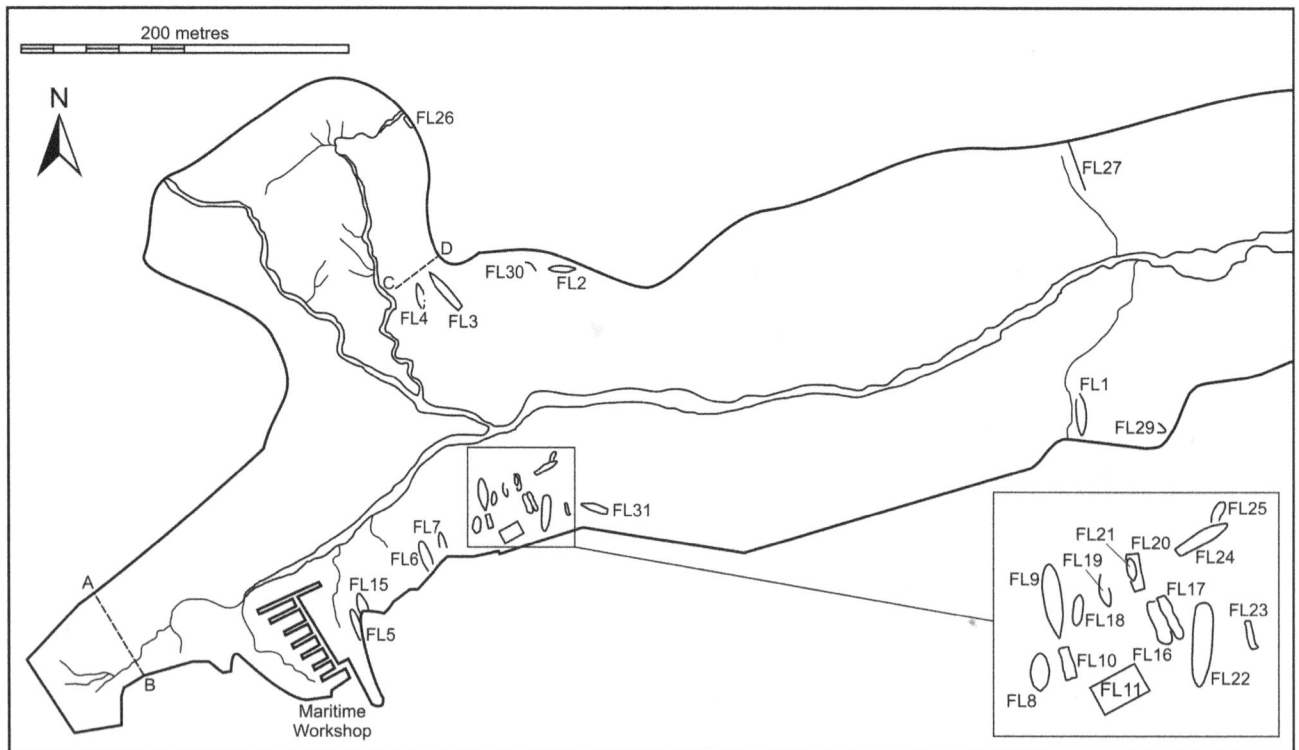

Fig. 4.1 Forton Lake. Location of hulks. A–B is the baseline for the 2006 auger survey; C–D the baseline for that of 2008 (page 6)

Project UID	National Grid Reference	HCC AHBR Record	Name	Type	Theme	Level of Record	Year	Pages
FL1	SU 461550, 100865		Unknown	Motorized Fishing Vessel	Fishing vessels	Measured survey	2007/2008	39–41
FL2	SU 461243, 100915	AHBR 53066	Unknown, possibly MFV *Lauren*	Motorized Fishing Vessel	Fishing vessels	Measured survey	2008	42–3
FL3	SU 461150, 100915	AHBR 53067	293	Motor Minesweeper	Military	Measured survey	2007	44–7
FL4	SU 461143, 100902		Unknown	Unclassified vessel	Unclassified vessels	Photographed	2006	63–4
FL5	SU 461107, 100678	AHBR 53069	Unknown	Wooden Barge	Transportation	Excavated	2007/2008	17–21
FL6	SU 461145, 100741	AHBR 53070	Unknown	Metal Barge	Transportation	Photographed	2006	28
FL7	SU 461158, 100747	AHBR 53071	704	Pinnace	Military	Measured survey	2007	47–9
FL8	SU 461181, 100747		Unknown	Possible Metal Barge	Transportation	Photographed	2006	28
FL9	SU 461187, 100761		Unknown	Motor Fishing Vessel	Fishing vessels	Measured survey	2008	43–4
FL10	SU 461190, 100749	AHBR 57862	Unknown	Landing Craft	Military	Measured survey	2006	49–54
FL11	SU 461193, 100748	AHBR 53074	Medina River Chain Ferry	Chain Ferry	Ferries and Lifeboats	Survey	2006	29–32
FL12–FL14	UIDs not allocated							
FL15	SU 461108, 100692	AHBR 53069	Unknown	Wooden Barge	Transportation	Excavation	2007	21–5
FL16	SU 461214, 100767	AHBR 57866	Unknown	Landing Craft	Military	Photographed / measured	2006	50–54
FL17	SU 461213, 100770	AHBR 57869	Unknown	Royal Air Force Ferry Boat	Military	Measured survey	2008	54–6
FL18	SU 461191, 100763	AHBR 53073	Unknown	Unclassified vessel	Unclassified vessels	Photographed	2006	64
FL19	SU 461199, 100770		Unknown	Unclassified vessel	Unclassified vessels	Photographed	2006	64
FL20	SU 461206, 100773	AHBR 57872	Unknown	Landing Craft	Military	Photographed / measured	2006	50–54
FL21	SU 461207, 100776		Unknown	Lifeboat	Ferries and Lifeboats	Photographed	2006	37–8
FL22	SU 461226, 100771	AHBR 57876	*Vadne*	Gosport Ferry	Ferries and Lifeboats	Photographed	2006	33–7
FL23	SU 461237 100757	AHBR 57878	Unknown	Royal Air Force Bomb Scow	Military	Measured survey	2008	56–9
FL24	SU 461225, 100790	AHBR 57879	Unknown	Pinnace or Harbour Launch	Military	Photographed	2006	59–61
FL25	UID not allocated							
FL26	SU 461138, 101005		Unknown	Unclassified vessel	Unclassified vessels	Photographed / measured	2006	64–6
FL27	SU 461558, 100954		Groyne	Groyne	Shoreside structures	Photographed	2006	68
FL28	UID not allocated							
FL29	SU 461608, 100872		Unknown	Wooden Barge	Transportation	Excavation	2007/2008	25–8
FL30	SU 461243, 100915		Unknown	Lifeboat	Ferries and Lifeboats	Measured survey	2008	37–8
FL31	SU 460519, 100985		Unknown	Possible Motor Gun Boat	Military	Measured survey	2009	61–3
Slipway site	SU 461114, 100652	AHBR 55067	Patent slipway		Shoreside structures	Excavation	2006	66–8

Table 4.1   List of hulks recorded on Forton Lake

FL5: Wooden Barge (NGR: SU 461107, 100678; AHBR 53069)
(Julian Whitewright, Paul Donohue, Daniel Pascoe and Julie Satchell)

Site description

The Maritime Workshop boatyard and slipway lies on the south side of Forton Lake (Figs 1.2 and 4.1). To the east of the slipway a small bank had been created by accretion of sediments within the hulls of FL5 and FL15. The 2006 assessment identified ship/boat timbers protruding from the ground surface associated with this mole (Plate 4.1). The nature of the site as a mole means that parts of it are accessible at all states of the tide. However, as excavation was undertaken, mid to low tide was needed

Trench	Year	Length in metres	Width in metres	Position	Location of trench on baseline (from datum)
FL5A	2007	3.8	2.5	Bow	21.9 m
FL5B	2007	4.8	1.2	Amidships	14.9 m
FL5C	2008	6.2	1.4	Amidships	8.9 m
FL5D	2007	1.8	1.0	Stern	0.4 m

Table 4.2   Summary of the excavation areas relating to FL5

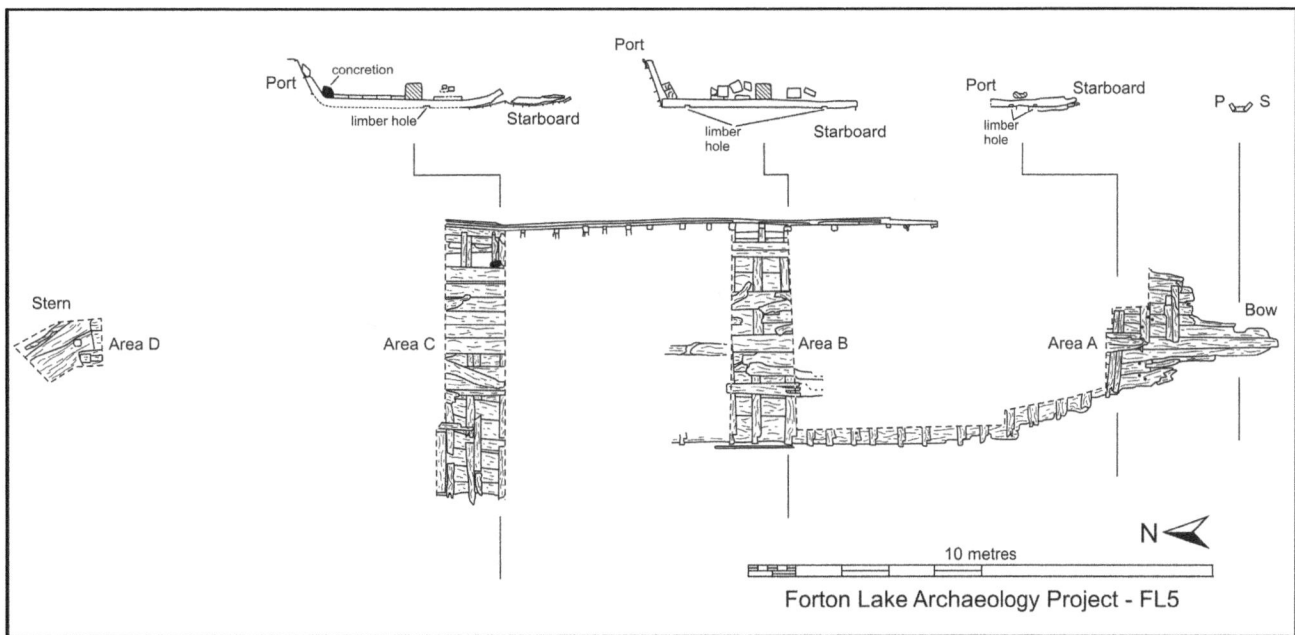

Fig. 4.2 Plan of the excavation areas of FL5 over the course of the 2007 and 2008 seasons

to allow work to progress without the trench filling with water, particularly at the lower areas of the site along the eastern and northern edges of the mole.

Survey approach and methodology

Although some timber ends are visible around the sides of the vessel remains, excavation, in conjunction with a survey of the extant timbers, was required to investigate FL5 fully. A baseline was established along the assumed centreline of the vessel, with the datum located on a post protruding through the sediments at the northern end of the mole, which was believed to be the stern of the vessel. Four trenches were excavated; two amidships, one in the bow area and one in the vicinity of the stern. These areas are identified as FL5A, FL5B, FL5C and FL5D; they are summarized in Table 4.2.

Survey Results

The results of the excavation of the four areas of FL5 are presented in Fig. 4.2. The archaeological investigation of the site revealed a wooden, carvel built, flat-bottomed, hard-chined vessel, measuring 25.3 m in length and 4.12 m wide across the bottom of the vessel. These characteristics indicate a vessel primarily designed for working in shallow waters and being able to take the ground at low tide. On this basis FL5 can be initially identified as a sailing barge or lighter barge. A summary of the characteristics of FL5 as detailed through its excavation and survey is presented in Table 4.3 and described below.

Planking

The hull of FL5 is flat-bottomed amidships, with the deadrise increasing towards the bow where the keel has been rabbetted to receive the garboard strakes. On the west side (lakeside) of the mole, floor timbers and hull planking were visible. At three points small lengths of longitudinal timbers were exposed. In one area of the east side of the vessel, towards what was presumed to be the bow, concrete had been deposited.

Trench		FL5A		FL5B		FL5C		FL5D	
Element		S'd	M'd	S'd	M'd	S'd	M'd	S'd	M'd
Planking	Garboard	18	8	–	–	–	–	40	–
	Outer (Bottom)	24	10	40	–	40	–	40	–
	Outer (Side)	–	–	–	–	38	3	–	–
	Ceiling	–	–	38	9	28	6	–	–
Framing	Keel	30	10	–	–	–	–	32	–
	Keelson	40	10	40	32	32	32	–	–
	Sternpost	–	–	–	–	–	–	20	24
	Chine keelson	–	–	14	30	–	–	–	–
	Floors	24–28	18–20	16	18	30	24	–	–
	Futtocks	–	–	18	14	30	24	–	–

Table 4.3   Summary of the constructional details of FL5. All dimensions are given in cm. S'd = Sided, M'd = Moulded. Where composite elements are present, the total dimension is given

The garboard strakes are 18 cm sided and 8 cm moulded.[2] In the bow area they are set at an angle of 45° (Fig. 4.3). By the time the plank runs reach the first surviving floor timber they are nearly horizontal. Other planks excavated towards the bow of the vessel are 24 cm sided and 10 cm moulded. Towards the midships section of the vessel (area FL5B) the hull is almost completely flat-bottomed. Four bottom-strakes were visible either side of the keel which have an average sided measurement of 40 cm. These dimensions continue towards the stern of the vessel (area FL5C) and were also observed in the stern area (area FL5D). The side strakes of the vessel were visible amidships (area FL5C) and were 38 cm sided and 3 cm moulded. The side strakes at this point were scarfed with a stepped lap-joint.

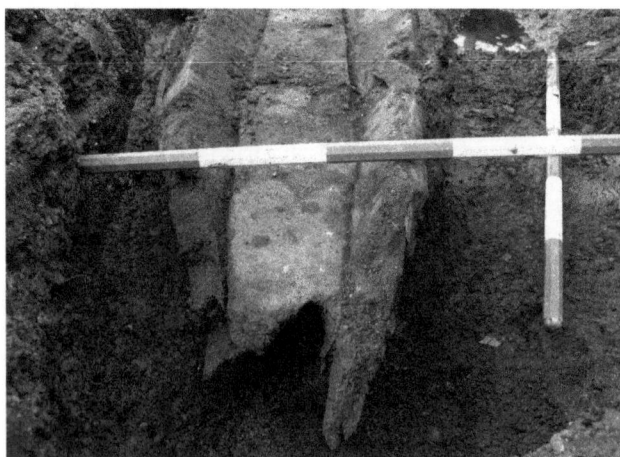

Fig. 4.3 The extent of the keel at the bow, with the angled garboard strakes and rabbetted keel clearly visible (scale=1 m)

2   The sided dimension of frames is in the fore-and-aft direction (width), whilst the moulded dimension is from inboard to outboard (depth). See Appendix C, page 98

Remains of the ceiling planking survive amidships (area FL5B). The excavated remains indicate that these are spaced 54 cm to port and starboard of the vessel's keelson. A well preserved example of this first ceiling plank from the port side is 38 cm sided, 9 cm moulded. Further aft (area FL5C) five strakes of ceiling planking were visible on the portside. These measured 28 cm sided by 6 cm moulded.

Framing

The framing of FL5 is relatively complex, in part due to its flat-bottomed hull form. As well as a keel, keelson, floor timbers and futtocks, FL5 is built with a chine keelson along either side of the vessel. This serves to define the angle of the hard chine of the vessel and also to provide additional support to the frames and planking at a point of potential weakness. This type of constructional feature is common in wooden vessels with flat bottoms and hard chines.

The keel of FL5 has a greater sided dimension than moulded. It either has the same moulded dimension as the bottom planking or is only very slightly thicker. Towards the bow of the vessel (area FL5A) the dimensions of the keel were 30 cm sided and 10 cm moulded. As noted above, the keel is rabbetted at the bow to facilitate the garboard strakes (Fig. 4.3). At the stern of the vessel (area FL5D) the keel had a moulded dimension of 32 cm. The sternpost of the vessel was 20 cm sided and 24 cm moulded.

In the bow area (FL5A) three floor timbers survived. In each case these comprised a pair of timbers, set side by side. A clear curvature is visible to the floor timbers in the bow of the vessel (Fig. 4.4). Their overall dimensions were 24–28 cm sided and 18–20 cm moulded. No floor timbers are visible in the first 2.10 m of surviving keel, although the outline of a number of treenails survives. The frames in this area, if surviving, are likely to have

Fig. 4.4 General view of FL5A, looking aft. Floor timbers comprised of two elements are visible, which have a clear curvature, in contrast to the floor timbers excavated amidships. The degraded keelson is visible towards the top of the picture (scale=1 m)

Fig. 4.5 The starboard (western) side of the bottom planking in area FL5B, looking aft. Three floor timbers with the exposed half-lap joints are attached to the outer planking with treenails. The degraded timber on the right of the picture is one of the starboard ceiling planks (scale=1 m)

Fig. 4.6 The port (eastern) side of the vessel, internal view (area FL5B). The staggered nature of the framing is clearly visible. In addition, port side ceiling planking can be seen on the floor timbers at the bottom of the picture. The chine keelson is located at the junction of floor timber and futtock. Side planks are fastened to futtocks with iron fastenings (scale=1 m)

Fig. 4.7 General overview of FL5B. From bottom right (port side) to top left (starboard side) along the exposed floor timber, the following elements are visible: chine keelson, ceiling plank and keelson. The timbers protruding from the baulk are loose and may represent the upper futtocks of the vessel (scale=1 m)

been cant frames. Moving aft (area FL5B), the floor timbers are comprised of single timbers, 16 cm sided and 18 cm moulded. These run across the full width of the vessel and the remains of a half-lap joint are visible at their ends on the western (starboard) side of the vessel (Fig. 4.5). This is the point at which the more vertically set futtocks would have formed the hard chine of the vessel at an angle of 110° to the bottom of the hull. These futtocks survive on the eastern (port) side of the vessel and are 18 cm sided, 14 cm moulded and extend to a height of 1.05 m. At their upper end are the remains of a half-lap joint, indicating the probable presence of a series of second futtocks. The second futtocks may be represented in the remains of the hulk by a series of loose timbers found amidships on the port side (area FL5B). These timbers were 22 cm square and were slightly curved, possibly indicating their use as framing timbers. Two similar timbers were found on the starboard side of the vessel. In the unexcavated section of the site,

between areas FL5A and FL5B, twelve floor timbers can be seen protruding from the sediment on the starboard (western) side of the vessel. These are all made from single timbers and are similar to the floor timbers excavated in area FL5B. On the port (eastern) side of the vessel sixteen futtocks are visible protruding from the mole. These futtocks extend from midway between areas FL5A and FL5B as far as area FL5C. They are all similar to the futtocks excavated in area FL5B.

Further aft (area FL5C), a second group of composite floor timbers were identified on the starboard side of the vessel. The individual timbers averaged 15 cm sided and 12 cm moulded. Their combined measurement of 30 cm sided and 24 cm moulded is comparable with the composite framing from area FL5A. The futtocks in this area, FL5C, were also composite, although they had broken off and splayed outwards following their deposition. The joints in these composite frames were staggered to increase their strength.

A further feature of the vessel's framing, identifiable following excavation, is that, where single timbers are used, the floors and futtocks are staggered as a result of the joint between them. This is visible in Fig. 4.6, where the futtocks are on the forward side of the floors. Further aft, in area FL5C, the floors and futtocks are composite and the combined framing element remains in line. Averaged across the length of the vessel, frame spacing (centre-to-centre) was 61 cm.

Limber holes have been cut in the underside of the floor timbers along the length of the vessel 8 cm wide and 25 mm deep. In the bow region (area FL5A) these are close to the keelson, amidships (area FL5B) they were observed closer to the chine than to the keelson and further aft (area FL5C) they are again close to the keelson.

A keelson runs the length of the vessel. Its remains in the bow area (FL5A) are badly preserved; it measures 40 cm sided and 10 cm moulded. It is degraded to the extent that it is no longer attached to any other elements of the vessel's framing in the bow area. The keelson continues for the length of the vessel, where it is better preserved (Fig. 4.7). Amidships (area FL5B) it is 40 cm sided and 32 cm moulded and is attached to the floor timbers. Further aft (area FL5C) the keelson measures 32 cm sided and 32 cm moulded. There is no indication of any form of scarf joint in either of the areas where the keelson has been exposed.

The hull of FL5 is given additional strength by the use of a chine keelson (Fig. 4.7). This rests upon, as well as being secured to, the junction of the floors and futtocks. In doing so it provides a great deal of strength to an area of potential weakness. The chine keelson on FL5 is well preserved amidships on the port side (area FL5B) and is comprised of two timbers placed one on top of each other. The uppermost of these is 14 cm sided and 12 cm moulded, the lower is 14 cm sided and 18 cm moulded. Their combined measurements make for a substantial longitudinal timber that is 14 cm sided and 30 cm moulded. It must be assumed that a similar timber was present on the starboard-side of the vessel.

Fastening

The outer planking is fastened to the framing elements using treenails and iron fastenings. The former are used to fasten the outer planking to the floors and the latter for attachment to futtocks. In the bow area of the vessel (trench FL5A) the remains of treenails are visible in the keel; these are likely to have secured the floor timbers to the keel. In trench FL5C the composite frames were fastened together with iron fastenings running fore-and-aft through both elements of the frame. The half-lap joints associated with the single timber floor/futtock joints must also have been secured horizontally through the joint. However, the exact fastening method remains unclear.

Interpretation

The constructional features of the vessel, particularly the flat bottom and hard chine are consistent with its identification as a sailing barge or lighter barge. In particular, the amidships section of the vessel bears direct comparison with many published examples of such vessels (McKee, 1983: 53; Leather, 1984: figs 32 and 37; Simper, 1997: 96; Milne *et al.*, 1998: figs 63 and 68; Dawkes *et al.*, 2009: fig. 16). In addition, there is no evidence in the excavated areas of the vessel for an engine mount, footing or propeller shaft housing. No mast-step was found during excavation; however, given the shape of the hull, this would probably have been located in the unexcavated section of the site between trenches FL5A and FL5B, if one had been present.

The remains of the bow of FL5, especially the angle of the garboard strakes and associated rabbet, indicate that the vessel was built 'stem-headed' with a conventional stem post. This method of construction, with a flat-bottomed box-like section amidships and rounded ends has been termed 'transitional' by McKee (1983: 89). It contrasts with the alternative 'swim-headed' bow that was also seen on sailing and lighter barges (for examples of both types see Milne *et al.*, 1998: 23–36; for swim-headed types see Dawkes *et al.*, 2009: 74–83). A discussion of the complexity of this type of construction is provided by Milne *et al.* (1998: 44–50). The characteristic 'transitional' construction of FL5 also provides an indication of the date of the vessel. This type of construction only began to be developed from the mid-19th century on the shipyards of the Swale and Medway (Childs, 1993: 3). By the late 19th century, such vessels (today termed Thames Barges) were built all around the south-east of England and traded as far afield as Ireland and the continent as well as the South Coast of England (Carr, 1989: 92). The overall dimensions of FL5 tally closely with the larger stem-headed sailing barges surveyed at Whitewall Creek on the Medway (Milne *et al.*, 1998: 19). This, in combination with the stem-headed construction, suggests that FL5 was a sailing barge, rather than a lighter barge. Stem-headed construction was more complex than the swim-headed form (Milne *et al.*, 1998: 44–45) and its main benefit would have been an improved sailing performance, while maintaining a shallow draft. It would seem strange to build a lighter, which has no requirement to sail, using this more complicated technique.

Based on its construction FL5 probably dates from between the mid-19th to early 20th century. During this period sailing barges were an integral part of the sailing trading fleet right around the south and east coast of England. Barges are documented as being used in the Solent area in this period, both locally built and from the south-east of England (Leather, 1984: 153). Locally built 'Solent barges' or 'Cowes ketches' seem to have been round-bottomed vessels (Simper, 1997: 120, 123), although Leather (1984: 153) records the building of a series of flat-bottomed sailing barges by John Crampton. He goes on to note that Crampton was possibly influenced by sailing barges from Kent. Other barges in

Crampton's fleet are described in terms that tally with the constructional details of FL5, namely that they were stem-headed and flat-bottomed. This would correspond with the Kentish influence noted above. Such vessels are also differentiated from 'Cowes ketches' (Leather, 1984: 153–156). Leather also notes other Solent merchants who built or imported Thames-style sailing barges (Leather 1984: figs 96 and 97). FL5 may therefore have been built within the Solent region in a manner borrowed from the sailing barges of the Thames region or it could have been purchased from that area for use in the Solent. During the decline of wooden vessels in favour of metal hulls there are many examples of former trading vessels being purchased for conversion for other purposes, local examples including hulks from the River Hamble.[3] It is possible that FL5 could have spent much of its active working life in another area of the south coast, with its final years spent in the Solent.

The hull of FL5 is fastened with treenails and iron bolts/nails. There are no indications that copper/copper alloy fastenings were used, despite the presence of these fastenings in other ship/boat types from the 18th century onwards. The treenail/iron fastening combination is consistent with the fastenings seen on other surveyed sailing/lighter barges from the mid-19th century onwards. Both the frame spacing and stepped lap-joint plank scarfs on FL5 are also consistent with features recorded on Thames barges of comparable dimensions (Milne *et al.*, 1998: 32–3). Of further interest is the absence of any evidence for the use of iron knees on FL5. These fittings are shown on contemporary plans of vessels built within the same tradition as FL5 (Leather 1984: fig. 37) and are recorded on some surviving comparative vessels (Milne *et al.*, 1998: 31; Dawkes *et al.*, 2009: 81). This absence may be due to the lack of upper hull elements surviving in the remains of FL5.

The excavated remains of FL5 also indicate that the vessel underwent a major repair/refit at some stage in its use. The composite frames visible in trenches FL5A and FL5C are notably different from the single timber floors and futtocks that are visible in the rest of the extant vessel. It can be suggested that the framing system in place in trench FL5B and visible in the frame ends of the unexcavated area is the original framing system of the vessel. Repairs at some stage in the vessel's use led to the replacement of a number of frames with composite floors and futtocks that utilized a number of timbers. The differences between the single timber framing elements in trench FL5B when compared to the composite framing used in the rest of the vessel must be indicative of this. The composite framing is fairly consistent in its size, suggesting it may have been added as a single piece of work. These frames are also much bigger that the single timber frames visible in the rest of the vessel. This further supports the notion that the composite frames represent a repair or refit with a view to strengthening certain areas of the vessel.

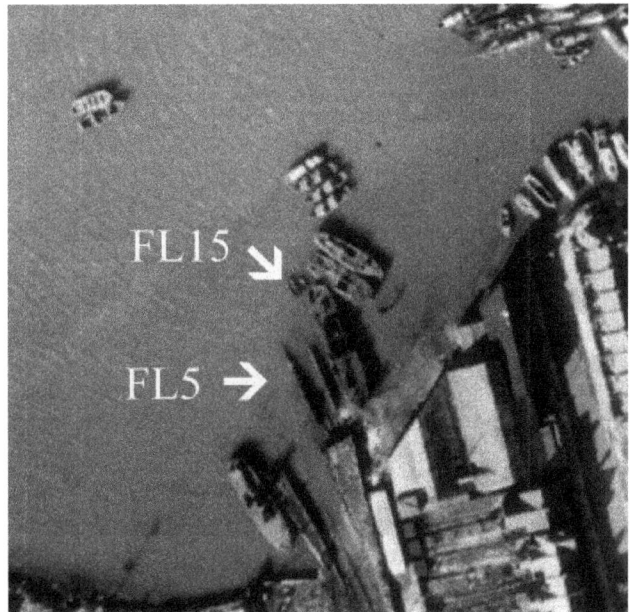

Fig. 4.8 Aerial view of FL5 in 1949 (second from the left in the bottom of the picture). Immediately alongside is FL15. North is to the top. Detail from Fig. 2.1

The information gathered during the survey and excavation of FL5 suggests that the vessel is a stem-headed sailing barge of the type commonly built on the south-east coast of England. It is possible that FL5 may represent a locally built equivalent of the same form of vessel. The vessel probably dates between the mid-19th century and the early 20th century. FL5 seems to have undergone a refit/repair at some point in which single piece timbers were replaced by composite timbers in two sections of the hull framing. Eventually FL5 seems to have outlived its usefulness and to have been laid up on the southern shore of Forton Lake. The RAF aerial photos of Forton Lake dating from 1949 and 1950 show FL5 in a considerably degraded state (Figs 4.8 and 4.15). The deck of the vessel has been lost, along with all cross-beams. The bow and stern of the vessel have also gone as far as the turn of the bilge. This evidence suggests the vessel may have arrived at Forton Lake some time before the late 1940s and have been subject to severe stripping of the useable materials.

FL15: Wooden Barge (NGR: SU 461108, 100692: AHBR 53069)

(Julian Whitewright, Paul Donohue and Julie Satchell)

Site description

FL15 is located to the east of The Maritime Workshop slipway, at the end of a north/south oriented grassy bank (Fig. 4.1). This location is immediately to the east of FL5. The orientation of FL15 is north/south, in line with the bank. The hulk is inundated at high tide, but is accessed relatively easily at other states of the tide. Its general date and identification remain uncertain. FL15 comprises the remains of a wooden vessel. The stern extends northwards into the lake and the sternpost of the vessel protrudes from the surrounding mud. Wooden frames, iron knees and a section of hull planking are also

---

3   http://www.hwtma.org.uk/uploads/documents/Archaeological %20Projects/HambleHLFProjectReport1.pdf, 2008: 53–77.

visible in this area. The forward section of the hulk is buried under the grassy bank. Between the sternpost and the beginning of the grassed area a number of other elements relating to the vessel can also be seen. These include frame ends, transverse timbers and iron knees.

Survey approach and methodology

Excavation was required to ascertain details of the vessel's construction and possible identification. A baseline was established running along the centre of the vessel, with the datum at the sternpost. Two trenches were located and both were excavated during the 2007 season. FL15A was located amidships, where the vessel continues under the grassy bank. FL15B was located at the stern of the vessel. These areas are summarized in Table 4.4. FL15A was recorded in plan and section; the latter was not possible in trench FL15B due to the nature of the mud. The sternpost was recorded in profile. During the excavation of FL15B a quantity of fuel oil was noticed and excavation was halted. Unstable sediment meant that it was not possible to excavate down to the keel of the vessel. A comprehensive photographic record was collected once excavation was complete.

Trench	Length in metres	Width in metres	Position	Location on trench on baseline (from datum)
FL15A	6.7	1.0	Amidships	10.15 m
FL15B	0.85	0.5	Stern	0.0 m

Table 4.4 Summary of the excavation areas relating to FL15

Survey results

The results of the excavation of FL15 are presented in Figs 4.9 and 4.10. The archaeological investigation of the site revealed a carvel-built wooden vessel. The length of the vessel, based on visual inspection, is uncertain due to the bow area being buried. The surveyed remains extend for 10.15 m forward of the stern post. The widest part of the vessel was visible in the southern section of FL15A. The vessel was 6.04 m wide at this point. Reference to the 2006 aerial photograph of the site (Fig. 1.2) indicates that the total length of the vessel is *c.* 30 m with a beam of *c.* 6.5 m. A summary of the characteristics of FL15 as detailed through its excavation is presented in Table 4.5.

Planking

Remains of the vessel's planking were uncovered in trench FL15A. On the port side, outer hull planking measured 30 cm sided and 8 cm moulded. On the interior of the hull the remains of lining planking were preserved; these measured 22 cm sided and 8 cm moulded. Inboard of the lining planking was a second run of planks. This comprised two planks, one on top of the other, 22 cm sided and 8 cm moulded. The pattern of the inner plank run, lining planking and outer planking was mirrored on the starboard side. Hull planking survived in the stern

Trench	FL15A		FL15B	
Element	Sided (cm)	Moulded (cm)	Sided (cm)	Moulded (cm)
Outer planking	30	8	40	–
Lining planking	22	8	–	–
Inner planks	22	8		
Sternpost	–	–	23	20
Futtocks	10–16	10–12	–	–

Table 4.5 Summary of the constructional dimensions of FL15

area of the vessel. However, it was too damaged and eroded for meaningful measurements to be recorded.

Framing

Problems with the stability of the trenches meant that excavation did not uncover the keel of the vessel in either trench. A number of futtocks were recorded on both the port and starboard side of the vessel in trench FL15A. These measured 10–16 cm sided and 10–12 cm moulded. The difference in sided dimensions probably results from erosion and degradation of the remains, rather than a real difference in the size of the vessel's framing, from frame to frame. In trench FL15B, the sternpost and inner sternpost of the vessel were uncovered (Fig. 4.11). The sternpost is exposed to a height of 1.26 m clear of the sediment. It is 23 cm sided and 20 cm moulded. The upper section is broken and the original post would have been taller. The inner sternpost seems complete. It rises to a height of 1.89 m, is 20 cm sided and 21cm moulded. A rudder gudgeon is attached 34 cm above the sediment, the gudgeon is 76 cm long and 8 cm wide.

In the unexcavated area between trenches A and B a number of protruding frames allow the shape of the vessel to be established (Fig. 4.12). In addition, a number of these frames have the remains of iron knees still attached to them. It may be assumed that such knees would have been present throughout the vessel to provide reinforcement in place of wooden knees. Other remains of iron knees can be seen in this area and can probably be identified as staple knees that were placed between deck or hold beams (Fig. 4.13). The remains of two athwartship timbers are located 5.7 m forward of the stern. Both of these have 90° metal corner pieces that must have been associated with their attachment to the vessel (Fig. 4.14). These cross-beams may represent the remains of a bulkhead or bulkheads towards the stern of the vessel. Forward of these, lying 7 m forward of the sternpost, on the starboard side, is a feature made up of two metal strips with the remains of timber between the two. There is no indication of the function of this object within the vessel.

Fastening

Little can be said about the fastening employed on FL15. All structural elements were fastened together with iron bolts/nails. Likewise, all of the planking elements were fastened to the framing using the same system of iron bolts/nails.

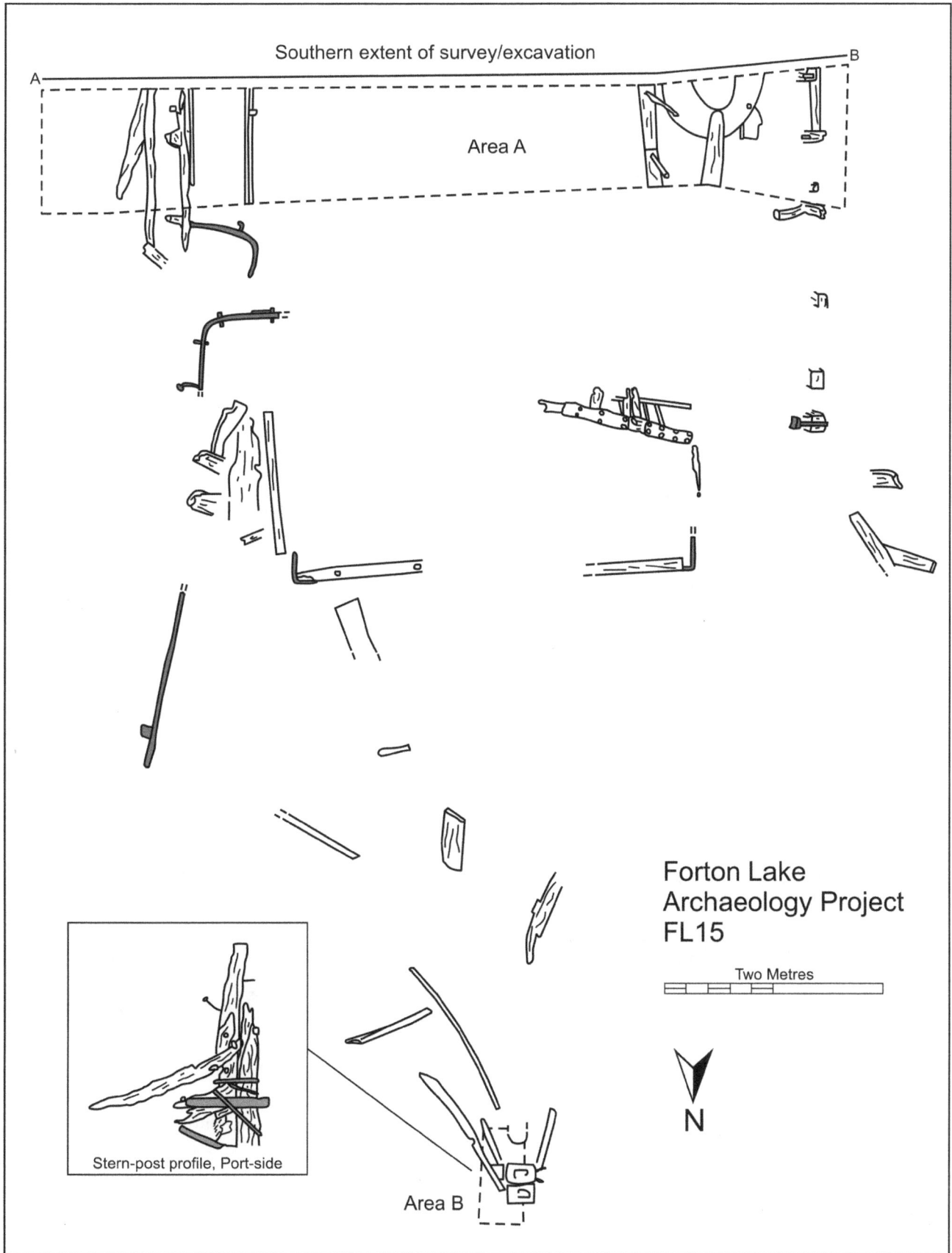

Fig. 4.9   Plan of the survey and excavation of FL15

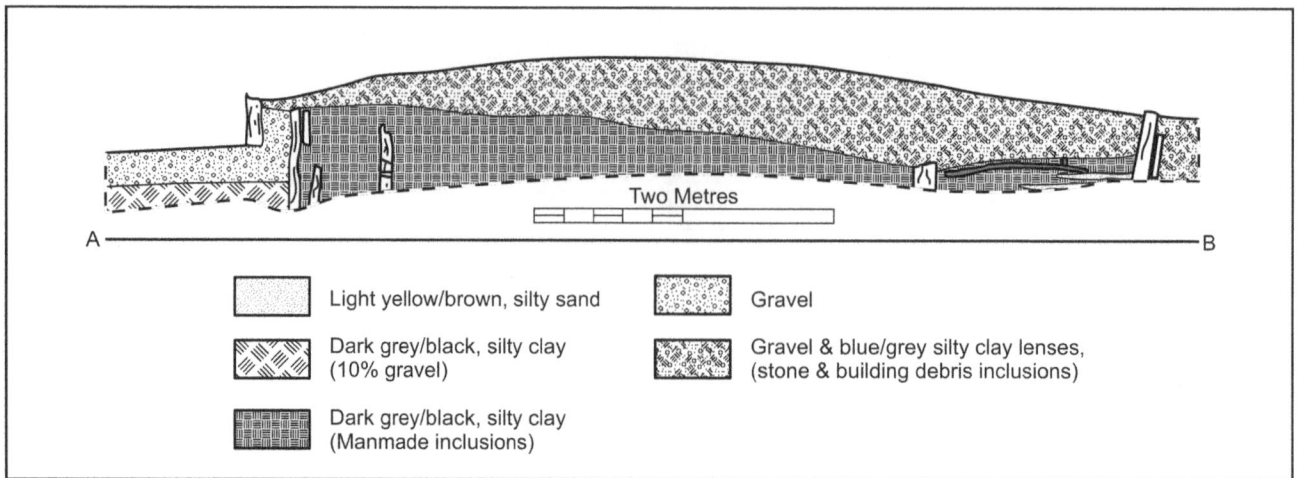

Light yellow/brown, silty sand

Gravel

Dark grey/black, silty clay (10% gravel)

Gravel & blue/grey silty clay lenses, (stone & building debris inclusions)

Dark grey/black, silty clay (Manmade inclusions)

Fig. 4.10   Section A–B, through southern limit of the excavations in trench A

Fig. 4.11   View of the port side of the stern, looking west. The taller of the timbers is the inner sternpost, the sternpost lies to the right of it. Degraded plank remains are also visible (scale=1 m)

Fig. 4.12   Unexcavated starboard-side frames protruding from the shoreline, looking north-east. The remains of an iron knee are visible fastened to the middle frame (scale=1 m)

Fig. 4.13   Unexcavated port-side area, looking south-west. A robust outer hull plank is fastened to the futtocks with iron fastenings; further iron elements are visible through a break in the plank. The remains of an iron staple knee protrude from the sediment. Starboard-side frames are visible in the background (scale=1 m)

Fig. 4.14   90° iron fitting on the port end of the one of the visible transverse timbers

Interpretation

Further analysis of FL15 is difficult due to the limited nature of the results obtained during the survey and excavation. The vessel is wooden and carvel built,

fastened with iron and utilizing iron knees for reinforcement. The keel and bottom of the vessel was not uncovered, so there is no indication if the vessel has a rounded hull or a flat bottom. Likewise, although the sternpost survives, there is no indication as to the nature of the upper stern; pointed, transom, etc.

The aerial photographs dating to the immediate post-war period shed further light on the nature of the vessel. In the RAF photograph from 1949 the vessel is relatively

Fig. 4.15   Aerial view FL15 in 1950. Detail from Fig. 2.4

well defined (Fig. 4.8). The upper decks are still in place and, as noted above, it is possible to establish the basic dimensions of the vessel: 30 m x 6.5 m. This is a length to beam ratio of 4.25, which could class FL15 as a wooden sailing barge. A 1950 aerial photograph taken from a more oblique angle allows a more interpretative view of FL15 (Fig. 4.15). This allows the main cargo hatch and fore hatch to be identified. The remains of the vessel's bowsprit are also visible along with a transom stern. The attributes of FL15, as visible in the aerial photographs strongly suggest that the vessel is a stem-headed sailing barge, similar to FL5 (for an example of a plan of such a vessel see Leather, 1984: fig. 22).

Local residents report that children used to play on the remains of FL15 in the late 1970s. This eventually led to Gosport Borough Council filling in the vessel with debris due to health and safety concerns (Fiona Richie, pers. comm.). This account is corroborated by the evidence of debris found during the excavation of the vessel.

FL29: Wooden Barge (NGR: SU 461608, 100872)

(Julian Whitewright, Paul Donohue, Daniel Pascoe and Julie Satchell)

Site description

FL29 is situated towards the eastern end of Forton Lake (Fig. 4.1). The vessel's remains lie at the upper end of Forton Lake's tidal range. Much of the sediment filling the remains consists of gravel/stones as well as the mud seen on many of the other vessels. Currently both the date and the identification of the vessel are unknown, although the vessel type is almost certainly a barge of some sort. Extant remains consist of a single longitudinal timber and a series of frame ends protruding from the overlying sediment; five to the east and six to the west of the longitudinal timber.

Survey approach and methodology

The visible remains of FL29 were surveyed in the 2007 season (Fig. 4.17). This provided an outline of the probable extent of the vessel and was followed by excavation in 2008. This excavation was successfully completed despite the presence of two mooring pontoons that were sitting on the site during 2008. A test trench was dug 4 m to the north of the exposed timbers on the foreshore. Only one longitudinal timber was found; so

the trench was extended to the south up to the exposed timbers and 3 m to the west. This was nominated as trench A. Trench B was then excavated running north/south along the starboard side of the vessel. On completion of trench B a baseline was established along this side with the datum origin located at the rudder pintle. FL29 was then recorded in plan and section.

Survey results

The excavation of FL29 revealed a vessel of unusual construction, unlike any of the other vessels present around the shores of Forton Lake (Fig. 4.16). The vessel is wooden, flat-bottomed, with no keel. Construction is based around a central keelson and two large chine keelsons. As a result, the vessel can be classified as bottom- or chine-built. Six strakes of bottom planking survive and one strake of side planking. The surviving remains represent the stern of the vessel, indicated by a rudder pintle. The stern area has been severed from the rest of the vessel and this process is visible in the saw marks that survive in the ends of the keelson and chine keelsons (Fig. 4.18). The surviving remains of FL29 measure *c.* 4.8 m long, with a width of *c.* 2.65 m. The basic dimensions of the vessel remains are given in Table 4.6.

Area	Trench A		Trench B	
Element	Sided	Moulded	Sided	Moulded
Bottom planks	20 and 34 cm	8–10 cm	–	–
Side planks	30 cm	9 cm	–	–
Keelson	40 cm	30 cm	–	–
Sternpost	–	–	12 cm	20 cm
Chine keelson	30 cm	26 cm	–	–
Frames	10 cm	10 cm	–	–
Stern knee (length=1.3 m)	–	–	22 cm	–

Table 4.6   Summary of the basic dimensions of FL29

Planking

The remains of FL29 provide evidence for the nature of the bottom planking of the vessel, as well as some indication as to the characteristics of the side planking. Two strakes of bottom planking are 20 cm wide and a further two are 34 cm wide. All measure between 8–10 cm in thickness and are laid athwartships, rather than in fore-and-aft runs. The width of the remaining two strakes at the very stern of the vessel could not be measured, but their thickness was 8 cm. One strake of side planking survives on either side of the vessel. In each case this strake measured 30 cm wide and 9 cm thick. Excavation of trench B revealed that the bottom timbers extend outwards until they are flush with the lower edge of the side planking.

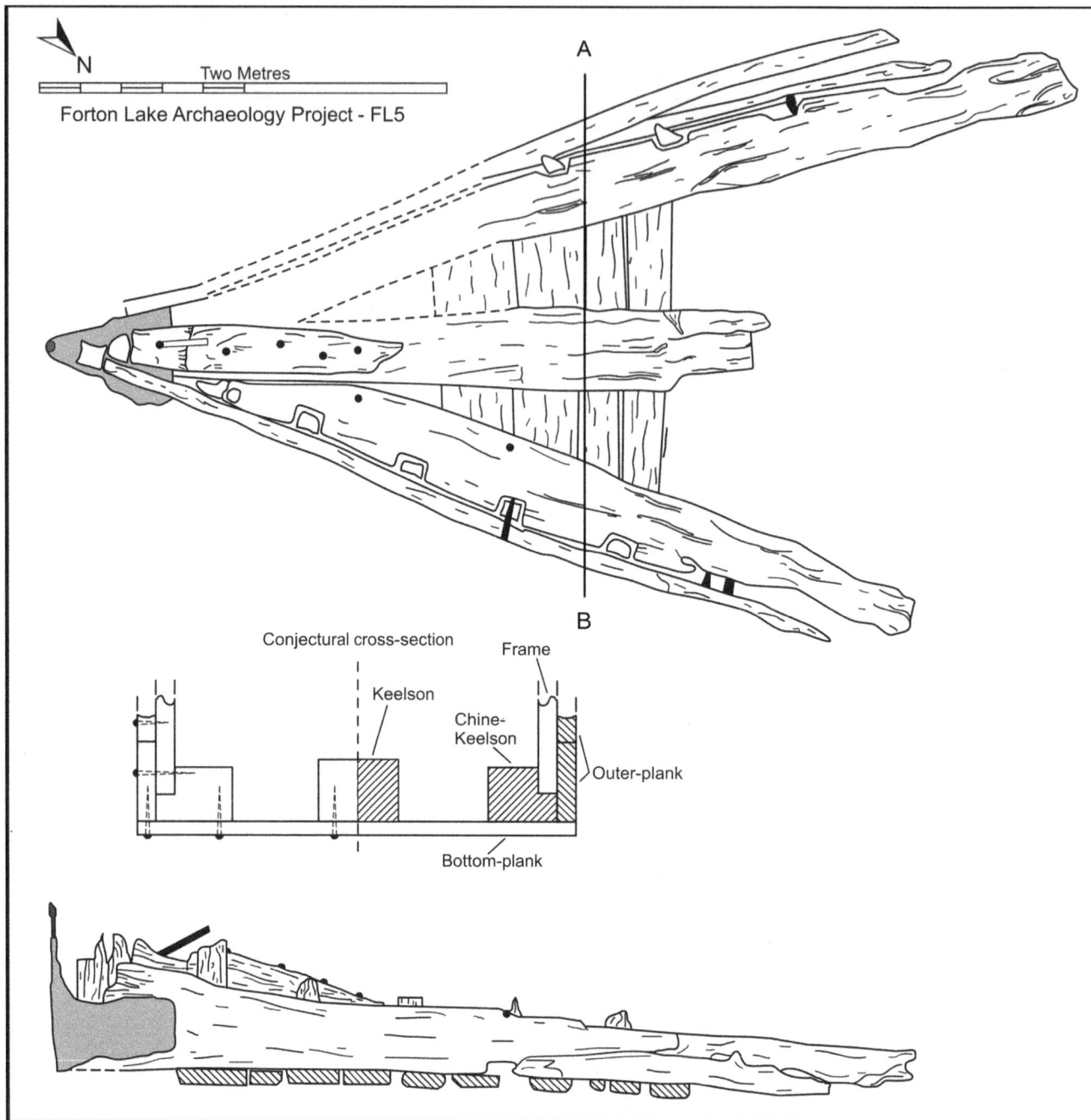

Fig. 4.16   *Plan and section of FL29 following excavation of the vessel remains.   A–B is the line of the conjectural cross-section*

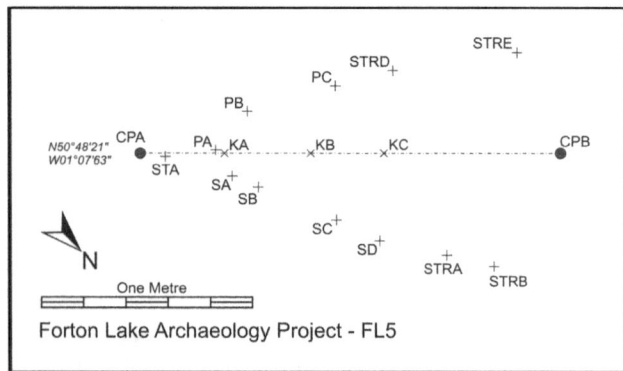

Fig. 4.17   *Results of initial offset survey of FL29*

Fig. 4.18   *Overview of the remains of FL29. The breaking up of the vessel by sawing can be seen from the clean cuts on the ends of the chine keelsons. The mooring pontoon lying across the vessel is also visible (scale=1 m)*

Fig. 4.19   The construction of FL29 is based around two chine keelsons and a central keelson. All three timbers meet at the stern of the vessel (scale=1 m)

Framing

The framing system used in the construction of FL29 is distinctive and very different from that of any of the other vessels present in Forton Lake. The vessel is built around a central keelson and two chine keelsons (Fig. 4.19). The latter run down either side of the vessel and provide the link between the bottom and side planking. The keelson is 40 cm sided and 30 cm moulded at its largest point. The chine keelsons measure 30 cm sided and 26 cm moulded. All three timbers come together at the stern of the vessel. The jointing/fastening that comprises this is unclear because of the position of the mooring pontoon. However, it seems likely that the keelson extends for the full length of the vessel and that the chine keelsons are cut to butt against the sides of the keelson (Fig. 4.20). All three elements are presumably fastened together at this point. The vessel's stern post, badly degraded, survives and measures 12 cm sided by 20 cm moulded. It is secured to the keelson by a stern knee. This extends for 1.3 m along the keelson and is 22 cm sided.

The frames of the vessel consist of vertical timbers only. Their function is simply to support the side planking. These frames are rebated into the outside of the chine keelson (Fig. 4.21). The rebates are between 12 cm and 15 cm wide. The frames are 10 cm square and fit snugly within the rebates. Frame spacing is 53 cm centre to centre.

Fastening

The fastening of FL29 is quite difficult to discern from the remains uncovered during excavation. The fastenings that are visible are either treenails or iron bolts/nails. Both of these fastenings are used to secure the single strake of surviving side planking; in particular, iron nails are used to fasten the planks to the frames in several places. Meanwhile the stern knee is secured using iron bolts/nails alone. The fastening of the bottom planks is invisible as it probably ends in the underside of the keelson and chine keelson. However, it can be suggested, based on the rest of FL29's remains, that it was probably fastened either by treenails or iron bolts/nails.

Fig. 4.20   Junction of chine-keelson and central keelson at the stern of the vessel. The stern knee, fixed to the central keelson, is visible on the right of the image (scale=30 cm)

Fig. 4.21   Frames are rebated into the chine-keelson and secured in place with iron nails driven through the outer planking (scale=1m)

Interpretation

FL29 represents the remains of a robustly built, flat-bottomed wooden barge. The vessel was laid up at the eastern end of Forton Lake, probably stern first. Following this event, the vessel was broken up and only the stern of the vessel remained on the banks of the lake. The construction of FL29 is chine/bottom-based with the chine keelsons playing a major role in determining the final shape of the vessel and providing much of its rigidity. Other surviving elements of the vessel, namely the planking, are constructed on a large scale. In contrast to this the frames of the vessel are relatively lightweight. This possibly suggests that the sides of the vessel do not extend very far in a vertical direction.

Comparative evidence for this type of vessel is limited. However, McKee (1983: 53) observes that the 'continuous transverse arrangement, where the bottom is cross-planked under chines, with or without a keelson along the centre line, is uncommon in Britain, but it is found in the once numerous narrow canal boats.' This is maybe suggestive of an origin for FL29 within the building traditions of Britain's inland, rather than coastal waterways. McKee (1983: 53) also records that the side planking is secured by nails hammered through the bottom planking into the ends of the side planking. A further comparative vessel to FL29 is the tub-boat, a cargo barge used on inland canal systems and particularly associated with the transport of coal. An example survives from the Bude Canal (Blue, 2004). This vessel is also chine-built with a cross-planked, flat-bottom. It has a swim-headed bow and stern, in contrast to the pointed stern of FL29 and does not have a central keelson. The Bude tub-boat also has the same system of frames, rebated into the chine keelson, as FL29. These are secured via iron nails hammered through the side planking, frames and into the chine keelson.

At present, little else can be said regarding FL29. While uncommon, the construction of FL29 is not unique within British watercraft and has parallels with canal barge construction related to the coal industry from the 19th century. There does not seem to be any evidence for a propeller shaft exiting the hull at the stern of the vessel.

So the vessel may predate such developments; it may have been a sailing barge of some sort or a 'dumb' barge that was towed from location to location as required. FL29 may well have been associated with the nearby naval dockyard at Portsmouth, before being broken up at Forton Lake.

Metal Barges

There are two metal barges within Forton Lake – FL6 and FL8; these represent more modern shipping and transport than the wooden examples.

FL6: Metal Barge (NGR: SU 461145, 100741; AHBR 53070)

(Julian Whitewright, Paul Donohue and Julie Satchell)

Site description

Fig. 4.22   Remains of FL6, looking north-east

The remains of FL6 are situated on the southern shore of Forton Lake, between the main cluster of vessels and The Maritime Workshop (Fig. 4.1). The vessel lies on a north/south orientation with the bow facing the creek and the stern lying embedded in gravel on the beach (Fig. 4.21). The port side of the vessel remains intact; however very little remains of the starboard side. The surviving length of the vessel measures 23.26 m and is constructed of steel plates and frames, riveted together. Surviving elements include bollards and ballast. The

latter consists of what is believed to be cylindrical blocks of concrete set into metal containers. There may also be the remains of solidified paint, in tins. Two bollards can be found on the starboard side of the vessel.

Fig. 4.23   Remains   of   FL8,   looking   north (scale=2 m)

Fig. 4.24   Remains of FL8 from one side, looking east

FL8: Possible Metal Barge (NGR: SU 461181, 100747)

(Julian Whitewright, Paul Donohue and Julie Satchell)

Site description

FL8 is located on the southern side of Forton Lake at the western edge of the main cluster of vessels (Fig. 4.1) where it becomes almost completely submerged at high tide. The vessel is the remains of a flat-bottomed steel barge (Fig. 4.23). Its date and identification are both unknown.

The vessel is double-ended, with no appreciable indication, including steerage or propulsion, of the bow or stern. It may be assumed that FL8 is the remains of an unpowered or 'dumb' barge. The surviving dimensions of the vessel are 10.71 m long and 4.72 m wide. In one area the hull survives to a height of 1.82 m. Three visible bulkheads remain in the vessel and four vertical rubbing timbers survive on the exterior of the eastern side (Fig. 4.24).

It was deemed that detailed survey would be unlikely to enhance the understanding of FL8. No further work was conducted other than to note the position of the vessel in Forton Lake and to record its basic dimensions. The function of the vessel is also unclear. It can be postulated that it may be related to naval activity in Portsmouth Harbour or at nearby Priddy's Hard.

Ferries and lifeboats

(Julie Satchell)

This section concentrates on the vessels which have been used for the transport of people – ferries and lifeboats. Ferries have developed in response to the need for particular transport routes, so their form has been dictated by the number of passengers and traffic to be ferried and the sea conditions faced. Lifeboats are designed for a very different eventuality, the rescue of passengers and crew in the event of a ship sinking, and so have evolved to be transportable on larger vessels, while fulfilling the basic needs of safety at sea. Within Forton Lake there are the remains of two ferries and two lifeboats, the former representing some of the largest vessels included in the survey, while the latter are some of the smallest.

Ferries

As the Solent region is characterized by tidal creeks and estuaries in addition to the main Solent waterway, ferries perform a vital service transporting people and goods on a regular basis. Locally there are historical references to ferries across the River Hamble from the medieval period onwards.[4] However, many services are likely to date back much further. Today there are key crossing points from the mainland to the Isle of Wight and also on a smaller scale across many of the harbours and tidal estuaries such as the Hayling Island ferry across Langstone Harbour mouth and the Hamble River service from Warsash to Hamble.

---

4 http://www.hamblelocalhistory.hampshire.org.uk/bhistory.htm

The two ferries abandoned in Forton Lake have a long history in the Solent Region; FL22, the *Vadne*, was a former Gosport ferry, while FL11 was a chain ferry which crossed the Medina River on the Isle of Wight. Both vessels have very strong historical connections with the area and are two of the best known hulks within the local community.

FL11: Medina Ferry (NGR: SU 461193, 100748; AHBR 53074)

(Julian Whitewright, Charlotte Pham, John Harbridge-Rose, Paul Donohue and Julie Satchell)

Site description

FL11 is situated on the southern side of Forton Lake. It is part of the main cluster of abandoned craft to the north-east of The Maritime Workshop boatyard (Fig. 4.1). It lies in the intertidal zone and access is restricted at high tide, but is straightforward at other states of the tide. The degraded nature of the hull means that water enters the vessel at high water. The mud on which the vessel sits becomes slightly deeper on the northern (lake) side of the vessel, but does not inhibit access.

FL11 is former chain ferry that operated on the Medina River, Isle of Wight, between 1896 and 1909. When replaced in service, the ferry remained at Cowes as a spare 'floating bridge' until 1925. Following a period of ownership by the boat designer and sailing enthusiast Uffa Fox, it was deposited in Forton Lake in 1948 where it was slowly broken up in order to be re-used to build other vessels. The current remains of FL11 consist of the basic hull form, one of the two boarding ramps, the four posts of the lifting gear, the chain ways and two water

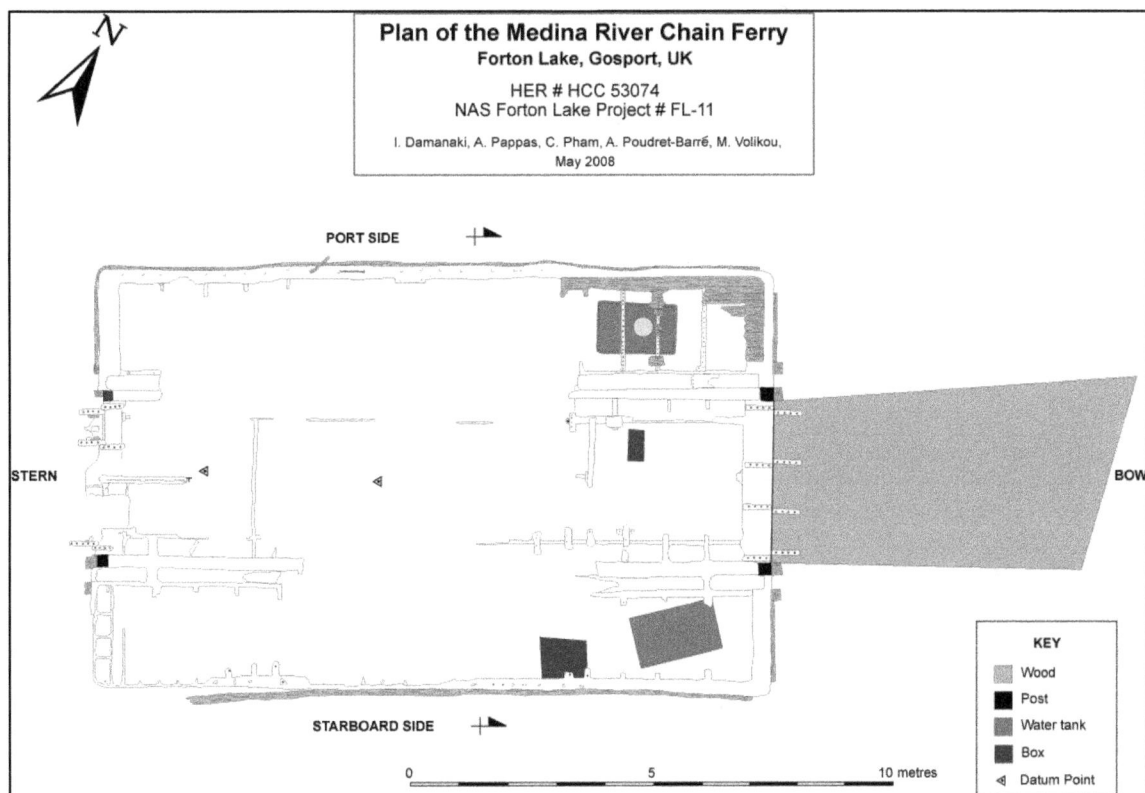

Fig. 4.25   Drawn plan of FL11

tanks. As a chain ferry, FL11 is a double-ended craft; for the purposes of the survey, the remaining boarding ramp was considered the bow of the vessel. Regular tidal action over the last sixty years has led to the hull of the vessel being badly degraded, in comparison to the areas above the tidal limit. Sediment has also become deposited within the hull. As a result of all of these factors the hull has become hogged and deformed.

Survey approach and methodology

The coherent nature of the remains of FL11 dictated that no archaeological excavation was required. A full survey of FL11 was conducted by Maritime Archaeology Masters Degree students from the University of Southampton (Charlotte Pham, Ioanna Damanaki, Maria Volikou, Alexandre Poudret-Barré and Apostolis Pappas). Their report forms the basis of this section covering FL11.

Two survey techniques were adopted. Firstly, a fully measured, drawn plan, using measured offsets from a baseline was produced at a scale of 1:40. Secondly, the site was surveyed digitally with a Leica TCR 703XR total station[5] to produce a 3D plan of the vessel, with the datum points of the total station recorded by Global Positioning System (GPS) using a Leica GPS 530. The results obtained from the total station survey confirmed the accuracy and detail of the drawn survey. Both surveys were conducted over a period of four days, working around the tide, with the full survey team of five people.

Survey results

FL11 comprises the remains a late 19th-century Medina chain ferry. Its overall length is 14.4 m, beam 8.93 m, total height 4.5 m and depth of hull 1.56 m (Plates 4.2–4.4; Fig. 4.25). The hull of the vessel is made from iron, fastened with iron bolts. The deck is constructed from wood and the boarding ramp from wood and iron.

Hull

The hull is rectangular in shape, with an overall dimension of 14.4 m x 8.93 m (length/beam). It is made from Lomore iron (Fox, 1966: 80), comprising several overlapping metal sheets riveted together. Lomore iron came from the Low Moor Iron Works near Bradford in Yorkshire and was known to be high quality and expensive 'Best Yorkshire' iron (Engvig, 2006: 110). Most of the hull is still present and has preserved some of its structural integrity, although it has high levels of corrosion. The aft starboard corner is missing as well as the stern part between the two posts where the ramp was positioned. The bottom of the hull is covered with seaweed and mud, the depth of which varies significantly. A timber wale runs along the hull, just below the shear and probably functioned as a rubbing strake (Plate 4.5). The wood has lost its physical strength due to the ongoing effects of the tide and its submerged/emerged state. It is cracked and splitting at different locations.

---

5 A total station is an electronic theodolite integrated with an electronic distance meter to read slope distances from the instrument to a particular point.

The inside of the hull is divided longitudinally and transversely into different compartments with bulkheads (Plate 4.6). These are only partially preserved and mainly towards the bow. Some segments of the longitudinal bulkhead on the starboard side are still present, and still have a small rounded door/opening. The bulkhead on the bow side is better preserved and presents a circular opening of *c.* 60 cm. There are remains of the same features on the bulkhead of the stern side. Two tanks are present within the bow compartments on either side of the vessel (Plate 4.7). It is suggested from Fox's description that they were water tanks, rather than fuel tanks. Fox stipulated clearly that he removed all parts of the engine from the ferry and that he collected rain water (Fox, 1966: 82), presumably in the vessel's water tanks. Three out of four mooring rings are still present (Plate 4.5). Two are on the bow and one on the stern. The absent ring must have been located on the missing part of the stern.

Only one of the two boarding ramps survives (Plate 4.8). It is 7.45 m long, 4.27 m wide and is made out of wooden transverse planks set on a metal frame. The hinge fastening system between the ramp and the hull is still visible. Four pairs of hinges are bolted to the metal frame at 50-cm intervals and are connected to a main hinge-pin (Plate 4.9). The ramp is almost entirely covered with seaweed and becomes completely submerged during high tide. There is a breach in the central part, which weakens the whole structure. The ramps were originally both flanked by two posts, one to either side, that were used to lift them. All four of these lifting posts are still standing. They are approximately 3 m high and 24 cm square. They are made of wood, covered by a three-sided metal case. Each post is mounted by a metal cap, slightly wider than the rest of the posts. The wood is quite dry and the metal is rusted.

The chain-ways are still visible and are located next to the ramps (Plates 4.10–4.11). The two chains attached to the river bank would go through the hull in the chain-ways on the port and starboard sides. The chain-ways are about 40 cm in width, and are set at a slight angle to the hull (*c.* 35°). Three of the four chain-ways are preserved to a length of *c.* 4 m, with the one on the port quarter being shorter, *c.* 1 m. On the outside of the hull, thick pieces of wood 24 cm in width are bolted around the opening of the chain way. On the inside, two U-shaped metal features are present on each side of the chain way, possibly supporting some sort of wheel used to help it stay in a straight line. They are situated near to the opening and are part of the mechanism.

Superstructure

The whole superstructure is missing. Only a small fragment of the wooden deck survives on the port bow corner, which indicates that the deck planking was 8 cm in width. It must be assumed that this deck originally extended along the entire length and width of the hull of the vessel. The deck was supported by a series of transverse iron beams. Some of these survive, but none is intact to its full length; they vary from 14 cm to 30 cm wide (Plate 4.7). The original nature of the superstructure

Fig. 4.26   FL11 landing on the Medina at Cowes, c. 1903 (courtesy of www.simplonpc.co.uk)

Fig. 4.27   Inside of the 'summer bridge', Uffa Fox's workshop (courtesy of Hampshire Magazine)

can be derived from old photographs showing FL11 in use (Fig. 4.26).

Framing

The hull is reinforced by L-shaped iron frames, placed every 40 cm (Plate 4.12). The overlapping metal sheets, the fastening and the frames are only visible from the inside. Iron knees are positioned every two frames to support the deck. Additionally, on the central part of the port side, four other knees protrude and are situated at the middle height of the same frames.

Fastening

The vessel is primarily fastened together with iron bolts

31

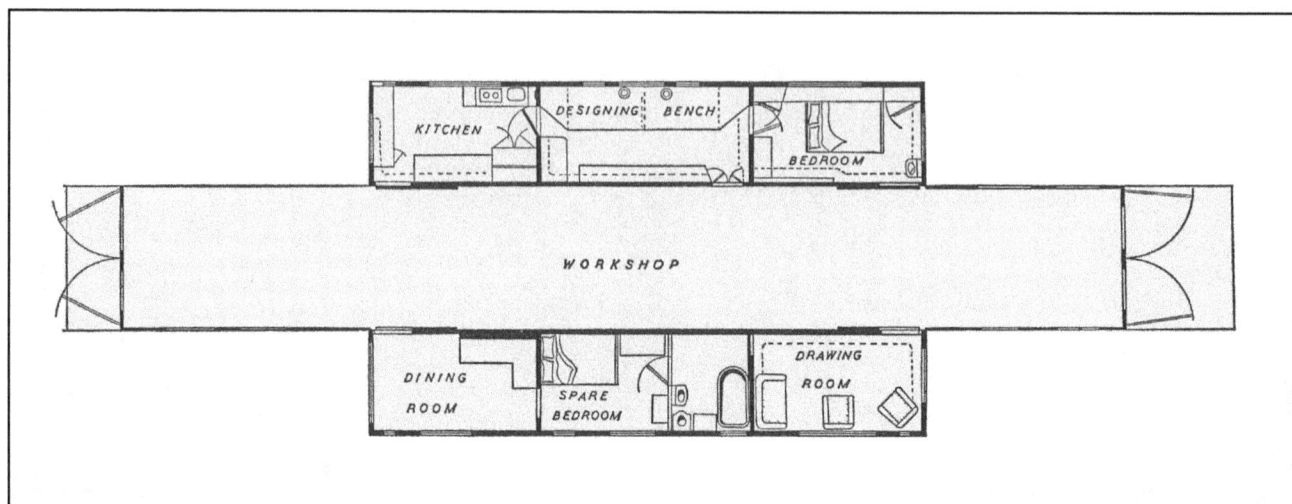

Fig. 4.28   Plan of Uffa Fox's converted workshop (Fox, 1966: 81). Reproduced by permission of Tony Dixon

and rivets. Sections of the iron sheets used to make the hull are riveted together. Meanwhile, elements such as frames, deck timbers and rubbing strakes are bolted into place (Plate 4.13).

Discussion

FL11 is former chain ferry that operated on the Medina River, Isle of Wight between 1896 and 1909. It was constructed by William White and Sons at Vectis Works, Cowes in 1896. Following its replacement in 1909, the ferry remained in Cowes as a spare 'floating bridge' until 1925. The vessel is flat-bottomed, with an access ramp at either end. A lifting system enabled these ramps to be raised and lowered to embark and disembark passengers, animals and vehicles. The deck of the ferry was open to the elements. On either side, at each corner of the deck, two cabins provided shelter to the passengers. The boiler and a small coal bunker were located between the two cabins on one side, while the other side hosted the steam engine and big copper pipes, through which the steam would circulate. Below, the iron hull hid the larger coal bunkers, the water and oil storage tanks, spare gear and a workbench (Fox, 1966: 80). The Medina ferry was steam powered. This would drive the two wheels located onboard the vessel. The cogs of the wheels would drag the ferry along the chain path. The chain itself was heavy enough to sink below the surface as the ferry moved away, allowing other vessels to use the river uninhibited.

Following the end of its useful life as a spare ferry in 1925, FL11 was sold for £150 to Uffa Fox (Fox, 1966: 79). As a prominent boat designer, Fox (1898–1972)[6] transformed the former chain ferry into a workshop and house that became known as the 'Summer Bridge'. He roofed the central part of the ferry and turned it into a workshop area (Figs 4.27 and 4.28). The ramp at one end formed a gangway to the shore and the other became a slipway for launching boats into the river. The boiler and steam engine were removed and sold. Where they were once located, he turned the space into a designing office and a spare bedroom. The passenger cabins were

converted into a kitchen and bedroom on one side, whilst on the other side they became a dining room and drawing room or lounge. The large tanks that held water for the boiler were cleaned and cement-washed and served as recipients for rain water used for domestic use.

In *c.* 1948 FL11 was sold to a Gosport shipbuilder (Adams, 1986: 116). The vessel was acquired in order to re-use certain parts for the construction of other vessels. At the same time it was moved to Forton Lake. By 1981 all the elements of the operating mechanism and superstructure had been removed and the vessel began to deteriorate.

Mechanical chain ferries have been utilized at twenty locations throughout the UK since their invention in 1799, with over 80 such vessels constructed in total. Only seven ferries are currently in operation, including one that crosses the River Dart at Dartmouth, the Windermere Ferry across Lake Windermere, the Torpoint Ferry across the Tamar River in Devon and the King Harry Ferry on the River Fal in Cornwall (Plate 4.14). Within the wider Solent region, examples still operate across the Medina River and the mouth of Poole Harbour, those at Southampton and Portsmouth being no longer in use. Chain ferries similar to FL11 are not a common vessel within the UK and no chain ferries are currently registered in the National Historic Ships Register.

The locations of three other chain ferries of late Victorian date are currently known within the UK. The Southampton floating bridge No.8 (built 1896) currently serves as a floating restaurant at Bursledon, Hampshire; its engines are cared for by Southampton City Council. Walney Island floating bridge No.1 (1878) is buried under a car park at Bursledon, Hampshire. Southampton floating bridge No.9 (1900) sank while under tow off Selsey Bill in 1974. The Reedham No.1 ferry (1914) is now abandoned on Reedham Marshes, Norfolk (John Harbridge-Rose, pers. comm.).[7]

---

6   http://www.uffafox.com/uffabiog.htm

7   John Harbridge-Rose is a maritime historian, who maintains his own detailed archive of all known United Kingdom chain ferries, including a complete history of FL11.

Fig. 4.29   General view of Vadne *(FL22), looking east*

Fig. 4.30   General view of Vadne's *(FL22) bow, looking north*

FL22: Vadne (Gosport Ferry) (NGR: SU 461226, 100771; AHBR 57876)

(Julian Whitewright, Daniel Karmy, Paul Donohue and Julie Satchell)

Site description

FL22 is located on the southern shore of Forton Lake at the eastern side of the main cluster of hulks (Fig. 4.1). It is one of the most prominent craft laid up on the shores of the lake because its hull is relatively intact and its location is adjacent to nearby residential housing. The vessel is beached bow first towards the top of the tidal range on a north/south alignment (Fig. 4.29). Identification of the vessel is straightforward because of the survival of the vessel's name on the bow (Fig. 4.30). FL22 is the *Vadne*, a former Gosport Ferry. As such it has an immediate link with many of the local residents who used it to travel to and from Portsmouth. Although it is in a seemingly complete condition, there has been substantial degradation of the hull from gradual rusting and the development of holes in the hull. The majority of the vessel's internal fittings have been removed.

Survey approach and methodology

A limited amount of archaeological recording was undertaken on FL22. This involved a record of the vessel's location, basic dimensions and a photographic survey for the purpose of long-term monitoring of the rate of decay of FL22.

Survey results

The dimensions of the hull are 23.32 m long, 5.75 m wide and a height to the sheer of 3.22 m. FL22 was propelled by a twin-cylinder steam engine and had a registered net tonnage of 33.84 tons. It is constructed from steel plates, fastened with rivets to a steel frame (Fig. 4.31). Large amounts of the superstructure remain, including the funnel (Fig. 4.32). Much of the wooden deck survives, particularly in the stern half of the vessel, and this deck remains accessible, having retained a large amount of its integrity. Other surviving elements include; keel, floors, hull exterior, metal knees, guardrails, bulkheads, rudder and rubbing strakes at the bow.

Inside the vessel, it is possible to gain access as far aft as the third and largest compartment directly below the funnel area. From what can be seen from this compartment, the aftermost area begins slightly aft of the skylight located near the funnel on the top deck. However due to extensive corrosion and rotting planks coupled with flooding and a large amount of debris, this area should be considered to be extremely hazardous and entry should not be attempted. In addition, the underside of the hull in particular has long since begun to rot and the curve of the bottom of the hull leaves the stern section of the vessel unsupported by the lake bed and therefore liable to collapse. No structural components are visible in the sternmost section.

Throughout the vessel numerous pipes and wires can be found running its entire length. The second compartment from the bow is divided lengthways into two sections by an iron bar, 5 cm wide. A second bar runs at right angles to this (athwartships), splitting the compartment into four areas in total. These bars may originally have been intended to aid the structural integrity of the vessel. Both bars are welded to larger iron strips which run around the inner hull. However, this arrangement is not evident anywhere else within the *Vadne*.

On the port side, between the second compartment and the third compartment, attached to the hull is a small fuse box and hanging from it are several white cables. The fuse box is constructed from plastic and therefore cannot have been part of the original vessel, which was built before plastic was universally used. It will have been added later on in *Vadne*'s career.

Overall the vessel has corroded extensively and is in an advanced state of decay, though this is not fully evident from the condition of the outer hull and upper deck. In due course, the state of the *Vadne* will worsen gradually; however at the present time the vessel retains a degree of its integrity. Being the most exposed, the upper structures and deck of the vessel are most vulnerable to the ongoing effects of weathering and human interference. When comparing a photograph of *Vadne* during the attempted restoration project in 1981–83 with more recent photographs, it is evident that a great amount of decay has occurred. Though what is left of the upper decking itself remains intact and has retained its integrity, the strength of the metal plates on which it is placed can be brought into considerable doubt. Years of neglect and constant weathering have led to gradual rusting which has weakened the structural integrity of the vessel. Holes have formed as a result of this rusting, which have allowed water into the vessel to the extent that all of its compartments are flooded at high tide (Fig. 4.33).

Discussion

Vadne was built in 1939 by Vosper of Portsmouth, the first of the Portsmouth Harbour steam ferries to be built by that firm as a foot passenger ferry. The vessel worked for a short time for the Port of Portsmouth Steam Launch and Towing Company (the 'New Company'), before being requisitioned by the Navy. The Navy used *Vadne* as an examination vessel until 1943 when it was shipped out to Freetown, Sierra Leone, to serve as a tender. *Vadne* remained in West Africa for three years before being returned to its owners in 1946, continuing to serve as a ferry. In 1963 ownership of *Vadne*, along with its three contemporaries (*Vita*, *Venus*, and *Vesta*) passed from the 'New Company' to the newly formed Portsmouth Harbour Ferry Company. *Vadne* continued to be used at peak periods only until 1965, when it was sold to the Gosport Cruising Club as a floating clubhouse. *Vadne* continued in this role until 1981, when corrosion of the hull resulted in it sinking at its moorings. Despite efforts to repair the breach with concrete during a

Fig. 4.31   Internal view of Vadne (FL22) illustrating hull and frame fastenings as well as accumulated debris

Fig. 4.32   View of the deck and superstructure of Vadne (FL22) on the starboard side, looking forwards. Note the missing deck in the bow area of the vessel

Fig. 4.33   *Photograph of the inner compartments of* Vadne *(FL22) flooded at high tide in February 2008, looking aft from the bow area (photo: Dan Karmy)*

Fig. 4.34   Vadne *ferrying passengers across Portsmouth Harbour*

restoration project which took place between 1981 and 1983, the vessel had become unusable. *Vadne* was initially abandoned near the Forton Lake bridge from 1983 until 2000/2001 when it was towed to its current location further up the lake.

For many of the inhabitants of Gosport this vessel would have played an important role in their daily lives, as a local ferry in the 1950s. During the survey and investigations at Forton Lake a number of people came forward with anecdotal evidence regarding this vessel. Much of this can be corroborated by references to photographs of the vessel and newspaper reports. Mr Eric Walker recollected that passengers used to stand on the upper deck of *Vadne* with their bicycles leaning against the vessel's railing. The scene is visible in one of the photographs of *Vadne* carrying passengers across Portsmouth Harbour (Fig. 4.34). Many of the passengers on the ferry, especially in the mornings and evenings, were employees of the dockyard across the water or workers at what was then the HMS Vernon naval training establishment. Mr Smith, who was one of those workers and travelled on *Vadne* during his career, noted that the journey was much more unsteady than at the present time. However he also pointed out that for himself and his fellow passengers, the only significance *Vadne* would have had was as a ferry boat; because of this, as a part of everyday life, it was not seen as particularly significant at that time.

Another resident recalled an attempt by the ferry company to increase the internal size of the *Vadne* by removing a bulkhead. However, this severely weakened the structural integrity of the vessel to the extent that it had to be removed from service. This modification signalled the end of the vessel's use as a ferry and *Vadne* was sold to the Gosport Cruising Club.

Mr George Akhurst also recalled the *Vadne*. He commented that '... the *Vadne* is the biggest size you can build a boat without a lifeboat'. This perhaps tallies with the perception of *Vadne* as being a slightly unsafe vessel for passengers. This was added to by two unfortunate incidents. In the early 1950s a passenger fell into the sea while boarding the vessel, but fortunately was saved. Later, *Vadne* was involved in the only fatality in the ferry company's 125-year history. This occurred early in the morning of 13 July 1957. *Vadne* was on the return trip to the Gosport pontoon, about a quarter of the way through the journey, when it struck the warship HMS *Redpole* (a Black Swan modified escort class). The force of the impact was great and many passengers, caught unawares, were flung towards the bow section of the vessel. Shortly after impact, the ferry *Vesta* answered calls for help, coming to the aid of passengers and taking them back to the Portsmouth pontoon, while dockyard workers helped tow the ailing vessel back to shore.

One of the passengers was Mr Reginald H. Bartlett, aged 65 years, who was standing at the sternmost end of the *Vadne* during the collision. On impact he was thrown forward and struck his head on the engine room skylight, knocking him unconscious. When the vessel was towed back to the Portsmouth pontoon, he was transported by ambulance to a nearby hospital, but suffered a heart attack and died (*Portsmouth Evening News*, 13 July 1957).

The collision with HMS *Redpole* severely damaged *Vadne's* bow section and a large hole was torn in the port bow, which caused the vessel to flood up to a foot below the upper decking. Over the next two weeks, the hole in the hull was repaired and the bows hammered and riveted back into shape. *Vadne* was returned to service by August 1957.

Lifeboats

An important aspect of life at sea is ensuring the safety of those onboard. The construction of larger ships in the late 19th- and early 20th-centuries meant more people could travel on individual vessels. However, requirements for safety were not as stringent as modern day, with the requirement for lifeboats being based on the tonnage of the vessel rather than the number of individuals onboard. In the early 20th century only vessels of 10,000 tons and over had to carry any lifeboats. This changed after the sinking of the Titanic in April 1912 when there was tragic loss of life due to the lack of sufficient lifeboats; this led to the requirement for all ships to carry enough lifeboat capacity for all passengers onboard.

Evidence of this is found in Forton Lake with the remains of two lifeboats, one is substantially intact (FL21) with very little of the other one surviving (FL30). Although these were boats carried on other vessels, their history is just as important, making them equally deserving of recording for the future.

FL21: Lifeboat (NGR: SU 461207, 100776)

(Julian Whitewright, Paul Donohue and Julie Satchell)

Site description

FL21 is located on the southern side of Forton Lake within the main group of vessel remains and rests inside the hull of FL20 (Figs 4.1 and 4.35; page 49). The vessel is totally submerged at high tide and the remains of both FL21 and FL20 are surrounded by deep sediments.

The vessel represents the remains of a ship's lifeboat; it is likely to be relatively modern in date. FL21 is 9.96 m long, 2.25 m wide and is constructed of riveted steel plate, reinforced with ribs. An internal bulkhead survives at the stern of the vessel. As access to the vessel was difficult because of the deep sediments, only its location and overall dimensions were recorded.

FL30: Lifeboat (NGR: SU 461243 100915)

(Julian Whitewright, Paul Donohue and Julie Satchell)

Site description

FL30 is situated on the northern side of Forton Lake, approximately 10 m to the west of FL2 (Fig. 4.1). The remains of the vessel lie near to the high water mark, making access relatively easy. The vessel itself is

Fig. 4.35   FL21, resting inside the remains of
FL20, looking north (scale=2 m)

virtually gone, leaving only the keel along with the lifting
gear at the bow and stern to survive (Fig. 4.36).
However, these were enough to indicate that FL30 is the
remains of a ship's lifeboat. The dating of the vessel is
uncertain, although it is likely to be relatively modern.

Survey approach and methodology

The vessel was recorded using the datum offset method to
produce a basic site plan.

Survey results

The results of the survey of FL30 are shown in Fig. 4.38.
The surviving length of the vessel is 7.60 m; this includes
a steel keel strip. The keel strip measures 5 m long and
4 cm wide. The remnants of concrete ballast are located
either side of the keel. At either end of the vessel, the
steel lifting hooks survive (Fig. 4.37).

Discussion

Little more can be said with certainty regarding FL30.
The vessel represents the remains of a ship's lifeboat, of a
type that was deployed using a davit. This was attached
to the vessel using the hooks that are located in the bow
and stern.

Fig. 4.36   Remains of FL30, looking south-east
(scale=1 m)

Fig. 4.37   FL30, remains of the bow lifting hook
(scale=1 m)

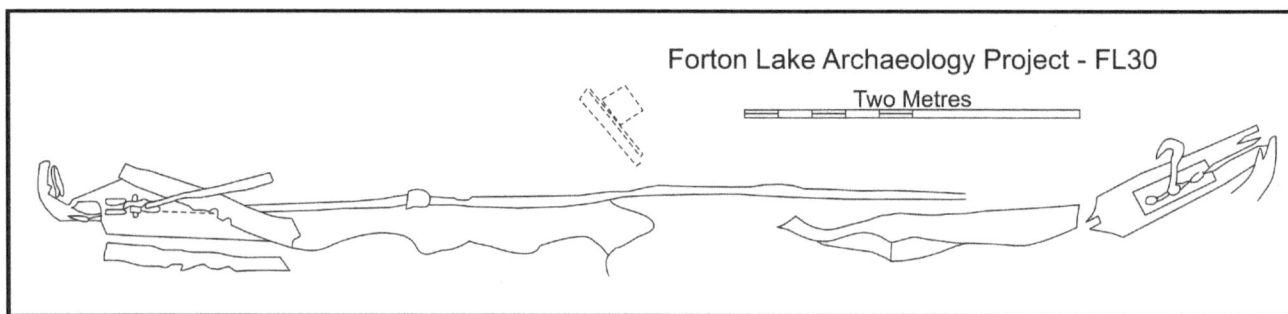

Fig. 4.38   Plan of the remains of FL30

Fishing vessels

(Jane Maddocks and Mark Beattie-Edwards)

From the survey work undertaken during the project and
from subsequent research it is believed that at least three
of the vessels at Forton Lake are the remains of
Motorized Fishing Vessels (MFVs). From both the
vessel dimensions and the boatyard sales records, it is
thought likely that some of these may be Admiralty
MFVs which were used during the Second World War
by the Royal Naval Patrol Service (RNPS), also known as

Harry Tate's Navy or Churchill's Pirates. As such they
would have carried out a variety of jobs, from acting as
fleet tenders, fireboats, coastal patrols to mine
countermeasures. Because the vessels were built in many
small boatyards around Britain, sometimes scantlings
would vary if the necessary material was not available.
Some MFVs were specifically built for use overseas with
several 90 ft (27.4 m) MFVs built for service in
Singapore and the South China Seas, which were given
copper sheathing.

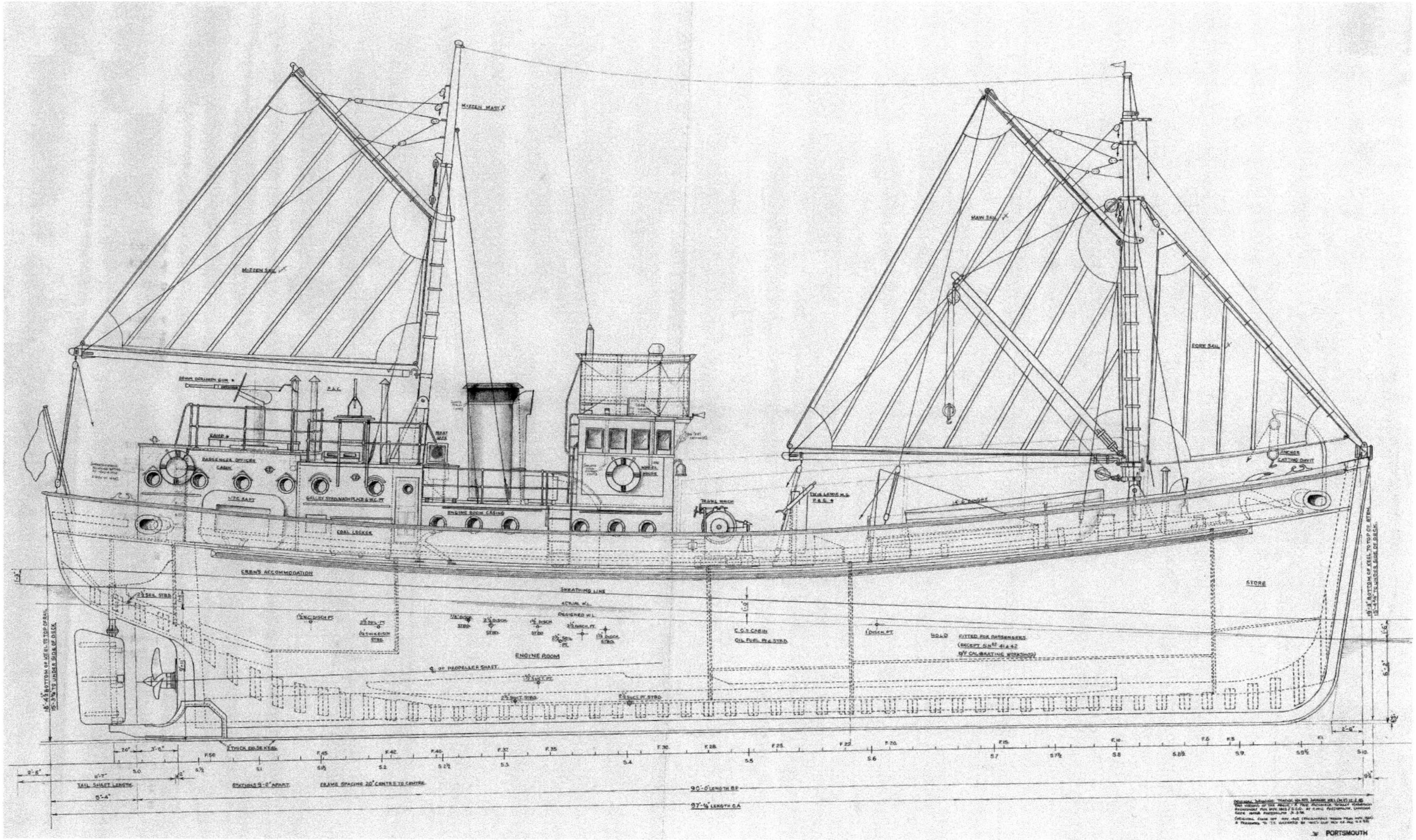

Fig. 4.39   General arrangement of a 90 ft MFV (courtesy of David Fricker, drawn from an original held by Charts Maintenance Unit, HM Portsmouth Naval Base in 1994)

Date	Vessel	Number	Engined	Price
Aug 54	61½ ft MFV	180	Engine unmentioned	£200
Aug 54	61½ ft MFV	29	Kelvin K4 88hp diesel	£800
Aug 55	45 ft MFV	995	Engine poor	£350
Oct 55	45 ft MFV	955	Engine Poor	£350
Nov 55	75 ft MFV	1132	Lister diesel 160hp	£1,200
Nov 55	75 ft MFV	1019	Lister diesel 160hp	£1,200
Jan 56	61½ ft MFV	41	Kelvin diesel seized	£700
Nov 56	75 ft MFV	1106	Lister dismantled	Offers
Apr 57	61½ ft MFV	49	Kelvin K4 diesel	Offers
Apr 57	61½ ft MFV	302	Lister diesel	Offers
May 57	61½ ft MFV	270	Waddop Engine	Offers
May 57	90 ft MFV	1564 *Sybella*	Crossley diesel 240hp	Offers
May 57	75 ft MFV	1204	Lister diesel 160hp	Offers
Jul 57	61½ ft MFV	201	Lister diesel	Offers
Oct 57	61½ ft MFV	106	Lister diesel 120hp	Offers
Feb 58	61½ ft MFV	179	Widdop diesel	Offers
Mar 58	75 ft MFV	1030	Lister diesel	Offers
Mar 58	75 ft MFV	1080	Lister diesel	Offers
Mar 58	75 ft MFV	1203	Lister diesel	Offers
Jul 58	45 ft MFV	669	Atlantic diesel	Offers
Aug 58	75 ft MFV	1029	Lister 4cyl diesel	Offers

Table 4.7   List of MFVs (including non-admiralty MFVs) on sale from the F.J. Watts Boatyard between 1951 and 1959

Admiralty MFVs were built in four sizes – 45 ft (13.7 m), 61½ ft (18.7 m) (often simplified to 60 ft (18.3 m)), 75 ft (22.9 m) and 90 ft (27.4 m) (Holt, 1946: 295; Fig. 4.39) and can be considered as the last type of wooden vessel built for a fighting or naval support purpose. MFVs were expressly designed to carry a large outfit of sails with some MFVs sailing under canvas on voyages of many thousands of miles. As such, they clearly represent the end of a direct line of the long tradition of carvel sailing craft (David Fricker, pers. comm.). One of the best known survivors of this Class, MFV Number 1502 was commissioned in January 1944, having been built by Richards Ironworks of Lowestoft (Fig. 4.40). From 1965, MFV 1502 was used by Royal Corps of Transport and became famous as RCTV *Yarmouth Navigator*. By 1976 MFV 1502 had been changed over to civilian manning and was attached to the Fleet Squadron 20 Maritime Regiment based at Gunwharf in Portsmouth. MFV 1502 is now been restored and is in private ownership and

recorded as vessel number 1384 on the National Register of Historic Ships (NRHS).[8]

In trying to determine the identity of the MFVs at Forton Lake it has been possible, from sale records of craft disposed of by the F.J. Watts Boatyard between 1951 and 1959, to identify three 45 ft MFVs, nine 61½ ft MFVs, one 90 ft MFV, as well as eight 75 ft (non-Admiralty type) MFVs (Table 4.7 and Appendix A).

FL1: Motorized Fishing Vessel (MFV) (NGR: SU 461550, 100865)

(Paul Donohue, Julian Whitewright and Jane Maddocks)

Site Description

FL1 is a large wooden vessel located on the southern bank of Forton Lake, 150 m to the west of the Millennium Bridge (Fig. 4.1). It lies stranded in the inter-

8   http://www.nationalhistoricships.org.uk/ships_register.php? action =ship&id=1384

Fig. 4.40   MFV 1502. In this photograph the wheelhouse has already been modified (courtesy of David Fricker)

tidal zone beside a small drainage culvert in the adjacent bank. The relatively intact nature of the hull construction presents good opportunities for survey. The vessel lies on its starboard side, partially buried in sediments, with the bow to the south, and the stern to the north. During the course of the project two large mooring pontoons intruded into the site and in 2007 lay partly within the vessel's structure (Plate 4.15). In 2008 the pontoons were no longer *in situ*, allowing a more detailed survey to be done.

Survey approach and methodology

The nature of the sediments meant that survey work was undertaken on the inside of the hull. A baseline was established in the centre of the vessel with the datum origin at the centre of frame five towards the bow. A further baseline was positioned between frame five and the stem post, to record the bow structure. The vessel was recorded in plan and section. Section lines were established along the baseline where the frames of the vessels crossed the baseline.   Seven sections were recorded in total to give an overall representation of the vessel from bow to stern and an extensive photographic record was made.

Survey results

The remains of FL1 measure approximately 27.6 m (90 ft 6 in) and approximately 6.0 m (19 ft 8 in) at the widest point, although it was not possible to confirm the overall width, as frames had been truncated by sawing through, probably for salvage. The vessel is carvel built with the timber strakes lying flush; the planks of these strakes are fastened to the frames by metal pins. The run of the strakes finishes at the stem post, which is narrow at the front. In front of the stem post a false stem has been attached. On the inside of the bow section there is a short run of ceiling planking. As the frames run directly into the keel at the bow the first four floor timbers have a higher vertical section than those found on the rest of the vessel and are attached to the aft side of the bow frames and the keelson. Concrete has been placed in the bow section to act as ballast (Plate 4.16; Fig. 4.41).

The frames of FL1 are composite, consisting of two timbers side by side that are vertically staggered to maintain strength (Plate 4.17). Between many of the frames there is evidence of concrete ballast. No ceiling planking is visible in the main section of the vessel aft of the bow. At the base of the hull there is a keelson that runs throughout the whole vessel. Beside this there is another sturdy longitudinal timber, which is a bilge keelson. This runs from the last of the four bow floor timbers, but it is not present at the stern.

At the stern, significant elements of the structure remain (Plate 4.18).   These include a curved stern post which

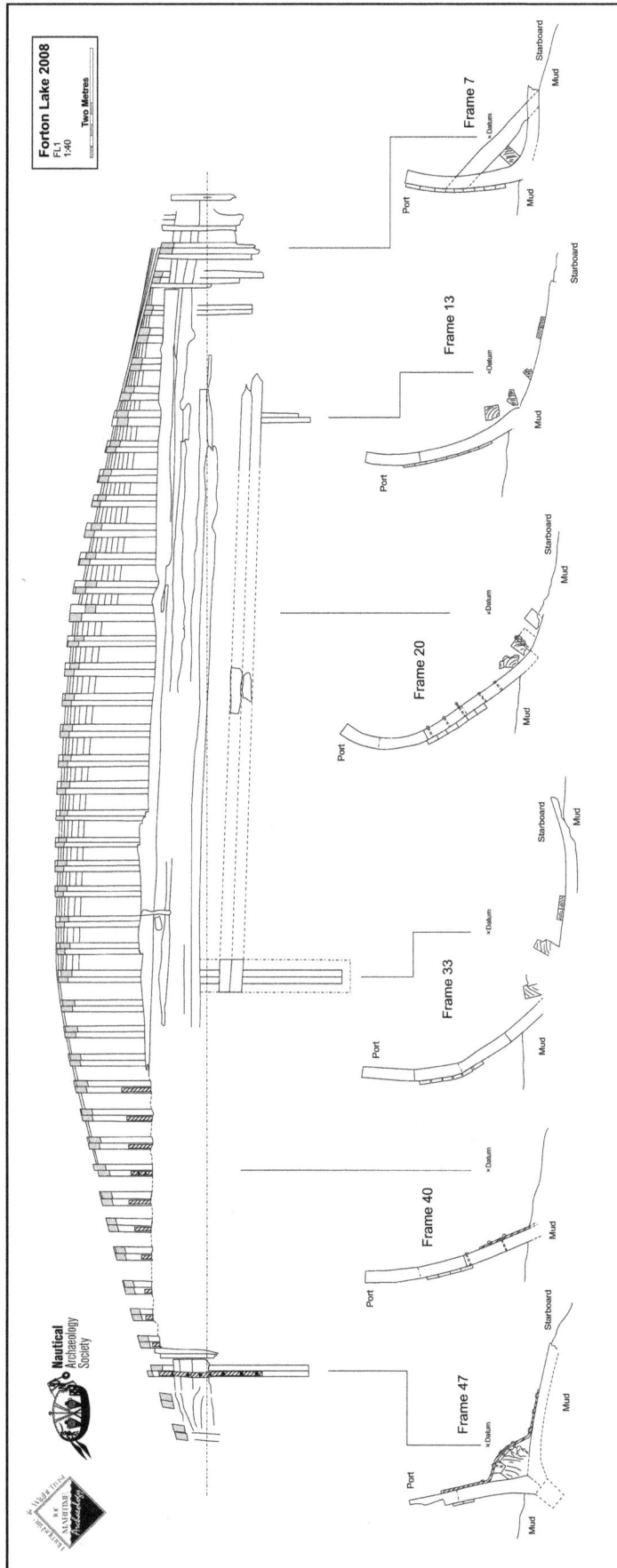

Fig. 4.41   FL1: Plan and section

gives an impression of how the buttock[9] of the vessel would have looked. Forward of this is the rudder stock. The rudder stock extends through the keel and underneath the vessel. Part of a rudder stay can be seen attached to the stock, but the rest of the rudder has disappeared. Forward of the rudder stock there is an inner post with a knee attached. The knee supports the inner-post and runs aft.

Planking

The outer planking is 18 cm wide and 3 cm thick and is fastened to the frames by large metal pins.

Framing

The vessel remains consists of 49 pairs of composite frames. The frames consist of floor timbers, futtocks and top timbers, which are sandwiched between the keel and the keelson. The individual timbers of the futtocks and top timbers making up the composite frames are 10 cm sided and 20 cm–22 cm moulded. The keelson lies on top of the floor timbers, its shape and dimensions changing from bow to stern. At frame seven, 4.60 m from the bow, it is 22 cm sided and 28 cm moulded. At frame 47, towards the stern, its maximum dimensions are 60 cm sided and 40 cm moulded. Unfortunately the keelson is not intact around the midships area of the vessel. The evidence from the remains of the keelson suggests it is more robustly constructed towards the stern. Aft of frame 37, iron strapping is fixed across the floor timbers and keelson providing reinforcement. The iron strapping is fixed to the keelson and floors by iron pins. The strapping is 10 cm wide and 1 cm thick. Beside the keelson is another timber, identified as a bilge keelson.

Other features

The physical evidence suggests that this vessel has been subject to salvage after being left in Forton Lake. The upper sections of the frames are flat, indicating they have been sawn off. There are other vertical saw marks at numerous locations around the hull (Plate 4.17). These marks seem to be common on vessels which have been partially salvaged and it is possible that these marks are associated with removing materials such as copper piping. The commercial value of copper makes it attractive to salvors and any wiring or piping is likely to have been sawn out.

Discussion

FL1 seems to conform to the design for a 90 ft Admiralty Type MFV. The records of disposal by the F.J. Watts Boatyard for May 1957 list one 90 ft MFV, identified as Number 1564 (*Sybella*), being sold with a 240 hp Crossley diesel engine. This is unlikely to be FL1, as a vessel of the appropriate size appears to be present in its current site in an aerial photograph from the RAF taken in February 1949. In this photograph the vessel seems

Fig. 4.42   *Possible MFV photographed in 1949 in the present location of FL1. The presence of the foremast is indicated by the shadow cast by the afternoon sun*

to have the decks intact; there is some evidence of superstructure and the foremast at least is still upright (Fig. 4.42). It has proved difficult to establish the identity of FL1, because of the lack of an identifying number and further research is ongoing.

A 90 ft MFV would be diesel powered, achieve a speed of just over nine knots, have sleeping spaces fitted for ten crew and have an operational endurance between 240 and 460 hours (Colin Poole, pers. comm.). There is no evidence of copper sheathing on the hull of FL1 and as such it is possible that the vessel may have served solely in the UK. Concrete was used routinely as ballast in Admiralty Type MFVs with a 90 ft MFV needing approximately nine tons of concrete ballast. The concrete ballast still evident in this vessel adds weight to the interpretation that FL1 is an Admiralty Type MFV. The location of FL1 is at least 600 m east of the F.J. Watts Boatyard and approximately 400 m from the main concentration of abandoned craft at the end of Parham Road. As yet the reasons for the vessel being abandoned here are unknown. Further investigation is needed to see if it is possible to establish the pennant number of this MFV and subsequently its service history.

There is one 90 ft MFV on the NRHS and there are at least three others still in private hands and capable of going to sea. Records of Admiralty Type MFVs are held by the Naval Historical Branch (NHB) in Portsmouth and log books from a number of vessels are held in the National Archives at Kew. Although it should be treated with caution, Wikipedia has a useful section on Naval Trawlers and some material, including an extensive reading list, is available from the RNPS web site.[10] There are also a number of ship models in its collection (Chris Broad, pers. comm.). The Institute of Naval Architects also has plans for MFVs of this class.

---

9   'That part abaft the after body, which is bounded by the fashion pieces, and by the wing transom, and the upper or second water-line' (Smyth, 1867: *Sailor's Word-bk.*, s.v. buttock).

10   http://en.wikipedia.org/wiki/Naval_trawler and http://www.rnps.lowestoft.org.uk/rnpsbooks.htm

FL2: Motorized Fishing Vessel (MFV) (NGR: SU 461243, 100915; AHBR 53066)

(Paul Donohue, Julian Whitewright and Jane Maddocks)

Site description

The remains of FL2 lie on the north side of Forton Lake in an east-west orientation (Fig. 4.1). The vessel remains lean to port, leaving that side of the hull mainly buried in soft sediments. These sediments allow access quite freely around the whole hull. The starboard side is fully visible with some degree of damage noted in the interior.

Survey approach and methodology

In 2006 a preliminary survey was undertaken on FL2. This survey included photographs, basic measurements of length and breadth, the observation of structural detail and the recording of position information. Following the preliminary 2006 research, local knowledge suggested that the remains were that of MFV *Lauren* (Bill Puddle, pers. comm.) and that, as the name of the hulk was believed to be known, a comprehensive survey was recommended. Following this recommendation, project volunteers undertook a detailed survey in 2008 under the direction of Julian Whitewright.

A baseline was established in the centre of the vessel from bow to stern, with the datum origin at the stern. The vessel was then recorded in plan and in section. Section lines were established where the frames of the vessel crossed the baseline. Three sections were recorded in total to give an overall representation of the bow, mid-ships and stern (Fig. 4.43).

Survey results

The measured dimensions of the vessel are 16.60 m long and approximately 4 m wide at its widest point. The keel, keelson, some futtocks and external planking are visible. The construction is carvel, with engine propulsion. The engine is no longer present, but the engine bed and footings can be seen, as can other structural elements including the mast, mast step, rudder and steering arc arms. There is evidence of a bench, identified as a machinist's bench, and a possible water tank. On the starboard side of the vessel, low down in the ship's hull is a hatch which has been covered in concrete and secured with stainless steel bolts (Plate 4.19).

Planking

FL2 is of carvel construction. The outer planking has a width of 20 cm and is 3 cm thick. The planks are fastened to frames with copper alloy coach bolts holding a screw thread on the inner side of the strakes, iron bolts and square shank copper nails.

Framing

The frames of the vessel have dimensions of 6 cm sided and 14 cm moulded. The spacing between the frames is 40 cm towards the bow, with the stern framing decreasing to 30 cm towards the mid-ship area. In the bow there is evidence of strengthening, as two framing elements from the port bow are sandwiched between iron reinforcements bolted through the timbers with screw-threaded bolts. This may have been a later modification strengthening the bows for tender work or a repair following a minor bow-on collision (Plate 4.20).

Other features

Concrete ballast lies between the frames and in the bow, which has a large area of concrete reinforcement. The ballast has been augmented at some stage by the inclusion of solid iron shells embedded in the concrete. The steering gear (transmission shaft and arms to take the steering lines) are still in place. Part of the propeller shaft is visible lying along the midline of the hull, but it is not attached, although it has a shaft bearing at one end and a flexible coupling at the other. The propeller is no longer present. The rudder is *in situ* and intact, and conforms to a shape generally associated with 60 ft MFVs. Immediately forward of the engine bed is the previously mentioned hatch which has subsequently been covered with concrete. On the outside of the hull opposite this concreted hatch there is a plate bolted across the external face of the strakes (Plate 4.21).

Discussion

The measured dimensions of 16.60 m by 4 m are taken from the extant remains which appear to be from the waterline to the keel. Some length is missing and it is possible that FL2 could be a 60 ft Admiralty Type Motor Fishing Vessel. The stern structure appears to be compatible with a canoe stern and the bow shows a post-1930s shape. There is some evidence of reinforcement to the bow which might be consistent with work as a tender or similar during the war. The distance between frames of 30–40 cm would suggest that the identification of the vessel as an MFV is correct, although the planking does not appear to conform to the usual size for a 60 ft boat. The rudder shape is also consistent with some Admiralty Type MFVs. As mentioned in the introduction to this section, some MFVs were built for overseas service, notably in Singapore and Australia, in which case they would have copper sheathing on the hull to guard against worm. There is no evidence of copper sheathing on FL2.

As a 60 ft MFV this vessel would have 5 tons of concrete fitted as ballast. The use of inert solid iron shells in FL2 to give added weight to the concrete ballast appears unusual and further investigation may be warranted. A 60 ft Admiralty MFV would have a water tank of either 90 gallons (410 litres) or 250 gallons (1140 litres); 60 ft MFVs numbered 1–160 had 90-gallon capacity tanks; later vessels had 250-gallon capacity water tanks. The possible water tank within the footprint of FL2 has an approximate volume of 900 litres, which is approximately 200 gallons. This may show that the tank, if it is a water tank, was later addition or it may be an intrusive element on the vessel.

The absence of the Admiralty number makes it difficult to identify where FL2 was built, what its service career might have been, and how it became hulked on Forton Lake foreshore. The Admiralty contracted for over 400

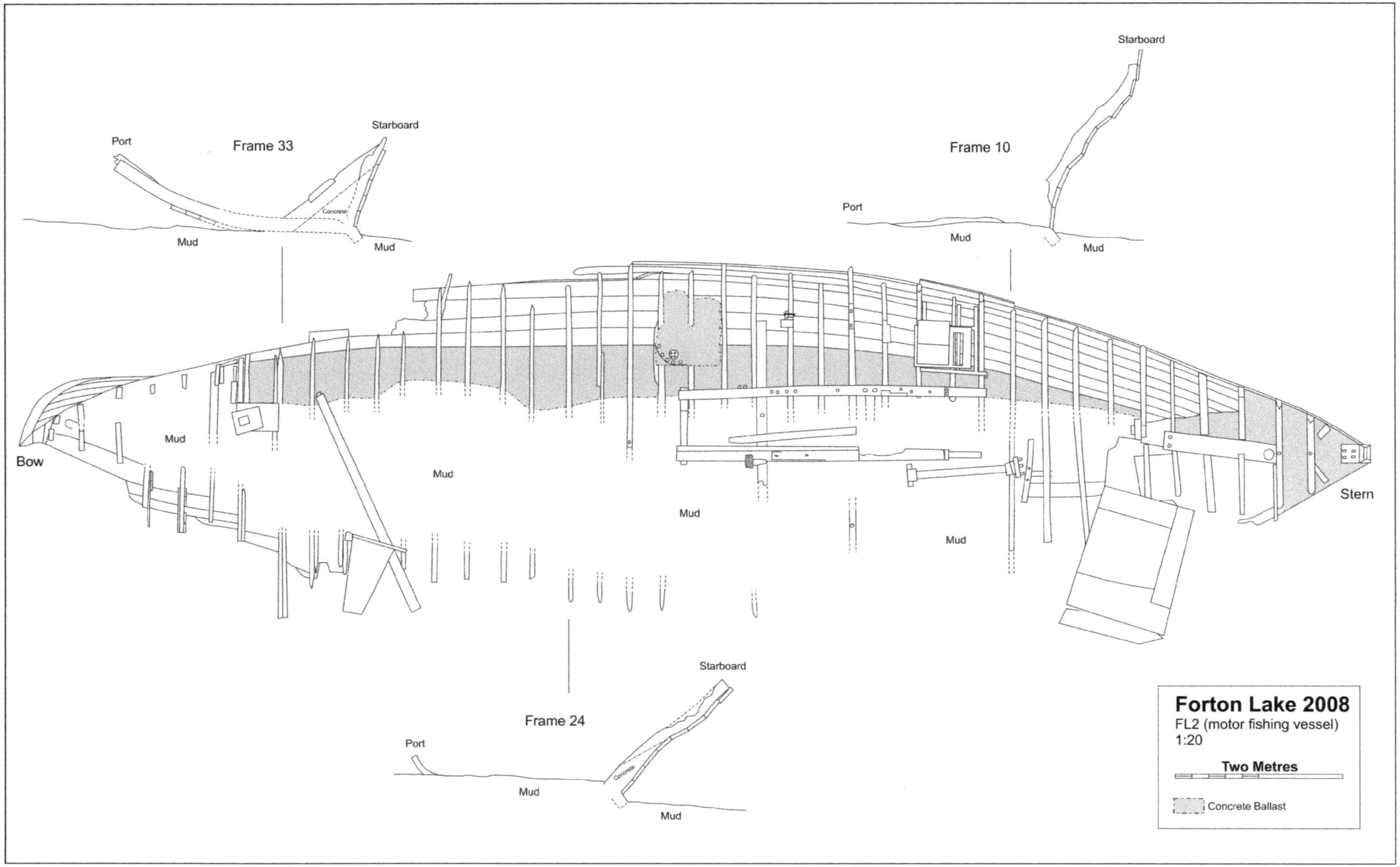
Port
Frame 33
Starboard
Concrete
Mud
Mud
Port
Frame 10
Starboard
Mud
Mud
Bow
Mud
Mud
Mud
Mud
Stern
Frame 24
Port
Starboard
Concrete
Mud
Mud
Forton Lake 2008
FL2 (motor fishing vessel)
1:20
Two Metres
Concrete Ballast

Fig. 4.43 Plan and sections of FL2

Available to download in A3 format from: http://www.barpublishing.com/additional-downloads.html

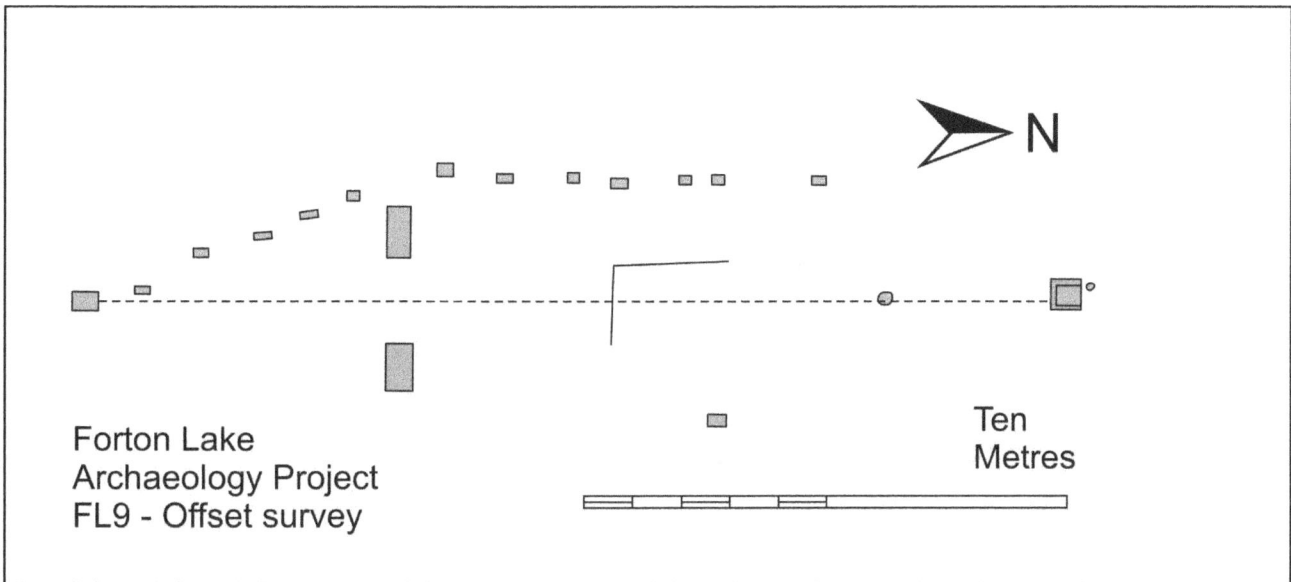

Forton Lake
Archaeology Project
FL9 - Offset survey

Ten
Metres

Fig. 4.44   Extent of FL9 as indicated by the offset survey conducted at the end of the 2008 survey season. Because of time constraints, the principal elements of the starboard side of the vessel were the main focus of the survey

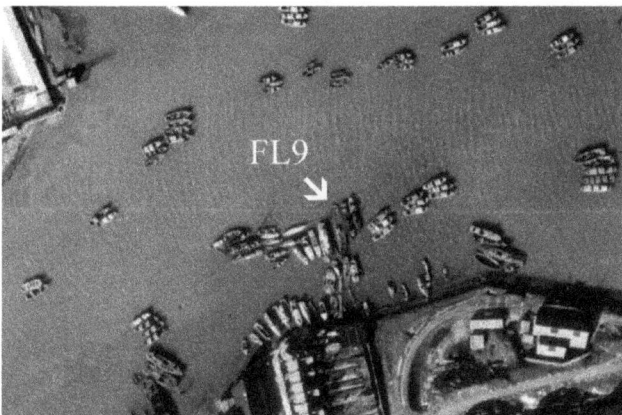

Fig. 4.45   FL9 recorded by an RAF aerial photograph in 1949. Detail from Fig. 2.1

60 ft MFVs during the 1939–1945 war (NHB) and small boatyards all over the country were involved in building them. At least one boatyard building 60 ft MFVs was Morris's Boatyard in Fareham (NRHS and Colin Poole, pers. comm.). Identification is further complicated because the MFV prefix is widely used for a range of Motorized Fishing Vessels and may not indicate that FL2 was built as part of an Admiralty contract or indeed is an Admiralty Type MFV at all.

There are a number of 60 ft Admiralty Type Motorized Fishing Vessels on the National Register of Historic Ships, as well as wooden 60 ft MFVs still in use from the period from the Second World War. MFV 119, built at the John Morris's Yard, is still operating in the Solent (NRHS and Sam Fulford, pers. comm.). Most of the existing MFVs have been modified for private use. The number of vessels of this general class still on the water means that FL2 cannot be considered particularly rare in terms of ship technology, although the remains may provide an opportunity to study an example of the class that has not been modified for modern use.

Documentary research undertaken so far has failed to confirm that FL2 is MFV *Lauren* or to find the original Admiralty number. Records of Admiralty MFVs are held by the Naval Historical Branch (RNHB) in Portsmouth and log books from the vessels are held in the National Archives at Kew. The RNHB records are accessed through the vessel's number and no MFV *Lauren* is identified.

FL9: Motorized Fishing Vessel (MFV) (NGR: SU 461187, 100761)

(Julian Whitewright, Paul Donohue, Daniel Pascoe, Julie Satchell and Jane Maddocks)

Site description

FL 9 lies on the southern shore of Forton Lake, at the northern edge of the main cluster of hulks (Fig. 4.1). The vessel has been hulked bow first in an area of relatively deep sediment and is almost completely submerged at high water. Although the vessel is badly degraded as a result of tidal action, the full extent of the remains is still visible. The bulk of the degradation has occurred to the vessel's planking, while many of the framing elements still survive (Plate 4.22). The date and identification of the vessel is unclear. A possible date to the inter-war period has been suggested, along with a tentative identification as a Motorized Fishing Vessel (MFV).

Survey approach and methodology

Full survey of the vessel was inhibited by its location in the tidal regime and deep surrounding sediments. In 2008 a basic survey of FL9 was conducted using the offset survey method. This concentrated on recording the structural relationship of the principal timbers on the starboard side of the vessel. A comprehensive photographic record of the vessel has also been conducted (Plate 4.23).

Survey results

The results of the basic survey conducted on FL9 are visible in Fig. 4.44. The measured dimensions of the vessel's remains are 20.7 m in length and 5.7 m in width. Reference to aerial photographs indicates an original length of *c*. 23.5 m and a breadth of *c*. 5.6 m. The vessel is predominantly of wooden construction, reinforced with iron knees. The remains of an engine mounting indicate that the vessel was motorized.

Planking

The vessel is carvel planked with planks fastened to frames with iron nails. The planking is badly degraded and little of it remains. Two deck planks survive in the bow area, immediately below the vessel's hawse holes. The planks are 15 cm sided and 12 cm moulded.

Framing

The framing of the vessel survives in a much better state of preservation, particularly in the bow (Plate 4.24). The stem, the knight-heads, hawse timbers, hawse holes, wooden breast hook and an iron crutch are all present. The stem post is 40 cm sided and 60 cm moulded. The knight-heads are formed by two timbers, one on each side of the stem post. Either side of the knight heads are hawse timbers; through these timbers hawse holes are cut. On the port side the partial remains of a hawse pipe remains. This is a cast iron pipe which would have prevented the anchor chain, which ran through these holes, from cutting the wood.

On the underside of the bow decking the breast hook survives. This is reinforced with an iron strap and gives an indication of the use of iron reinforcements throughout the rest of the vessel. The surviving frames are badly degraded. The average is 30 cm sided and 20 cm moulded. What appears to be the stern post of the vessel also survives; it is 40 cm sided and 50 cm moulded.

Other features

There are two metal boxes, possibly coal bunkers, 6.5 m aft of the bow, one on either side of the vessel (Plate 4.25). Both of these boxes are situated immediately forward of a large cross-beam. Next to the starboard tank there is a hatch and a boiler. Aft of the cross-beam there is another tank that lies slightly starboard of the centre line.

Discussion

Little is known regarding the history of FL9. However, reference to aerial photographs of Forton Lake taken after the Second World War indicates that the vessel was hulked in its present position in the earliest available image, dating to 1949 (Fig. 4.45). The vessel's upper decks and hatches are visible which may suggest relatively recent deposition at that date. The overall length of 23.5 m and breadth of 5.7 m established from aerial photographs would suggest that FL9 may originally have been a 75 ft MFV with a beam of 19 ft 8 ins, thus conforming with the overall measurements of a 75 ft Admiralty Type Motorized Fishing Vessel.

Military

(Mark Beattie-Edwards)

As has already been discussed, the appearance of military craft in the collection at Forton Lake is linked to the presence of the Royal Navy Dockyard in Portsmouth and to three very active boat yards, including the disposal yard owned by Frederick J. Watts from the 1930s to the late 1950s. The remains of at least nine vessels (FL3, FL7, FL10, FL16, FL17, FL20, FL23, FL24 and FL31) with a likely military function are now located within Forton Lake. These represent some of the most modern vessels that have been recorded as part of the project.

FL3: Motor minesweeper (NGR: SU 461150, 100915; AHBR 53067)

(Paul Donohue, Colin McKewan and Mark Beattie-Edwards)

Site description

The remains of FL3 lie towards the eastern end of Forton Lake, on the northern bank near to where the channel turns north into Mud Cottage Lake (Fig. 4.1). The wreckage lies on a north-west/south-east axis, approximately parallel to the shore at this part of the lake. The bow of FL3 is pointing north-west and is the most accessible part of the hulk (Plate 4.26) as the sediment in this area is gravel rich. However, the sediments become increasingly softer and more hazardous further aft. These conditions make any external survey of FL3 precarious, especially on the offshore port side of the vessel. During the project the inside of the vessel was entered only with a great deal of care and supervision and wearing personal protective equipment.

Ted Sutton's survey in 1997 identified FL3 as a minesweeper and in 2006 as part of the first year of the project local knowledge also suggested FL3 was the remains of a Second World War Motor Minesweeper (Eric Walker, pers. comm.). This identification was supported by the presence of a large sweep drum at the rear of the vessel and was subsequently verified by photographic evidence.

Survey approach and methodology

As part of the 2006 fieldwork programme the remains of FL3 were subjected to a photographic survey combined with the measurement of some general dimensions. In 2007 a detailed survey of the vessel was undertaken, although this survey did not aim to produce a site plan, but rather made detailed observations and measurements of particular constructional features and artefacts remaining in the wreckage. This was due to the size and complexity of the remains and the number of fieldwork days that would have been required to complete a full survey.

Survey Results

The upper deck and superstructure of FL3 have completely disintegrated or have been removed, leaving the lower hull, which is intact up to the sheers for a small section amidships and to just above the bilge at the fore and aft sections. The hull dimensions are 33.46 m long and 6.88 m wide. The hull itself is constructed from carvel laid planks attached to composite frame timbers (Plate 4.27). The planks are fastened to the frames with metal pins. The composite frames comprise two timbers side by side that are vertically staggered to maintain strength. These frames are in varying states of decay. Ceiling planking, attached to the inside of the frames, remains in sections throughout the vessel.

At numerous positions around the hull vertical saw cuts up to 15 cm wide provide evidence of salvage. At the bow the stem post has been reduced on its front face so that it is angled to receive the hull strakes. In front of this there is a false stem. The stem post and the false stem appear to be much shorter than their original height, and have broken off at a scarf joint. Within the bow the floor timbers are different to those found in the rest of the vessel as they are narrower and have a higher vertical face, and are attached to the fore and aft sides of the frames (Plate 4.28). There is evidence of burning through fire damage to the upper sections of the hull and local inhabitants remember FL3 being on fire (Fiona Ritchie, pers. comm.).

Inside the hull the bilges are buried beneath sediments and it was not possible to see the construction of this area. However, amidships there are large timbers forming a frame which extends above the sediments. These large timbers have long metal pins protruding from them and some have metal plates attached to the top. Between these frames and the hull there are supports made from diagonal timbers creating triangular structures. It is believed that the large timber frames, large metal pins, metal plates and triangular supports are all related to the engines; together they would have formed the mounts for the engines that have since been removed. Within FL3 there are a number of metal structures, some of which are *in situ*, while others are no longer in their original position. The foremost of these are four heavily rusted large tanks with associated fittings. Sections of these tanks have collapsed, but appear to be in their original location; they were likely to have been used for storage of fuel or fresh water. Aft of the tanks lies the partial remains of a timber bulkhead (Plate 4.29) which consists of laminated diagonally opposed timber strips.

In the central section of the hull, beside what would have been the engine mounts there is evidence of further metal structures. On the starboard side there is also a large cylindrical feature, with a flange at one end. This feature is not *in situ,* but may represent a large pipe that was once related to the engines. The other metal features may represent the remains of tanks, although they are much smaller than those found in the forward section. These tanks are in a poor condition, the tops have collapsed, as

have sections of the tank's bulkheads. Aft of these tanks, in the stern section is the sweep drum (Plate 4.30). This is a large metal cylinder, with two large circular metal plates at either end. The drum would have originally been located at the aft of the ship on the upper deck (known as the 'sweep deck'). The sweep deck is no longer present and the drum is lying in the stern bilges.

Much of the stern of the vessel is missing, showing more evidence of salvage. The rudder is not present and the keel runs to a point where the rudder post would have been. Forward of this there is a knee supporting an inner post (Plate 4.31). At the top of the inner post there are the remains of a transverse knee that would have supported the sweep deck. The inner post extends through the keel, and connects to the propeller shaft. Beneath the hull, between the inner post and the keel, the deadwood is present. At the end of the propeller shaft there is a large propeller shaft bearing.

Discussion

Through local knowledge and analysis of the fixtures and fittings FL3 has been identified as the remains of a motor minesweeper (MMS). Photographic evidence found during the course of research into the hulks of Forton Lake has indicated that FL3 is the wreckage of MMS 293 (Plate 4.32). In one photograph taken in the 1980s it is possible to see the pennant numbers 293 on the port bow (Plate 4.33). This identification is contrary to Melvin's identification of FL3 as MMS 298 – another Frank Curtis built MMS (Melvin, 1992: 159)

MMSs were wooden vessels designed to carry out inshore, shallow-water minesweeping of 'influence mines' (magnetic and acoustic mines) (Williams, 1994: 153). A total of 402 MMSs were constructed for the Royal Navy in 1942 and 1943. MMSs were built in two classes, the larger vessels (MMS 1001 class) were 127 ft long (38.7 m), displaced 360 tons (366 tonnes) , and were numbered MMS 1001 through to MMS 1090, while the smaller vessels were 105 ft long (32 m) (MMS 1 class), displaced 256 tons (260 tonnes) and were numbered MMS 1 through to 312. The two types of standard MMS were nicknamed as 'Mickey Mouse Sweepers', due to their type abbreviation, with the smaller ones known as 'Short Mickeys' and the larger class known as 'Big Mickeys' (David Fricker, pers. comm.; Melvin, 1992: 123). The vessels of these classes served under their pennant numbers and did not have individual names.

Minesweepers were vessels specially designed or adapted to sweep or explode mines laid at sea. Many minesweepers were originally fishing trawlers which were requisitioned in wartime and converted as minesweepers to tow an underwater sweep of serrated wire with explosive cutters inserted at intervals. These were designed to catch and cut the mooring wire of a mine, so that it came to the surface where it could be destroyed. Due to their wooden construction and thus low magnetic signature these vessels were ideal for sweeping for magnetic mines. As time passed and the two world wars continued to develop, so did the mines that were being used and new technologies were able to produce mines that were activated by contact, pressure, acoustics and magnetism, which meant that minesweepers and the art of minesweeping also needed to be adapted (Williams, 1994: 154).

Melvin states that by 1951 of a total of 60 MMSs still in service with the Royal Navy, 26 were active, two were with the Royal Naval Volunteer Reserve Service (RNVR), two were in training roles and 30 in reserve, most of them being laid up at Chatham on the River Medway. By 1956 this had been reduced to 25 craft with the numbers gradually reduced until there were no operational MMSs in any part of the world after 1963 (Melvin 1992: 205).

MMS 293 was of the MMS 1 class, built for the British war effort under the 'Lend Lease' scheme whereby the United States of America supplied many of the allied

nations with vast amounts of war material between 1941 and 1945 (Melvin, 1992: 135). The draught of an MMS 1 class MMS was 8 ft (2.5 m) with a beam dimension of 22 ft (6.7 m) (Melvin, 1992: 22). This beam dimension corresponds very closely to the recorded 6.88 m beam of FL3. The slight difference can be attributed to sagging, as the hull of FL3 collapsed.

Royal Navy records of motor minesweepers are held at the National Archives at Kew and also held by the Naval Historical Branch (NHB) in Portsmouth. There are also a number of comprehensive publications on the role of the Royal Navy's minesweepers during the Second World War, perhaps most notably Michael Melvin's *Minesweeper: The Role of the Motor Minesweeper in World War II* published in 1992. The Royal Navy records held at the National Archives and also those supplied by the NHB have been able to shed some light on the career of MMS 293 (Table 4.8):

Ordered:	21.08.1942 (part of batch MMS 288–306, all ordered on same date)
Built:	Frank Curtis Ltd, at Par in Cornwall
Launched:	10.01.1943
Completed:	03.06.1943
Commissioned:	07.06.1943
Service Record:	
1943	Joins 138th Minesweeper Flotilla – Nore Command – Yarmouth Area
13.06.1943	Plymouth
20.06.1943	Portsmouth
27.06.1943	Lowestoft
13.08.1943	Taken in hand at Lowestoft for repairs, completed 26.08.1493
1943	Joins 132nd Minesweeper Flotilla – Western Approaches Command, Liverpool Area (Commanding Officer Temporary Lieutenant A.M. Goodwin)
3-31.10.1943	Lowestoft
07.11.1943	On passage to Liverpool
14.11.1943–14.05.1944	Liverpool
30.11.1943	Taken in hand at Liverpool for repairs
16.02.1944	Taken in hand at Liverpool for repairs, additions and alterations, completed 05.03.1944
21.05.1944–04.06.1944	Plymouth
11.06.1944	Portsmouth
18–25.06.1944	Portland
01.07.1944	Taken in hand at Devonport for docking and repairs, completed 08.07.1944
30.07.1944	Portland
13–27.08.1944	Plymouth
03.09.1944	Operating from Portland
	Joins 132nd Minesweeper Flotilla, Portsmouth Command – Portland Sub-Command
10–24.09.1944	Operating from Portland
	Joins 132nd Minesweeper Flotilla, Western Approaches Command – Liverpool Area
01.10.1944–12.11.1944	Operating from Portland
	Joins 205th Minesweeper Flotilla, allocated to ANCXF (Allied Naval Commander Expeditionary Force)
19–26.11.1944	Operating from Portland

28.11.1944	Taken in hand at Portland
	Joins 147th Minesweeper Flotilla, allocated to ANCXF (Allied Naval Commander Expeditionary Force)
14.01.1945–18.03.1945	Operating from Ostend
25.03.1945–08.04.1945	Tamise, repairs
15.04.1945–03.06.1945	Operating from Ostend
10.06.1945–29.07.1945	Ostend, repairs
05.08.1945–09.09.1945	Operating from Ostend
16–23.09.1945	Ostend, repairs
	Joins 147th Minesweeper Flotilla allocated to NORE Command – Sheerness
30.09.1945–18.11.1945	Sheerness
	Joins 101st Minesweeper Flotilla (or 102nd Minesweeper Flotilla)
23.11.1945	Taken in hand at Sheerness for repairs, completed 07.12.1945
8–30.12.1945	Sheerness (Commanding Officer Temporary Lieutenant J. Cornock, RNVR)
1947	Portsmouth, relegated for duty as a Degaussing Vessel (DGV)
	Renumbered MMS 1793
02.05.1950	Handed over to Mr F.J. Watts of Gosport for care and maintenance pending sale
20.11.1950	Sold to L. Storham and Partners Ltd, London, SE2

Table 4.8   Service record of MMS 293 (source: Royal Navy records held at the National Archives and at the NHB)

Fig. 4.46   MMS 293; thought to be taken at Forton Lake (The Jack Smale Collection, courtesy of Philip Simons)

Interestingly in 1947 MMS 293 was renumbered MMS 1793. A photograph of MMS 293 included in the Jack Smale Collection (Fig. 4.46) believed to be taken at Forton Lake in or after 1950 shows the vessel still with its original pennant number on the port bow, and illustrates that the renumbering of MMS 293 to MMS 1793 was purely a paper exercise and that the new pennant was never added (David Fricker, pers. comm.)

The historical accounts demonstrate that after final paying-off from service, MMS 293 was handed over to the F.J. Watts Boatyard in Gosport in June 1950 and then sold on in November 1950. Therefore the only question still remaining is why MMS 293 is still at Forton Lake?

Did the vessel leave after being sold to L. Storham and Partners Ltd in 1950, did collection of MMS 293 never take place or did the vessel come back to Forton at a later date? Perhaps further research may shed further light on how MMS 293 came still to be lying in the mud at Forton Lake over half a century after it was meant to have been sold.

Despite 402 MMSs being built it appears that no examples are currently on the National Register of Historic Vessels. Towards the north of Priddy's Hard in Gosport there are the remains of another minesweeper located in the intertidal zone (AHBR 53061). However the number of other examples of MMS 1 class vessels surviving in the world in a similar derelict state is unknown and merits further study.

FL 7: Pinnace (NGR: SU 461158, 100747; AHBR 53071)

(Paul Donohue, Colin McKewan and Mark Beattie-Edwards)

Site description

On the southern bank of Forton Lake amongst the main cluster of hulks to the east of Parham Road lie the remains of a highly degraded metal boat (Fig. 4.1). The vessel lies on a north–south axis, approximately perpendicular to the shore, with the bow of the wreckage pointing towards the shore and being most accessible

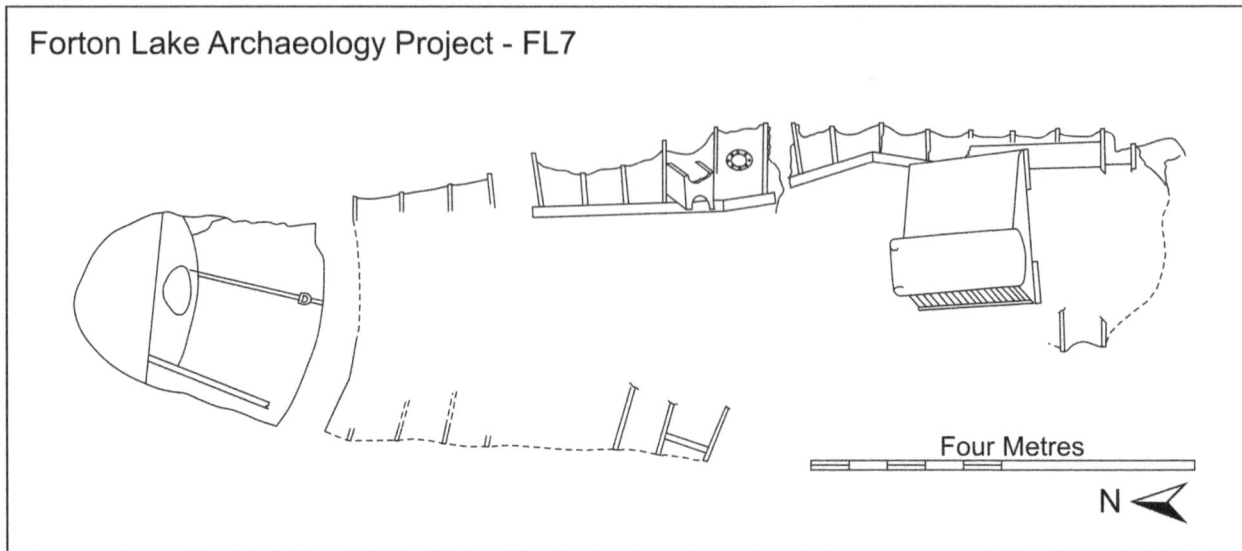

Forton Lake Archaeology Project - FL7

Four Metres

N

Fig. 4.47   Site plan of FL7

(Plate 4.34). The aft section of this vessel lies within an area of softer deep sediments with restricted access. At high spring tide FL7 is completely submerged. Most of the upper structure of the hull has disappeared, leaving only the bottom plating, a section of the stern and the engine boiler towards the bow.

Survey approach and methodology

In 2006 the wreckage of FL7 was surveyed as part of the first year of the project. This involved a simple photographic survey, taking basic length and breadth measurements, observing the structural remains and recording positional information. Following the 2006 survey it was recommended that additional diagnostic information would be required to identify the class of vessel represented by FL7. Following this recommendation, project volunteers undertook a detailed survey of the vessel in 2007, as well as taking additional photographs of component parts and measurements of particular features. The 2007 survey of FL7 was achieved using the datum offset method to produce a site plan (Fig. 4.47)

Survey Results

The 2007 survey demonstrated that the vessel remains are 11.60 m long and 3.52 m at its widest point. Its remains are significantly corroded, especially towards the bow which means the vessel is shorter than its original length. The lower sections of the port hull are visible, as is the port side, but only in the forward sections. The bilges are not visible as they are buried within the sediments. The vessel is constructed of metal plates riveted to a metal frame. The frames are 5 cm wide and are spaced 40 cm apart. Seven metres forward from the stern on the port side there is a circular riveted opening, which has a diameter of 18 cm, believed to be the remains of bilge pump outflow.

The most complete section of the vessel is the stern section, which remains up to the sheer. Above the stern the partial remains of a small deck survive. Forward of

this there is a small amount of coaming, which could have belonged to a hatch or part of the superstructure. On the forward side of the stern there is a bulkhead through which there is a circular access hole measuring 50 cm in diameter. Towards the bow of the vessel the engine boiler is present. This comprises of a central steam drum at the head of the boiler with two diagonal steam chambers off to the side (Plate 4.35). Part of the casing is missing from the starboard side chamber revealing the water pipes inside. To the back of the boiler there is a small rectangular opening, which could be the firebox.

Discussion

Following the surveys undertaken in 2006 and 2007 during the project the identity of FL7 remained uncertain and it had been considered that FL7 may be the remains of a Motor Gun Boat (HWTMA/NAS, 2006: 24–25). However the presence of the surviving boiler of FL7 has meant that, thanks to photographic evidence, it has been possible to witness the deterioration of FL7 and to identify it as the remains of a Royal Navy Pinnace (Fig. 4.48)

Pinnaces were communication vessels that were used by the Navy for the transfer of small stores and personnel to larger ships that lay at anchor. Towards the end of the 19th century and into the 20th century they were of steam propulsion with later versions built with internal combustion engines. Research undertaken in 2009 has demonstrated that the remains of FL7 had been photographed in the 1970s and the 1980s; this showed just how much the vessel had deteriorated over the years (Plate 4.36; Fig. 4.49).

Jack Smale identified FL7 as the remains as Pinnace number 704. Information on Pinnace 704 supplied by the NHB has indicated that it was part of batch order of 1915, built by Camper & Nicholson, with machinery built by Allen & Son of Bedford. It was delivered on 16 August 1917 measuring 50 ft (15.24 m) between the

Fig. 4.48   A Royal Navy Pinnace

Fig. 4.49   FL7 in the 1970s from the Jack Smale Collection (courtesy of Philip Simons)

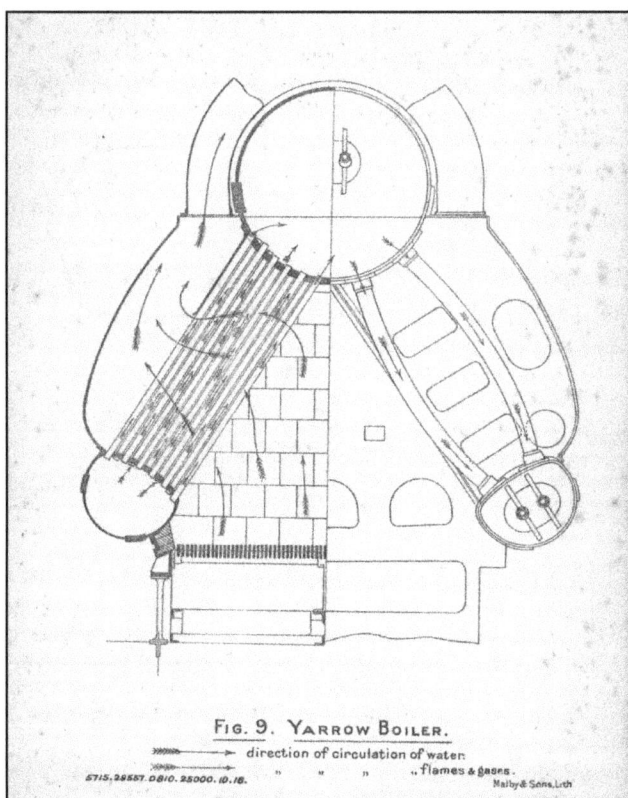

FIG. 9. YARROW BOILER.

→ direction of circulation of water
„   „   „   „   .. flames & gases.

6715.26557.0810.25000.10.18.   Malby & Sons. L.th

Fig. 4.50   End view of a Yarrow Boiler (Stokers' Manual 1912, Admiralty, HMSO)

perpendiculars, with a gross tonnage of 17 and a net tonnage of 8. Unusually the hull of Pinnace 704 was built from steel. Similar 50 ft steel pinnaces built by Camper & Nicholson measured 9 ft 9 in (3.0 m) in breadth and had a mean draught of 3 ft 1½ in (0.95 m).

Pinnace 704 was appropriated to Royal Clarence Yard in Gosport on 27 August 1919 and the limited records confirm it was still at the yard in 1924, 1925, 1934, 1936, 1938, and 1947. Disposal records demonstrate that it was disposed of on the 31 May 1948 (Iain MacKenzie, NHB, pers. comm.). The notes from the Jack Smale archive provided by Philip Simons suggest that the Pinnace 704 was 'beached at Fred Watts' Yard' in 1950 and that the remains were 'finally cleared by the local authorities'.

In the 1980s photograph it is possible to see the boiler of Pinnace 704 starting to appear as the decking and bulkheads surrounding it have begun to collapse. It is believed that this is a Yarrow Water Tube Boiler (Fig. 4.50)

This type of boiler was first fitted to the Royal Navy destroyer, HMS *Hornet*, in 1893. HMS *Hornet* went on to set a speed record of 28 knots during trials. The Yarrow Water Tube Boiler had the advantage of being lighter than traditional boilers and could generate steam much more quickly. It was fitted to many vessels, including those of the Royal Navy, for a long period of time and was still being used during the Second World War (Borthwick, 1965: 37). A similar Yarrow Water Tube Boiler was fitted to the Steam Pinnace 199, restored by the Royal Naval Museum and the Steam Launch Restoration Group in 1984 (Plate 4.37).[11] During the period of restoration of Pinnace 199, now known as *Treleague*, the remains at Forton Lake were visited in order to collect photographs of the boiler on FL7 for research (Peter Tunbridge, pers. comm.).

At present it is not known how many other examples of this type of vessel or boiler survive in the world. In 2009 16 pinnaces were registered on the UK's National Historic Ships Register dating from the *Collie* which was built around 1890 by Thornycroft as a sailing pinnace for the Royal Navy to the Pinnace *Diligence* built in 1946 by J. Samuel White of Cowes on the Isle of Wight. Based on the numbers of this vessel type registered with the National Historic Ships Register FL7 is not considered rare.

FL10: Landing Craft (NGR: SU 461190, 100749; AHBR 57862)

(Mark Beattie-Edwards and Paul Donohue)

Site description

The remains of FL10 lie towards the eastern end of the main concentration of hulks on the southern bank to the east of Parham Road (Fig. 4.1). Orientated on a north–south axis, perpendicular to the shore, what is believed to

---

11   http://www.royalnavalmuseum.org/collections_boats_pinnace.htm and http://www.royalnavalmuseum.org/collections_boats_pinnace mach.htm

be the stern of the vessel points towards the shore and is most accessible (Plate 4.38). The fore section of this vessel lies within an area of softer sediments with restricted access around the outside perimeter of the vessel. Like many of the hulks at Forton, FL10 lies reasonably high up on the bank of the lake and is partially submerged at high tide (Plate 4.39). The wreckage is made of steel, but the deteriorated hull has left it in a precarious state. The bow area to the north is collapsed and open, the engine room has also collapsed and no internal mechanics remain.

Ted Sutton's survey in 1997 identified FL10 as a Landing Craft Assault (LCA) and in 2006, as part of the project's first year, FL10 was also identified and listed as an LCA (HWTMA/NAS, 2006: 29).

Survey approach and methodology

In 2006 the wreckage of FL10 was surveyed as part of the first year of the project. This involved a simple photographic survey, taking of basic length and breadth measurements, observing structural remains and recording positional information using a handheld GPS. Following the 2006 survey it was suggested that additional survey would be of little archaeological value and that enough photographs had been collected to give an indication of rates of decay (HWTMA/NAS, 2006: 31).

Survey Results

In 2006 the remains of FL10 measured 8.71 m in length, 2.94 m wide and stood 0.94 m above the mud of Forton Lake. Its construction is composite, comprising of a steel plate outer hull and a wooden inner skin. A substantial amount of the hull remains, but all of the propulsion system has been removed. Internally, the forward engine compartment bulkhead is missing. The engine compartment deckhead remains and three access hatch coamings can be seen, although no hatch covers are in place. At the four corners of the main hull, on the upper side, four lifting strong points can be seen. These strong points are diagnostic of a LCA. Much of the stern section, which would have comprised a housing for the propulsion shafts and the rudders, is now missing. Towards the forward section the bow door can be seen although this has collapsed into the mud.

FL16: Landing Craft (NGR: SU 461214, 100767; AHBR 57866)

(Mark Beattie-Edwards and Paul Donohue)

Site description

The remains of FL16 also lie at the eastern end of the main concentration of hulks on the southern bank to the east of Parham Road (Fig. 4.1). They rest on a north–south axis, perpendicular to the shore, between the hulks of the *Vadne* (FL22) and the RAF Ferry Boat (FL17). The bow of FL16 points towards the shore and is therefore the most accessible part of the wreckage (Plate 4.40). The aft section of this vessel lies within an area of

softer sediments with restricted access around the outside perimeter of the vessel. Like many of the hulks at Forton, FL16 lies reasonably high up on the bank of the lake and is partially submerged at high tide. The wreckage is made of steel, but the deteriorated hull has left it in a precarious state with many sharp edges and would suffer damage if substantial weight was placed upon the upper part of the hull. In 2006 as part of the project, FL16 was identified as an LCA.

Survey approach and methodology

As with FL10, the wreckage of FL16 was surveyed as part of the first year of the project in 2006. This involved a simple photographic survey, taking basic length and breadth measurements, observing structural remains and recording positional information with a handheld GPS. Following this survey it was suggested that additional survey of FL16 would be of little archaeological value (HWTMA/NAS, 2006: 36).

Survey Results

The remaining hull of FL16 was measured in 2006 with a length of 8.73 m, with a width of 2.66 m. The visible remains include the hull on both the port and starboard sides as well as the upper decking on the port and starboard sides. Much of the external metal plating of the vessel is present and inspection of the hull demonstrated the presence of an internal timber skin. It is possible to see that it comprises of diagonally opposed layers of plywood (Plate 4.41).

The hull and decking of FL16 are in a poor condition and as witnessed on FL10 the stern engine covering has disappeared. In the cargo bay of FL16 there are five steel tanks with associated pipe-work. It is believed that these tanks would not have been part of the original construction. Much of the bow has also disappeared, as can be seen when comparing the extant remains with the wreckage in a photograph taken in 1987 by David Fricker (Plate 4.42).

FL20: Landing Craft (NGR: SU 461206, 100773; AHBR 57872)

(Mark Beattie-Edwards and Paul Donohue)

Site description

The remains of FL20 lie at the eastern end of the main concentration of hulks on the southern bank to the east of Parham Road (Fig. 4.1), on a north–south axis at right angles to the shore, just north of the remains of FL16 and FL17 (Plate 4.43). FL20 lies in an area of deep sediment with restricted access. Lying within FL20 are the remains of FL21 which has been identified as a lifeboat, which has no other association to FL20 (page 36).

Being located further into the channel of the Lake than most of the vessels at Forton, FL20 becomes completely submerged at high tide. Very little internal structure of this vessel remains, but enough of the outer hull remains to indicate that this vessel was once an LCA similar to FL10 and FL16 (HWTMA/NAS, 2006: 38).

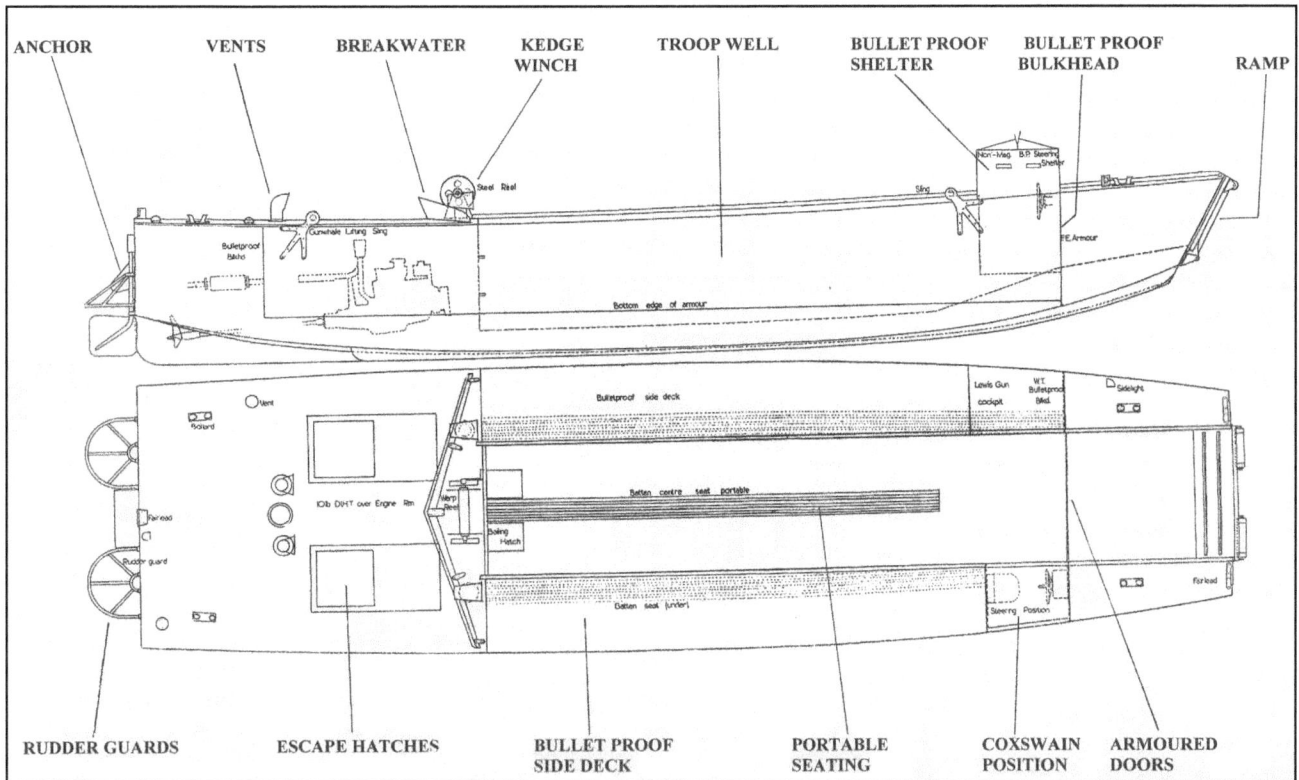

ANCHOR   VENTS   BREAKWATER   KEDGE WINCH   TROOP WELL   BULLET PROOF SHELTER   BULLET PROOF BULKHEAD   RAMP

RUDDER GUARDS   ESCAPE HATCHES   BULLET PROOF SIDE DECK   PORTABLE SEATING   COXSWAIN POSITION   ARMOURED DOORS

Fig. 4.51   General layout of a standard form Landing Craft Assault (from Holtham, 2009: 3)

Survey approach and methodology

As with FL10 and FL16, the wreckage of FL20 was surveyed in 2006 as part of the project's first year. This involved a photographic survey, taking basic measurements of length and breadth, observing the structural remains and recording positional information with a handheld GPS. Following this survey it was suggested, as with FL10 and FL16, that additional survey would be of little archaeological value (HWTMA/NAS 2006: 38).

Survey Results

In 2006 the remains of FL20 were measured as being 10.10 m in length including the propeller frames, with the main hull measuring 8.83 m and 2.73 m in width. As with FL16, the construction of FL20 is of riveted steel with an inner wooden layer. The level of sediments surrounding FL20 makes it difficult to determine exactly what features remain. However, it was possible in 2006 to report that there was no engine. At the stern the propeller frames do remain, although the housing has now disappeared and at the bow a small section of the collapsed bow door can be seen in the sediments.

Discussion for FL10, FL16 and FL20

As already stated, FL10, FL16 and FL20 have been identified as the remains of Landing Craft Assault (LCAs). These craft were built to transport and land troops during amphibious assaults on beaches. Nearly two thousand LCAs were built between 1939 and 1945 in 39 boat yards in the United Kingdom, as well as 154 built

in India and 24 built in Australia (Holtham, 2009: 3–11). LCAs, called Assault Landing Craft (ALC) prior to 1942, have been described as 'the humblest vessel in the wartime Royal Navy during the Second World War ... commanded by a rating rather than an officer ... they did not appear in the Navy List ... and had a number rather than a name' (Lavery, 2009: 7).

The first batch order for production craft was placed with Thornycroft of Woolston, Southampton, who had already built the prototype ALC 2; Thornycroft sub-contracted many of the orders to other smaller boatbuilding companies, such as Morgan Giles at Teignmouth, Devon, in order to speed up delivery (Holtham, 2009: 1–8). Thousands of LCAs were built over five years with the last ones being completed in the last months of 1945.

A directory of Royal Navy Landing Craft Assault produced by the World Ship Society (WSS) Small Craft Group lists the principal particulars for LCAs (Holtham 2009: 3; Table 4.9).

The construction of the hull of the landing craft was of wood, mostly being of African mahogany, as well as obechi, pine, teak and spruce. The hull was built on a Canadian rock elm keel and was shaped by 24 mahogany frames. These frames were covered by double diagonal planking (as evidence on FL16) to provide strength and fastened by copper rivets, brass bolts and brass screws. The armour plating was then added pre-drilled by the manufacturer (Lavery, 2009: 20). This armour protection of the hull was provided by D1HT, a heat treated steel

Operational use:	For raiding operations or large-scale landings of troops from transports
Builder:	Various
Displacement:	9.0 tons (9144 kg) (Light); 13.0 tons (13,208 kg) (Loaded)
Burthen:	4.0 tons (4064 kg)
Hull Dimensions:	
Length Overall.	41 ft 6 in (12.65 m) with propeller guards
Beam	10 ft (3.05 m)
Draught Loaded	1 ft 9 in (0.53 m – fwd), 2ft 3in (0.69 m – aft)
Draught Light	1 ft 1 in (0.28 m – fwd), 1 ft 9 in (0.53 m – aft)
Main Machinery:	Two x 65 hp FORD V8 engines – twin screwed
Maximum speed:	10.0 knots (16.1 kph – light), 7.0 knots (11.3 kph – loaded), 11.5 knots (18.5 kph – maximum)
Total fuel carried:	64 Imperial gallons (291 litres) petrol
Range:	50–80 nautical miles (80–130 km) @ 7.0 knots (loaded), 65 nautical miles (105 km) at full speed
Crew:	1 Coxwain, 1 Gunner-bowman, 1 Seaman, 1 Mechanic
Troop space:	18 ft x 8 ft 10 in (5.5 m x 2.7 m)
Capacity:	35 troops and 800 lb (363 kg) of equipment
Armament:	1 x Bren gun in port cockpit
	2 x .303 Lewis guns
	2 x 2 in mortars fitted aft (to some craft)
Armour protection:	10 lb D1HT to bulkheads and hull sides
	7.8 lb D1HT to hold decks
	10 lb D1HT to parapets could be fitted

Table 4.9   Principal particulars for LCAs (Holtham 2009: 3)

based on the chemical composition of D1 quality steel (Ministry of Defence, 2000: 12.2 (110)).[12]

From the general layout of the LCA (Fig. 4.51), it is possible to see the long central open well that was fitted with three wooden benches, – one each on the port and starboard sides and one along the centre for seating troops. The benches on the port and starboard sides were covered by the top deck to provide increased protection. The central well was divided from the bow section by a bullet-proof bulkhead fitted with two vertically hinged doors. These doors lead to the ramp, which was lowered and raised by a simple pulley and wire. The ramp was made from a steel frame with a double mahogany planked skin. Immediately behind the bulkhead on the starboard side was the steering shelter which was protected by non-magnetic bulletproof plate and a hinged double-door roof. The gas operated .303 calibre Lewis gun was located opposite the steering shelter on the port side.

In trying to determine the identity of the actual LCAs at Forton Lake it is possible, from sale records of craft disposed of by the F.J. Watts Boatyard between 1951 and 1959, to see that only one LCA is listed in November 1951 (see Appendix A for full list):

Month/Year	Vessel type	Pennant
November 1951	40 ft Landing Craft (LCA)	1841

LCA 1841 was the post war re-designation of LCA 842 which was built by Bolson's at Poole. Bolson's shipyard was acquired by Marine Sales UK Ltd in 1998 from Poole Harbour Commissioners and interestingly was also the shipyard that built Cowes Floating Bridge no 4, one of the successors of the 1896 chain ferry now at Forton Lake (FL11). LCA 842 was completed on 1 September 1943. On 5 June 1944 it was one of two stationed at Scapa on Orkney for special service under Admiral Command Orkneys and Shetland. A year later on 13 August 1945 the same craft was one of dozens in Operational Reserve at HMS Monck in the Clyde area.

---

12   ftp://217.17.192.66/mitarb/lutz/standards/dstan/02/706/
     00000100.pdf

Month/Year	Vessel Type	Pennant	Engined	Reserve price
May 1957	40 ft Naval Servicing Boat	(ex LCA) 335	No engines	Offers
November 1957	40 ft Naval Servicing Boat	(ex LCA) 338	No engine	Offers
November 1957	40 ft Naval Servicing Boat	(ex LCA) 340	Ford V8	Offers
November 1957	60 ft Naval Servicing Boat	(ex LCM) 347	2 x Hudson Invaders	Offers

Table 4.10   NSBs purchased by the F.J. Watts Boatyard in 1957

In 1946 it was one of eight craft stowed on the Landing Ship Tank (LST) 3002 as Replacement Reserve still in the Clyde Area. LCA 842 was re-designated as LCA 1841 on 19 August 1949 and then had pennant number L 1841. The service record of L 1841 from 1949 to1951 when it was sold to the F.J. Watts Boatyard on 26 November is not yet known (Terry Holtham, pers. comm.). Unfortunately because of the lack of records from the F.J. Watts Boatyard it is not possible to determine if L 1841 was sold or whether it never actually left Forton Lake.

Historical records show that the F.J. Watts yard purchased four Naval Servicing Boats (NSBs) from the Admiralty Small Craft Disposals Department in 1957 (Table 4.10). Maritime historian Terry Holtham from the WSS Small Craft Group has identified that three of these were formerly LCA 335, 338 and 340 and one was formerly a Landing Craft Mechanized (or Mechanical) 347 which was slightly longer at 60ft and was designed to carry vehicles as well as infantry troops.

Finally, from listings complied by the late Dick Dennison, it is possible that one other landing craft appears to have been handled by F.J. Watts (Danny Lovell, pers. comm.). This was a Landing Craft Infantry (Small) (LCI (S)), at 105 ft (32 m) length overall a much larger vessel than the LCA. The LCI (S) – or Fairmile H Landing Craft – was designed by Fairmile Marine of Cobham Fairmile, Surrey, who had already designed a number of small military vessels, and was supplied as kits for construction by boatyards around the coast (Lambert and Ross, 1990: 125–6). LCI (S) 503 was sold to the F.J. Watts Boatyard on 15 November 1950. Prior to the sale, LCI (S) 503 was used by the Royal Marines at the Amphibious School at Fort Cumberland, Portsmouth, for a couple of years. Normally moored in Langstone Harbour LCI (S) 503 would have had a mixed Royal Marine and Royal Navy crew. It took part in the Normandy landings carrying troops from No 6 Commando and in November 1944 it also served as a rescue craft in 'Operation Infatuate', the codename for the allied forces landing on the Dutch island of Walcheren in November 1944 (Danny Lovell, pers. comm.). Again unfortunately because of the lack of records from the F.J. Watts Boatyard it is not possible to

Fig. 4.52   10 November 1945: a sailor salesman talks to intending purchasers of a landing craft moored at Westminster Pier, London. (Photo: William Vanderson, licensed by Fox Photos/Getty Images)

determine if any of the ex LCAs, the ex LCM or the LCI (S) was sold on or whether they are the hulks still lying in the mud at Forton Lake, though, because of its size, FL10, FL16 and FL20 are unlikely to be the remains of LCI (S) 503.

It is known that quite a number of LCAs still survive in the United Kingdom and may well also survive in India and Australia where they were also built. As might be expected all of them are either in a dilapidated condition on the foreshore or have been converted into houseboats. A couple of houseboat-converted LCAs can be found on

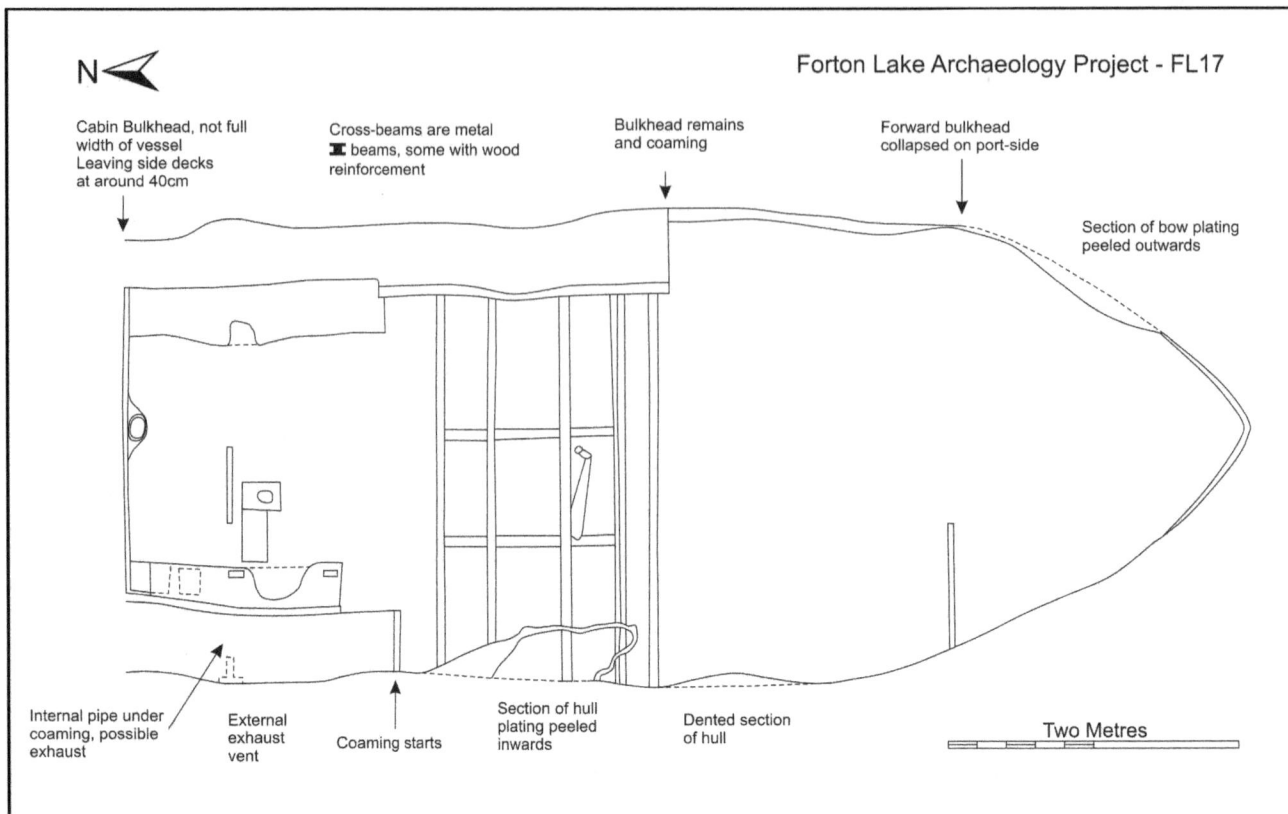

Fig. 4.53   Site plan of bow of FL17, drawn by Tim Parker

the Isle of Wight and recently several appeared for sale on the auction website eBay. Most of these have had their armour removed and have been extensively modified. This is not surprising as at the end of the Second World War it was possible to purchase surplus LCAs from the Admiralty for around £46, including plans on how to convert it into a home (Danny Lovell, pers. comm. – Fig. 4.52).

FL17: Royal Air Force Ferry Boat (NGR: SU 461213, 100770; AHBR 57869)

(Mark Beattie-Edwards, Paul Donohue and Tim Parker)

Site description

The remains of FL17 lie amongst the main concentration of hulks on the southern bank to the east of Parham Road (Fig. 4.1). The vessel lies on a north–south axis, approximately at right angles to the shore, with the bow of the wreckage pointing towards the shore and being most accessible (Plate 4.44). The aft section of this vessel lies within an area of soft, deep sediments with restricted access. At high spring tide FL17 is completely submerged. The vessel is made of steel, but the deteriorated hull has left it in a precarious state with many sharp edges and, if weight is placed upon the hull, it is liable to collapse.

During fieldwork in 2006 and 2007 this vessel was believed to be a Motor Gun Boat or Motor Torpedo Boat. However, subsequent research and photographic evidence has shown it most likely to be the remains of a 40 ft Royal Air Force (RAF) Ferry Boat.

Survey approach and methodology

In 2006 FL17 was surveyed as part of the project's first year. This involved a simple photographic survey, taking basic length and breadth measurements, observing structural remains and recording positional information. Following the 2006 survey it was recommended that additional diagnostic information would be required to identify the class of boat represented by FL17. Following this recommendation, project volunteers undertook a detailed survey of the vessel in 2008, as well as taking additional photographs of component parts and measurements of particular features. Project volunteer Tim Parker undertook this survey with the assistance of three other volunteers as part of his participation in the NAS Part II certificate.

The 2008 survey of FL17 was achieved using the datum offset method to produce a site plan (Fig. 4.53). Unfortunately since 2007 the vessel's condition had deteriorated and the stern area of FL17 was deemed too hazardous to record safely. Therefore the vessel was recorded in plan from the bow to the cabin bulkhead. In addition to the plan drawing a profile of the outer hull was undertaken at the bow using the offset survey method. Although the stern was not surveyed in detail, a photographic survey was undertaken in 2008 from the outside using the hard standing provided by an adjacent landing craft, FL16.

Survey Results

The survey revealed that, although most of the upper works of FL17 have deteriorated, the lower hull remains

Fig. 4.54 RAF Ferry Boat schematic, from Holtham, 2003

Fig. 4.55 FL17 in the 1980s (courtesy of David Fricker)

reasonably intact and it was possible to discern a number of features on the vessel. The complete length of FL17 was measured at 12.93 m and the width at 1.75 m. The vessel is constructed of metal plates welded to a metal frame. The corroded frames are between 3 cm and 5 cm wide and have spacings ranging from 30 cm to 46 cm. At the bottom of the vessel cross beams are riveted to the frames. There is external iron sheeting which has been welded and thin wooden planking in the interior of the vessel.

There are at least two main bulkheads surviving with a third, the forward bulkhead, having partially collapsed between the 2007 and 2008 fieldwork sessions, demonstrating how quickly the hulks at Forton degrade. Towards the stern there is a small amount of superstructure remaining on the port side, within which there are two square openings where windows would have been located. At the stern on the port side there are two rectangular openings for windows that measure 32 cm by 24 cm. Other features associated with the stern are cleats, bollards and a distinctive rail or bar running across the transom from port to starboard sides (Plate 4.45). Some side decking still remains at the stern, in length 8.83 m on the port side and 6.93 m on the starboard side. The width of this side decking is approximately 40 cm. None of the forward decking or cabin super structure has survived. From the stern there is a doorway through a bulkhead into the engine room behind the main cabin. The doorway measures 45 cm wide by 85 cm high.

Either side of it are two rectangular ports or vents that measure 40 cm wide and 18 cm high. A number of features within the hull of FL17 were found during the course of the survey including the remains of a fuel or cooling pipe in the engine compartment, an electrical supply junction box and a possible flywheel (Parker, 2009: 12).

Discussion

The characteristic hull shape of the remains had initially suggested that FL17 was the remains of a Second World War Motor Gun Boat (MGB) or Motor Torpedo Boat (MTB). However, Maurice Cocker (2006: 110–62) indicated that all MTBs and MGBs had wooden hulls and nearly all were in the region of 70 ft (21 m) in length, which is nearly twice the length of FL17. Although there are a small number of 35 ft to 40 ft (11 m – 12 m) prototype boats listed, which were consistent with the length of FL17, these prototypes were all wooden construction rather than metal, as seen in FL17 (Parker, 2009: 14).

During the course of research the photographs of FL17 taken during the 2008 fieldwork were provided to members of the (WSS) Small Craft Group and in May 2009 a member of the group, small craft historian Philip Simons, was able to identify FL17 as an ex-RAF Ferry Boat of either the Mark II or Mark III type (Fig. 4.54). The distinguishing features on FL17 were the tug bar at the stern, the rounded edge to the transom with the rubbing strake around the edge, the position of bollards and lifting eyes. Philip Simons also confirmed that there are no other known survivors of this type of craft. David Fricker, also a member of the WSS Small Craft Group, was able to provide a photograph, taken in the 1980s, of an RAF Ferry Boat at Forton Lake. The position from which this photograph was taken corresponds with the current location of FL17 (Fig. 4.55).

Within the collections of the National Archives at Kew there is a maintenance publication for Mark III 40 ft RAF Ferry Boats which provides further evidence of the identity of FL17. Features illustrated in this publication include the stern bar, the forward watertight bulkhead with the bolted access panel, the engine bay in the centre

Hulk catalogue

RAF Boat Numbers:	4001, 4004, 4006–4009
Builder:	Carrier Engineering Ltd, Wembley, London
Displacement:	Loaded: 10.75 tons (10,922 kg); light: 8.5 tons (8645 kg)
Hull Dimensions:	
Length over all:	44 ft 6 in (13.6 m)
Beam:	12 ft (3.7 m)
Draught Loaded:	2ft 10in (0.86 m – fwd), 3ft 1 in (0.94 m – aft)
Draught Light:	2ft 7in (0.79 m – fwd), 2ft 9in (0.84 m – aft)
Hull Construction:	
Material:	Steel
Method:	Welded hard chine
Main Machinery:	Twin Ford Vosper Thornycroft Conversion Mk 6 each 30/90hp
Maximum speed:	10.0 knots (16.1 kph)
Total Fuel carried:	100 gallons (446 litres)
Endurance:	11 hours
Crew:	4
Maximum Passengers:	40
Alternative Weight of cargo:	3 tons (3050 kg) (approx)

Table 4.11   Specifications for Mark II 40 ft RAF Ferry Boats (Holtham, 2003: 16F/127)

of the vessel and rear cabin structure.[13] A directory of marine craft produced by the WSS Small Craft Group lists the details for Mark II 40 ft RAF Ferry Boats (Table 4.11).

Only 18 Ferry Boats were ever in service with the RAF; one Mk I (no 4000), eight Mk II (nos 4001–4004, 4006–4009), and nine Mk III (nos 4005, 4010–4017). These vessels were built by a number of builders, including Carrier Engineering Ltd from 1944 (nos 4000–4009), Brooke Marine Ltd from 1948 (nos 4010–4013) and Aldous Successors Ltd (nos 4014–4017). All vessels in service with the RAF Marine Branch are detailed on individual Marine Craft Records, held by the RAF Museum at Hendon.[14] Unfortunately the Marine Craft Records for RAF Ferry Boats do not reveal significant details of where the Ferry Boats served. Most of them appear to have had limited careers and many ended up at RAF Calshot on the Solent. Records of RAF Calshot illustrate that a Marine Craft Section (Ferry Pool) was based there from December 1941. No 1102 Marine Craft Base Unit was stationed at RAF Calshot from August 1949 until October 1952 and No 238 Maintenance Unit from October 1953 until May 1961. No 238 Maintenance Unit supported RAF Marine Craft and the Marine Craft Records held by the National Archives confirm that many of the Ferry Boats ended up at the 238 Maintenance Unit, often as a final step before disposal in the late 1940s and 1950s (Parker, 2009: 17). Enquiries made with the Ministry of Defence Disposal Agency suggest that records of these disposals would no longer exist.

All the evidence obtained to date therefore suggests that FL17 came to Forton Lake after ending its service at the 238 Maintenance Unit at RAF Calshot and then on disposal from service was purchased by the F.J. Watts

Boatyard either for resale or for scrapping. If this is the case, FL17 probably arrived prior to August 1951 as no Ferry Boats are listed as being for tender or sale at the F.J. Watts yard between August 1951 and February 1959 (Appendix A).

FL23: Royal Air Force Bomb Scow (NGR: SU 461237 100757; AHBR 57878)

(Mark Beattie-Edwards, Paul Donohue and Dan Pascoe)

Site description

The remains of FL23 lie at the eastern end of the main concentration of hulks on the southern bank to the east of Parham Road (Fig 4.1). As with FL17 they lie on a north–south axis, approximately at right angles to the shore, with the bow of the wreckage pointing towards the shore and being most accessible (Plate 4.46). The aft section of the hulk lies within an area of softer sediments with restricted access around the outside perimeter of the vessel. It lies reasonably high up on the bank of the lake and is partially submerged at high tide. The wreckage is made of steel, but the deteriorated hull has left it in a precarious state with many sharp edges and it would suffer damage if substantial weight was placed upon the hull. The bow area is collapsed and open, the engine room has also collapsed and no internal mechanics remain.

Following the 2006 initial investigation it was suspected that the remains of FL23 were those of a Landing Craft Assault (LCA). However, subsequent research and evidence obtained in 2008 has indicated that it is most likely the remains of an RAF Mark III Bomb Scow.

Survey approach and methodology

In 2006 the wreckage of FL23 was surveyed as part of the first year of the project. This involved a simple photographic survey, basic measurement of length and breadth, observations of structural remains and recording

---

13 http://www.nationalarchives.gov.uk/catalogue/displaycatalogue
   details.asp?CATLN=6&CATID=4136880; Catalogue reference:
   AIR 10/4986.

14 http://www.rafmuseum.org.uk/london/collections/archive/
   marine_craft_records.cfm

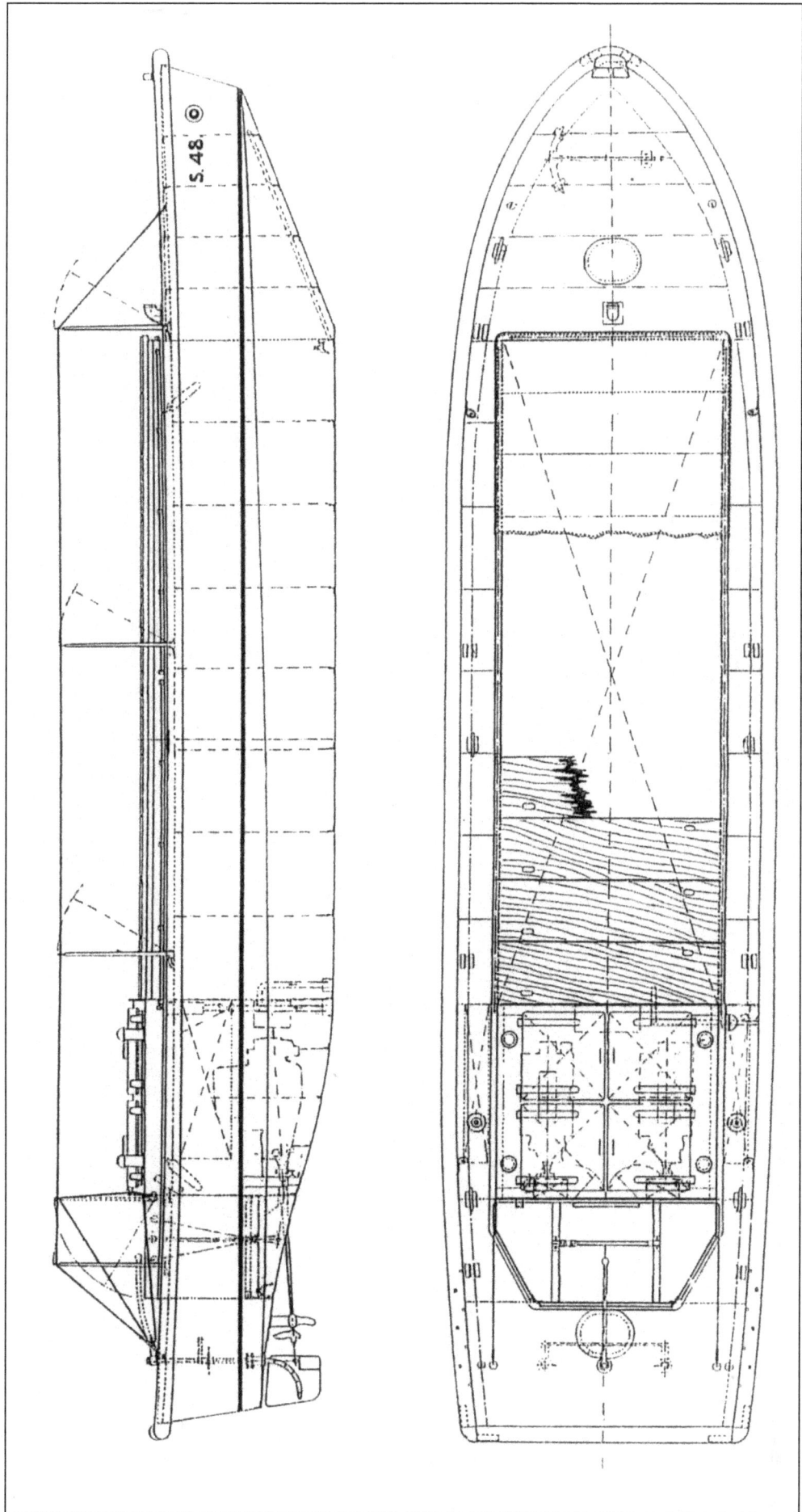

Fig. 4.57   *Bomb scow 33ft lines (from Holtham, 2003)*

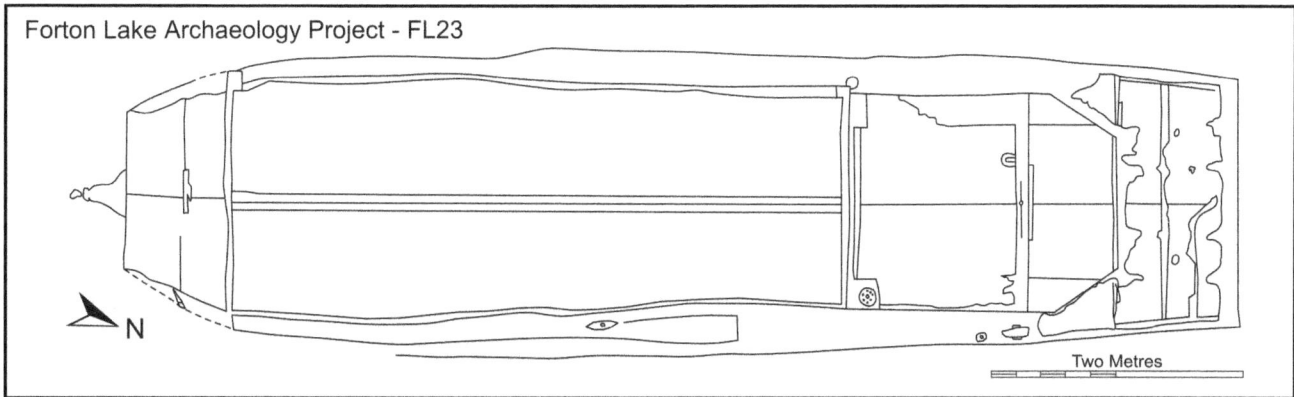

Fig. 4.56   Site plan of FL23

Fig. 4.58   Bomb scow 10 loaded at Calshot (courtesy of the Trustees of the Royal Air Force Museum)

positional information. Following the 2006 survey it was recommended that additional diagnostic information would be required to identify the class of boat it represented. Following this recommendation, project volunteers undertook a detailed survey of the vessel in 2008, as well as taking additional photographs of component parts and measurements of particular features.

This 2008 survey produced a site plan using the datum offset method with a baseline being established down the centre line of the vessel (Fig. 4.56). However, no excavation was undertaken on the wreckage and, therefore, the plan view does not include any features on the floor or lower hull.

Survey Results

The archaeological survey recorded FL23 as 9.20 m (30 ft 2 in) long and 2.40 m (7 ft 10 in) wide. The vessel

Fig. 4.59   S80 bombing up (courtesy of the Trustees of the Royal Air Force Museum)

is constructed of a steel plate outer hull, but the wooden inner skin is no longer present. A substantial amount of FL23's hull is extant, but all the propulsion system has been removed.

The vessel has three main transverse bulkheads and one main longitudinal bulkhead; however, very little remains of the forward bulkhead. It is the presence of this forward bulkhead that precludes the remains of FL23 being a LCA. The main hold of the vessel is 4.90 m long by 2.40 m wide. Behind the aft bulkhead are the engine compartment and the coxswain's position, which have a raised coaming above them. The engine compartment measures 1.70 m by 1.50 m. A top hatch over the engine compartment no longer survives, but there is an entrance from the coxswain's position which measures 0.6 m wide. The coxswain's compartment is 0.7 m by 1.74 m. Behind this compartment there is another compartment approximately 1.0 m by 2.10 m which would have housed the steering gear.

Discussion

Following the detailed recording of FL23 in 2008 the vessel has been identified as most likely being a Mark III RAF Bomb Scow (Fig. 4.57).

Bomb Scows were used for ferrying bombs and depth charges to and from marine aircraft at their moorings

Displacement:	Loaded: 7.6 tons (7722 kg), light: 5.6 tons (5690 kg)
Hull Dimensions:	
Length overall:	33 ft 0 in (10.1 m)
Beam:	7 ft 6 in (2.29 m)
Draught Loaded:	1 ft 8 in (51 cm – fwd), 2 ft 5 in (74 cm – aft)
Draught Light:	1 ft 4 in (41 cm – fwd), 2 ft 1 in (64 cm – aft)
Hull Construction:	
Material:	Welded Steel (listed as riveted by Holtham, 2003: 16F/67)
Method:	Welded hard chine
Main Machinery:	Twin Meadows 8/28 Marine Engines each 12/28hp
Maximum speed:	7 knots (13 kph)
Total Fuel carried:	28 gallons (127 litres)
Endurance/range:	11 hours/65 miles (120 km)
Crew:	2–6
Maximum Passengers (in lieu of cargo):	30
Weight of cargo:	2 tons (2032 kg)

Table 4.12   Technical specifications of 33 ft Mark I Bomb Scows

during the Second World War. The craft had a low freeboard to enable it to be manoeuvred under the wings of the aircraft to be bombed up (loaded). The bombs were stowed on racks in the bomb well and were hoisted out of the scow by the bomb winches on the aircraft (Air Ministry, 1952; Fig. 4.58).

The first prototypes of Bomb and Torpedo Scows were built in 1935 by Thornycrofts at Woolston, Southampton (Yard No 1142) and numbered RAF 1, RAF 2, RAF 3 and S1. Whilst based in Calshot near Southampton in 1935, RAF 1 and RAF 3 were sold to the F.J. Watts Boatyard at Gosport on 8 September 1936 for £25 and £26 respectively, with RAF 2 being sold to Belsize of Southampton on 15 April 1937 for £10. S1 went on to become the prototype for the 31 ft Bomb Scow. It was powered by twin Meadows 8/28 hp petrol engines costing a total of £790 to build. Following the successful sea trials S1 was transferred to Oban in 1937 and continued to spend the rest of its career in Scotland before being sold in March 1943 (Holtham, 2003: 16F/67).

Following the 1935 sea trials of S1 the Marine Craft Policy Committee proposed modifications to the design of the Bomb Scow to allow improved performance and the ability to bomb up underneath flying boats in all conditions (Fig. 4.59). The first order for 31ft Mark I Bomb Scows was placed in December 1937 with Philip & Son of Dartmouth, Devon, who went on to build 34 (S2–S35) from 1938 until 1940. Philip & Son also built three Mark I Bomb Scows for the Royal Australian Air Force Marine Craft Section (Holtham, 2003: 16F/67).

The technical specifications of 33 ft Mark I Bomb Scows produced by the Air Ministry (Air Ministry, 1952) are listed in Table 4.12.

In 1939 the minutes of the Marine Craft Policy Committee record that due to ballasting problems the Mark I Scows were having difficulty bombing up under high winged flying boats and consequently ballasting arrangements had to be altered. Subsequently 12 Mark II Bomb Scows (S36 – S47) were built by Philip & Son between 1940 and 1941, providing the company with a profit of £6,082 (Holtham, 2003: 16F/67). All craft built from S48 would be 33ft long to allow for the extra ballasting and extra height to the deck.

From 1941 to 1954 over 200 33 ft Bomb Scows, also known as Mark IIIs were built by five different shipyards around the country including Yarwood & Sons of Northwich (S48–S53 and S106–S125 and S194–S214), Grant & Livingstone of Ilford, Essex (S126–S137, S164–S193, S215–S222 and S243–S269), Radfords Ltd (S138–S143), John Harker Ltd of Knottingley in Yorkshire (S270–S274) and Philip & Son of Dartmouth (S54–105 and S223–242) (Holtham, 2003: 16F/67).

In total 204 Mark III type Bomb Scows were built between 1941 and 1954 and were disposed of over the world from Japan, Gibraltar, West Africa, Madras, Seychelles and all over Britain including Pembroke, Birkenhead, and Calshot in Southampton. No 238 Maintenance Unit based at Calshot was responsible for the care and repairs for all RAF Marine Craft. Badly damaged craft would be taken to No 238 Unit for necessary work to be undertaken. Of all the Mark III Bomb Scows built only nine vessels are recorded in the RAF Marine Craft Section cards as located at Calshot, Southampton, when they were transferred to the Admiralty for disposal. These Bomb Scows are listed in Table 4.13.

RAF Number	Builder	Date taken on charge	Date for disposal	Date for sale
S66	Philip & Son	20.11.1941	Struck off charge and to DNC 26.07.57 (238 MU)	09.1957
S88	Philip & Son	11.01.1943	Transferred to Admiralty for disposal 20.07.1948	
S104	Philip & Son	24.11.1942	Transferred to Admiralty for disposal 19.08.1947	
S165	Grant & Livingstone	23.09.1942	Transferred to Admiralty for disposal 20.07.1948	
S175	Grant & Livingstone	08.01.1943	Struck off charge 22.10.53 (238 MU)	03.1955
S178	Grant & Livingstone	15.02.1943	Struck off charge and to DNC 27.07.57 (238 MU)	09.1957
S243	Grant & Livingstone	15.06.1944	Struck off charge and to DNC 26.07.57 (238 MU)	09.1957
S258	Grant & Livingstone	22.12.1944	Struck off charge and to DNC 20.07.57 (238 MU)	09.1957
S271	J. Harker Ltd	06.05.1954	Struck off charge and to DNC 11.05.60 (238 MU)	07.1960

Table 4.13   List of Mark III Bomb Scows recorded at Calshot, Southampton, at the time of their disposal. In the fourth column the disposal of individual scows is recorded in the exact terms used on the respective Marine Craft Section cards for each boat. It is not known how the phrase 'Transferred to Admiralty for disposal' differs procedurally, if at all, from 'Struck off charge and to DNC' (Director of Naval Contracts – an official based in the Admiralty), but it is perhaps noteworthy that this change in terminology occurred after c. 1950 when surplus craft were disposed of by a tender process (craft being advertised in Motor Boat and Yachting *magazine – see Appendix A)*

It is believed that one of these nine Bomb Scows is most likely to be FL23 and to have been purchased by the F.J. Watts Boatyard and now to lie in Forton Lake. Only four other Bomb Scows are known to exist in Great Britain: the Motor Yacht *Margareta,* last reported at Titchmarsh Mill near Thrapstone, on the River Nene, known to be a Mark III built by Philip & Son; the *Millie II* in Bristol; the *Lowrie M* in the Forth Canal (thought to originally be a dumb scow[15]) and another unnamed workboat at Broadness Creek on the River Thames (Philip Simons, pers. comm.).

FL24: Pinnace or Harbour Launch (NGR: SU 461225, 100790; AHBR 57879)

(Mark Beattie-Edwards and Paul Donohue)

Site description

FL24 lies on the southern bank of Forton Lake amongst the main group of hulks, just north of the *Vadne* (FL22) (Fig. 4.1). The vessel lies on a north-east/south-west axis, approximately parallel to the shore at this point with the bow pointing towards the north-east (Plate 4.47). It lies on its starboard side within an area of softer deep sediments making access difficult. At high spring tide it is partially submerged. Most of the structure of the hull appears to be in good condition, but because of the

restricted access it is not known what internal features survive.

Survey approach and methodology

In 2006 the wreckage of FL24 was surveyed as part of the first year of the project. Because of the restricted access, this involved a simple photographic survey and the recording of positional information. Following the 2006 photographic survey it was recommended that additional diagnostic information would be required to identify the class of vessel it represented. It was also recommended that basic dimensions and an in-depth photographic survey be undertaken to enable a full interpretation (HWTMA/NAS, 2006: 43). Unfortunately because of the overwhelming health and safety implications it did not prove possible to act upon these recommendations.

Survey Results

From the results of the 2006 photographic survey of FL24 it is possible to identify some characteristics of the vessel (Plate 4.48). The wooden hull is carvel built with a flat transom. The rudder is still present and clearly visible at low tide. On the port side a rubbing strake or whale is partly intact and still attached to the hull.

The framing of FL24 is clearly visible at the bow of the vessel and along the starboard side where decking has rotted away. The metal framed skeleton of the

15   That is to say unengined.

Month/Year	Vessel Type	Pennant	Engined	Reserve price
Pinnaces				
Jun 1953	36 ft Pulling Pinnace	6798	Dumb	£40
Oct 1953	42 ft Sailing Pinnace	7413	Dumb	£75
Oct 1953	36 ft Rowing Pinnace	3068	Dumb	Offers
May 1957	35 ft Motor Pinnace	41590	Dorman diesel	Offers
Sep 1957	36 ft Motor & Pulling Pinnace	41818	No engine	Offers
Harbour Launches				
Aug 1951	36 ft Harbour Launch	43608	No engine	£120
Feb 1952	45 ft Motor Launch	No Number	No engine	£205
Aug 1952	52½ ft Steam Launch	HL(S) 169 *Musket*	Steam	£250
Aug 1952	42 ft Motor Launch	1204	Vosper petrol	£150
Jun 1954	45 ft Motor Passenger Launch	421214	Atlantic diesel	£200
Aug 1954	42 ft Launch	151/46	Dumb (no engine)	£70
Jan 1957	36 ft Harbour Launch	441194	Vosper V8 petrol	Offers
Jan 1957	45 ft Motor Passenger Launch	421191	Atlantic diesel	Offers
May 1957	45 ft Motor Passenger Launch	45635	Atlantic diesel	Offers
Nov 1957	45 ft Motor Launch	41117	Gardener 4 cyl diesel	Offers
Jan 1958	42 ft Dumb Launch	159/49	Dumb (no engine)	Offers
Apr 1958	52½ ft Harbour Launch Diesel	39450	No engine	Offers
Apr 1958	45 ft Motor Passenger Launch	421201	No engine	Offers
Apr 1958	45 ft Motor Launch	43321	No engine	Offers
Jul 1958	52½ ft Harbour Launch Diesel	3546	6 cyl diesel	Offers
Feb 1959	52½ ft Harbour Launch Steam	295	Steam engine	Offers

Table 4.14   Pinnaces and launched listed for tender at F.J. Watts Boatyard between 1951 and 1959

wheelhouse is still standing, although very little coaming survives. It has been suggested by the current manager of The Maritime Workshop on Parham Road at Forton that this metal frame was added in the 1980s by the owner (Bill Puddle, pers. comm.).

Discussion

In the 2006 project report the hulk of FL24 was thought to possibly be a Royal Navy Pinnace (see FL7 for background information on pinnaces – pages 48–9). It is not certain whether it is actually a pinnace or not, since because of its location it has not even proved possible to measure accurately the dimensions of the remains. Philip Simons (pers. comm.) has suggested that, as well as a 52 ft (15.8 m) steam pinnace, FL24 could be an early 52½ ft (16 m) Steam Harbour Launch (HL(S)) or a later Diesel Harbour Launch (HL(D)).

The first 52½ ft Harbour Launches were built as steam pinnaces at the end of the nineteenth century. They

adopted the acronym HL(S) and served the fleet all over the world until the mid 1920s when the diesel powered variety started to be built. Over 230 diesels were subsequently launched, with the last batch being produced in 1971. They operated in every corner of the globe where the Royal Navy was based with each boat given a unique pennant number which began with the year of build, followed by the consecutive boat number for that year. The boat number included all boats built for the Navy and not just HL(D)s, which for example explains that HL(D) no 56140 was the 140th boat (of all types) ordered for the Service in 1956 (Philip Simons, pers. comm.).

Looking to the records of the vessels from the tender lists of F.J. Watts Boatyard between 1951 and 1959 it is possible to find five pinnaces listed, as well as 16 launches (Table 4.14). Only four of these launches are listed as being 52½ ft (corresponding to the length of FL24 estimated by Philip Simons), with two steam and

Fig. 4.60   The remains of FL31 on the southern shore.   Only the bottom timbers remain in the foreground (photo: Julian Whitewright)

two diesel types. Additional work will be needed to measure the length of FL24 to confirm this, as well as an examination of the internal features to help determine if it was originally steam or diesel driven.

At present it is unknown how many other examples of this type of vessel survive in the world. As mentioned in the case of FL7, 16 pinnaces were registered in 2009 on the UK's National Historic Ships Register. In the context of surviving pinnaces FL24 is not considered rare. There are, however, currently no Harbour Launches listed on the Historic Ships Register. It is not known how many pre-Second World War Harbour Launches still exist, but a number have been found for sale with a simple internet search, including Motor Vessel *Saracen*, a 52 ft 1939 Harbour Launch.

FL31: Possible Motor Gun Boat (NGR: SU 460519, 100985)

(Julian Whitewright)

Site description

FL31 lies on a west/east orientation at the eastern edge of the main concentration of vessels on the southern shore of Forton Lake (Fig. 4.1). The coherent remains consist of the lower elements of the vessel (Fig. 4.60). Other elements, probably associated, are scattered in the immediate vicinity. The vessel remains are fully submerged at high water and fully exposed at low water.

Although some sediment has accumulated on the vessel, access is relatively straightforward. FL31 was located at the very end of the 2008 survey season, consequently only limited time was available to record the remains of the vessel.

Survey approach and methodology

FL31 was subjected to a basic survey in 2009, which concentrated on recording the relationship of the framing elements and any other features that were subsequently recorded during this work. A note was also made of the general constructional features of the vessel. A baseline was established along the keel line of the vessel and offsets were taken at each frame station.

Survey Results

The results of the basic survey of FL31 are presented in Fig. 4.61. It is a wooden, frame built vessel, with diagonal planking. The coherent remains measure 18.7 m (61 ft 4 in) in length with a maximum width of 4.1 m (13 ft 5 in). The transom stern of the vessel is present; however, the bow is more degraded and the stem post has been broken at the scarf with the keel indicating that the overall length of the original vessel would have been slightly greater than the current remains. Similarly, although the lower elements of the hull survive, the sides of the vessel do not extend above the turn of the bilge. The overall width of the original vessel would therefore

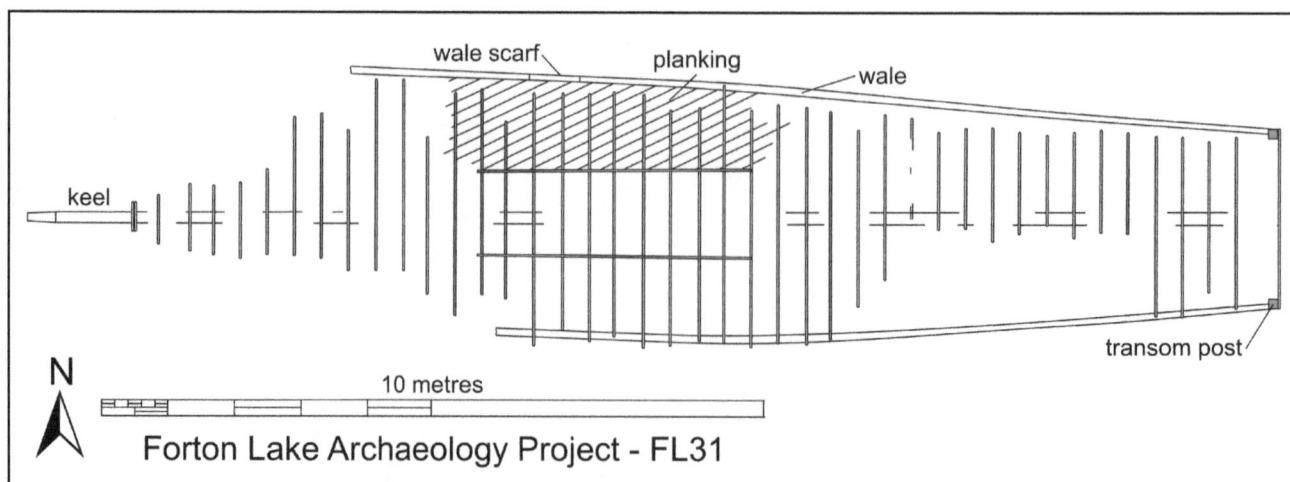

Fig. 4.61   Basic survey plan of the remains of FL31 (drawing: Julian Whitewright)

Fig. 4.62   Double-diagonal planks of FL31 (scale=30 cm) (photo: Julian Whitewright)

also have been greater than the current remains. The form of the hull, along with its construction indicates that the vessel was motorized. This feature, in conjunction with the characteristics described below, suggest that FL31 was a type of motor launch dating from the Second World War.

Planking & Fastening

The hull of FL31 is wooden and planked with diagonally laid planks. These survive in good condition in some areas of the vessel and a recorded area is shown in Fig. 4.62. These planks are 15 cm in width, 5 mm thick and are laid at an angle of 65° to the vessels frames (25° to the keel-line). This form of planking is often applied using two layers of diagonally laid planks running in opposite directions, termed 'double-diagonal'. Only a single layer of diagonal planking survives *in situ* on FL31. This is attached to the frames with screws, *c*. 5 mm in diameter.

Framing

The framing of FL31 is very uniform in nature, suggesting a regularized form of construction. Frames are 15 cm moulded and 25–30 mm sided and are sawn to

shape. In some places they are reinforced with thin layers of wood, attached to either side, possibly the remains of a bulkhead. Although difficult to establish, the frames seem to be bolted to the keel of the vessel. The frames do not survive beyond the turn of the bilge. This area is delineated on either side of the vessel by the remains of a wale. This element is characteristic of fast motor boats constructed in the mid-20th century. The surviving planking of the vessel stops at the wale, indicating that the wale was probably fitted prior to the planking. The wale is trapezoidal in section, the widest edge (attached to the frames) measuring 11 cm sided and the moulded dimension being 7 cm. One scarf was noted on the starboard wale (Fig. 4.61). This took the form of a half-lap scarf measuring *c*. 75 cm in length.

The vessel is transom-sterned, with posts on each quarter that form the edges of the transom. The remainder of these elements are buried, so their shape and relationship to the keel of the vessel is unknown. Two longitudinal timbers survive in the centre of the vessel. These are 35 mm sided; it is unclear if these are rabbetted over the frames or simply sit on top of them. The outer sides of these timbers are clad in thin wood, which extends downwards into the sediment and consequently its relationship to the keel and planking is unknown. This pair of timbers is likely to be related to the engine mounts or possibly to the fuel tanks.

Discussion

The dimensions and constructional features of FL31 fit closely with those of the fast motor launches utilized by the Royal Navy and RAF during the Second World War, such as Motor Gun Boats (MTBs) and Motor Torpedo Boats (MTBs). A great number of these vessels were built by the British Power Boat Company at their shipyard at Hythe, on Southampton Water, and by Vospers at their yard in Portsmouth. Many of these classes of vessels had an overall length of between 60 ft and 75 ft (18.3 m and 22.9 m). FL31 probably fits into the upper range of this bracket. Such vessels were

Fig. 4.63   FL31 in 1950. Detail from Fig. 2.4

Fig. 4.65   Vessels   of   a   similar   size   and construction to FL31

generally built of wood, with double- or triple-diagonal planking. The remains of only a single layer of planking on FL31 are, therefore, strange. However, it is possible that the outer layer was removed before the vessel degraded to its present state or has rotted and so was not observed during the brief period of the survey. The absence of the upper elements and superstructure of the vessel means that exact identification of the type and class of vessel is difficult on the basis of the coherent, surviving structure.

The RAF aerial photographs of Forton Lake from April 1950 show a vessel in the position now occupied by FL31 (Fig. 4.63). This vessel measures just over 20 m in length and *c.* 5 m in width, which corresponds to the likely complete length of FL31. The same vessel is present in the aerial photograph from February 1949 (Fig. 4.64). In an RAF aerial photograph from April 1953 (RAF/82/766 Frame 0311) the superstructure has disappeared and it resembles the remains that can be seen in modern aerial photographs. The photographic evidence strongly suggests that this vessel corresponds to FL31. Furthermore, it reveals that it was in roughly its current state of survival by 1953. The sudden degradation between 1949 and 1953 is most likely the result of a sudden event, for example a fire.

Fig. 4.64   FL31 in 1949. Detail from Fig. 2.1

Vessels of a similar size and construction to FL31 are still utilized as house boats, although very few survive in their original form (Fig. 4.65). Two such vessels can be seen on the west bank of the River Itchen in Southampton, immediately to the north of Cobden Bridge. A restored vessel of similar size (numbered MGB 81) is currently berthed at Buckler's Hard on the Beaulieu River in Hampshire. Several hundred of this type of vessel were originally built and nine Second World War fast motor launches of comparable size were listed on the National Register of Historic Ships in 2010. Further historical research into local archives or oral history has the capacity to reveal more about the disposal of FL31 at Forton Lake and its previous career.

Unclassified vessels

(Julie Satchell)

As has already been demonstrated in this chapter, when survey and research enabled the name of an individual vessel to be identified, it opened up a wider range of historical sources which allowed the full interpretation of the vessel. There are a number of vessels within Forton Lake for which a specific name is not known, but for which it is possible to identify a probable function from the hull form and construction. However, there are also a number of vessels, which have been recorded, but for which it has not been possible to ascribe a name or function. These have been recorded as 'unclassified'.

There are four unclassified vessels within Forton Lake; FL4, FL18, FL19 and FL26. It is possible that future research will enable these craft to be identified and hence their contribution to history more fully understood.

FL4: Unclassified vessel (NGR: SU 461143, 100902)

(Julian Whitewright, Paul Donohue and Julie Satchell)

Site description

FL4 composes the remains of an unidentified vessel located on the northern side of Forton Lake, 13 m to the west of FL3 (Fig. 4.1). The bow of the vessel lies to the north. It is located in an area that is completely inundated at high tide. Consequently it is surrounded by very deep

Fig. 4.66   Remains of FL4, looking south, 2007

sediments and access to the vessel is both difficult and hazardous.

Survey approach and methodology

This hulk was recorded by Ted Sutton in 1997, but it has since deteriorated considerably as can be seen when comparing the remains in the foreground of Plate 4.49 taken in 1984 with the condition of the vessel in 2007 (Fig. 4.66). A large amount of hull structure, including planking and framing elements have disappeared, highlighting a rapid rate of decay. The nature of the vessel and the lack of an adequate identification would normally recommend the remains of FL4 for a full survey and possibly archaeological excavation. However, the deep soft sediment surrounding the vessel made access problematic; consequently only a photographic survey was undertaken.

Survey results

Based on the 2006 aerial photograph of Forton Lake (Plate 4.50) it is possible to establish the approximate dimensions of FL4. The vessel is *c.* 17 m in length and *c.* 4.5 m wide. The vessel is wooden, carvel built, with a rounded bilge and was probably propelled by an engine. The vessel is thought to date from the early twentieth century. Surviving elements of the vessel include: keel, floor timbers, hull planking, stringers, timber knees and a metal skylight thought to form part of the deck structure (Fig. 4.67).

Hull remains

The visible framing elements of the vessel on the port side are composite, consisting of two timbers set alongside one another. The ends of these timbers are staggered to maintain strength and the two parts of the frame are fastened horizontally. A series of horizontal transverse timbers run across the vessel and provide a flat floor in the bottom of the vessel. The remains of a large stringer are also located on the remaining port side structure. All the fastenings visible on FL4 are iron bolts. These are used in the frame fastenings and also to secure the planks to the frames.

Discussion

Further analysis of FL4 is difficult because of the lack of information, both from historical sources and from survey of the vessel. The combination of wooden hull and engine propulsion probably serves to confirm the date of

Fig. 4.67   FL4: internal vessel remains, looking south.

the vessel as early 20th century. However, even with the earlier photograph in which the vessel is in a much better state of preservation it is still difficult to suggest a vessel type. The dimensions and shape of FL4 suggest that the remains are unlikely to be those of a cargo vessel. FL4 could be the remains of a small passenger vessel or a fishing vessel, the latter possibility being more likely.

FL18: Unclassified vessel (NGR: SU 461191, 100763; HER: HCC 53073)

FL19: Unclassified vessel (NGR: SU 461199, 100770)

(Mark Beattie-Edwards)

Site description

The remains of FL18 and FL19 lie in the middle of the main concentration of vessels on the southern bank to the east of Parham Road, just to the east of FL9 and the west of FL20 (Fig 4.1). They are located in an area that is completely inundated at high tide and consequently they are surrounded by very deep sediments and access to the vessels is both difficult and hazardous (Plate 4.51).

Survey approach and methodology

Because of the hazardous conditions around the remains of FL18 and FL19, they were only subjected to a photographic survey from the closest area of safe access.

Survey results

FL18 and FL19 appear to represent the hull remains of wooden built vessels. Both vessels lie in a generally north/south orientation, probably with their bows to the south. FL18 is *c.* 20 m in length and FL19 is *c.* 13 m in length. Only the bottom and sides of either vessel survive.

FL26: Unclassified vessel (NGR: SU 461138, 101005)

(Julian Whitewright)

Site description

FL26 is located in the northern area of Forton Lake (Fig. 4.1). Its remains lie in two portions. The larger comprises 0the stern and substantial part of the starboard

Fig. 4.68   Principal hull remains of FL26 (2006), looking north towards the stern of the vessel. The bow section is located in the drainage channel on the left of the picture. The main surviving structural elements are all visible: keel, keelson, hull planking, riser, engine footings, gunwale, hanging knee and propeller shaft log (scale=50 cm)

Fig. 4.69   Volunteers recording the basic measurements of FL26 in 2007. Note the missing hull structure on the left of the picture, when compared to the previous year

side of the vessel and is located at the high water mark (Fig. 4.68). The smaller comprises the bow of the vessel and is located in a nearby drainage channel. Access to both elements of the vessel is possible. Both the date and the identification of the vessel are unknown. Overall, the remains of the vessel are in poor condition, owing to the fact that it is broken into at least two sections and other sections are missing. However, the surviving sections are

Fig. 4.70   FL26, framing elements, engine footings and propeller shaft log. Frames are composite in the floor of the vessel and extend as far as the engine footing after which they are single timbers (scale=50 cm)

coherent enough to give a good impression of the main constructional characteristics of the original vessel.

Survey approach and methodology

Basic measurements were recorded (Fig. 4.69) and the vessel was subject to a photographic survey.

Survey results

FL26 represents the fragmentary remains of a wooden clinker built boat, with a recorded length of the surviving starboard side of the hull being 5.33 m. The complete vessel seems likely to have been less than 10 m in length. The width of the vessel cannot be estimated because of the distortion evident in the surviving starboard side. The footings for an engine and the propeller shaft log both survive, indicating that the vessel was motorized.

Planking and fastening

The planking of FL26 is clinker laid from wooden planks. The exterior of the vessel has been covered with a layer of fibreglass. This has been facilitated by the laying of wooden batons in the exterior channel of the clinker strakes to smooth the profile of the planking. The complete starboard side comprises eighteen strakes, fastened together with roved copper nails. The same fastening is used to secure the frames to the planks. The planks are 10 cm in width and 1 cm thick. The sheer strake has been fitted with a filler strake on the outside, giving the impression of a carvel laid plank. A rubbing strake is fastened to the exterior of the sheer strake.

Framing

The framing of FL26 is lightweight. In the bottom of the vessel the frames are set in threes, with two frames used together to make a floor timber (Fig. 4.70). This pattern extends to the longitudinal engine mount timbers, *c.* 25 cm either side of the centreline of the vessel. Thereafter, the frames continue in threes past the rounded turn of the bilge, but each frame is comprised of a single piece of wood. Once the sides of the vessel reach a vertical plane,

Fig. 4.71   FL26: Overview of floor frames and engine footings. The bottom of the picture is the starboard side of the vessel (scale=50 cm)

the central frame in each set also stops, leaving evenly spaced single frames along the upper works of the vessel (Fig. 4.70). The centre to centre frame spacing along the upper portion of the vessel is 14.5 cm. Individual frames are 2.3 cm sided and 1.25 cm moulded. Wooden chocks are located between each floor timber and the garboard and first strake to fill the gap and to form the limber holes of the vessel (Fig. 4.70).

The keelson of the vessel is plank-like and is 17 cm sided and 3 cm moulded. Iron bolts are used in the vessel with steel bolts fastening the keel and keelson together. These look to have been added after the original construction. The rigidity of the vessel is further increased by a pair of longitudinal timbers that act as the engine mounts, and which run along the surviving length of the vessel (Fig. 4.71). These are located 23 cm from the centreline of the vessel and are 5 cm sided and 10 cm moulded. Iron fittings survive which would have provided the attachment for the engine block to these footings.

A riser runs along the side of the vessel, 20 cm below the bottom of the gunwale (Fig. 4.72). A surviving hanging knee associated with this (Fig. 4.68) indicates that there may originally have been thwarts running down the side of the vessel, at the stern. There is no visible evidence for conventional thwarts or cross-beams set into the riser.

Discussion

FL26 represents the remains of a wooden clinker built boat. Although the vessel remains unidentified, a few comments can be made regarding its use. The remains suggest that it underwent a major refit at some point. This entailed the replacement of keel bolts and the sheathing of the exterior of the hull with fibreglass. This was evidently a considered undertaking as the sheathing required the laying of wooden batons in the external clinker channels to smooth the distinctive shape of the clinker planking. The present condition of the vessel, in several pieces, is probably the result of deliberate action. The severed ends of the bow section and the stern section are clean and straight, suggesting that the vessel was

Fig. 4.72   FL26, starboard side upper hull. The scale rests on the riser; the hanging knee can be seen in the lower right of the picture. The clean line of the break-up of the hull can also be clearly seen on the left of the picture (scale=5 cm)

sawn up, rather than broken down gradually. The construction and size of the vessel points to a possible identification as a fairly small motorized fishing vessel.

4.2: Shoreside structures

Although the project concentrated on the abandoned vessels, it was acknowledged that broader aspects of the historic marine environment were evident within the area. Two sites subject to survey were a slipway at the boatyard on Ferrol Road and a groyne structure to the north-east of the lake (Fig 4.1).

Slipway Site (NGR: SU 46114, 100652; HER: HCC 55067 (Boatyard and slipway))

(Ian Barefoot, Julie Satchell and Mark Beattie-Edwards)

Site Description

Access to the slipway site can be gained directly off Ferrol Road (Fig. 4.73). This site was not assigned an FL code, but is referred to as the 'slipway site'. There is a covering of sediment on the slipway which varies in depth along its length, but is generally less than 8 cm deep at the higher end, getting progressively deeper towards the low water mark. The visual and photographic survey undertaken demonstrated that the rails, rail bed, and the central rack system were still *in situ* on the slipway. The rails appear to be in good condition, although the central rack may be displaced at one point along its length.

Survey approach and method

The investigation of the slipway was undertaken in 2006. This work included a site inspection, a limited excavation which cleared the covering mud from a section of the slipway and a photographic survey.

Survey Results

The slipway was constructed of four parallel rails on a hard, two close-spaced in the middle (Plate 4.53). The rail used is believed to be a British Standard 40 lb/yard commonly used on light railway systems. All four rails

Fig. 4.73   *Aerial photographs of the slipway in 1950 and 2006. Detail from Figs 1.2 and 2.4*

seem to have been laid on longitudinal baulks (i.e. the timbers run longitudinally to support the rail, rather than being laid at right angles to it), similar to the method used by Brunel on his broad gauge system for the Great Western Railway. The Brunel system gained further stability from piles driven into the ground supporting the longitudinal timbers. Whether or not these were present on the slipway could not be determined during the course of the excavations in 2006.

A rack system lying immediately to the east of the central pair of rails would have carried a pawl mechanism to prevent the slipping cradle running back while being hauled in (Plate 4.54). Between these rails there is a short length of rack, possibly used to provide a safety locking system once the vessel was fully slipped, though the possibility that this has been displaced from its correct position should not be discounted. Immediately to the west of the central rails part of the winching cable survives running up the slipway. This cable would have run from the winch at the head of the slip to a pulley mounted on the cradle, then to a secure point at the head of the slip.

In use the cradle would be let down into the water and the vessel to be slipped would be manoeuvred over it. Once secure on the cradle, the vessel could be winched up the rails, in a manner similar to that used by rope-worked inclines common on early mineral railways. This resulted in a much easier slipping of the vessel, as the carriage wheels of the cradle supporting the load induced significantly less friction than the vessel's hull resting directly on the slipway

Discussion

The proximity of the slipway to The Maritime Workshop enabled consultation with local residents about its known history. Mr Hollins, secretary of The Maritime Workshop, stated that it was a 'patent railway slip' or patent slip (Peter Hollins, pers. comm.). This refers to a patent for the design of a method of bringing ships ashore granted to Thomas Morton, a shipbuilder based in Leith, in 1818 in Scotland and in 1819 in England, Wales and the Colonies (patent no GB 4352).[16] The patent describes the 'carriage' on which a ship may be brought ashore with copious detail of its construction and of the mechanisms designed to settle the vessel securely onto the carriage. The carriage runs up and down the slip on 'trucks, wheels or rollers' or may 'slide with grease or other unctuous substance'. The use of rails as such is not specified, but the patent says that it is 'of advantage' to lay 'ways ... of wood, iron or other fit substance' beneath each of the longitudinal beams of the carriage. Morton also recommends the use of a rack and pawl to prevent the carriage running back in case the chain or rope used to haul the carriage up breaks.

In the event Morton did not make much money from his patent; although at least 45 slips had been installed, for the first six years of the patent, Morton had made no profit and only £5,737 profit over the whole period of the patent. He therefore petitioned House of Commons to extend its duration and in 1832 a Select Committee under the chairmanship of Rt Hon Sir George Cockburn was convened to adjudicate the question. In the event, although sympathetic, the Committee felt unable to support Morton's petition because of the precedent that it would create, but their report from April of that year provides some interesting facts about the early history of the patent slip, including a comparison with other means of bringing ships out of the water for repair, such as dry docking. The comparative costs for the time were stated

---

16   http://www.ipo.gov.uk/about/contact.htm

Fig. 4.74　　　FL27: line of posts stretching towards the main entrance/exit channel of Forton Lake. Looking south-east

Fig. 4.75　　　FL27: detail of protruding timber posts in the intertidal zone (main scale=50cm).

as £170 for dry docking compared to £3 for hauling out on a slip (Prosser, 2004).[17]

At one time this type of slip would have been a common sight in dockyards, but it has now virtually disappeared. Slow to be accepted, the House of Commons Select Committee reported that by 1832 there were over one hundred in use in Britain, including one 'in Portsmouth'. Whilst this probably refers to the Naval Dockyard, the possibility of the Ferrol Road site being its location should be explored further.

During the 2006 project, contact was made with several boat owners based at The Maritime Workshop on Ferrol Road. They commented on the loss of the slipway situated adjacent to Ferrol Road, which appeared to be in the process of being covered with accumulated rubbish. Subsequent conversations with Mr Hollins revealed that this was indeed the case. A photograph supplied by local maritime artist Colin Baxter, showing the ex-Admiral's barge *Janet* on the slipway at Forton in June 1992, demonstrates that the infilling of the slipway with rubble and rubbish must have happened sometime between 1992 and 2006 (Plate 4.52).

FL27: Groyne Structure (NGR: SU 461558, 100954)

(Julian Whitewright, Paul Donohue and Julie Satchell)

Site description

FL27 appears to be the remains of a groyne, located on the northern side of Forton Lake towards the eastern end of the lake (Fig. 4.1). The groyne is situated in the intertidal zone on a north/south orientation (Fig. 4.74).

Survey approach and methodology

The site was subject to a basic photographic survey.

Results

The visible remains of the structure consist of a series of wooden posts over a length of 29 m, stretching out into the channel. The posts are placed 14–20 cm apart between centres (Fig. 4.75). The exposed wooden posts have clearly been subjected to degradation from physical, chemical and biological processes.

Discussion

An indication of the historical presence of FL27 on the shores of the lake first appears on an annotated map of Gosport and Portsmouth from 1922. The path of FL27 extends into Forton Lake from the land boundary of the nearby Priddy's Hard. It is therefore possible that FL27 was constructed to act as a physical extension to this boundary designed to prevent unwanted access along the shore of the Forton Lake at all states of the tide. FL27 is the only such structure present with Forton Lake. However, aerial photographs of the wider Portsmouth Harbour area show the presence of several other structures that are probably similar to FL27.

17　http://www.oxforddnb.com/view/article/19374 – subscription website.

Plate 3.1   Volunteers undertaking hulk recording using the offset survey method taught during the NAS Introduction course (photo: Colin McKewan)

Plate 3.2   The Mayor of Gosport presents an award in the 2007 fancy dress competition

Plate 3.3   Schoolchildren meet the archaeologist on the foreshore

Plate 3.4   Being a 'Maritime Archaeologist for an Hour'

Plate 3.5   Front cover of the 'Forton's Forgotten Fleet' popular booklet

Plate 3.6   A visitor to the exhibition at the Local Studies Centre in Gosport High Street

Colour Plates

Plate 4.1   The exposed frames of FL5 as they appeared in 2006

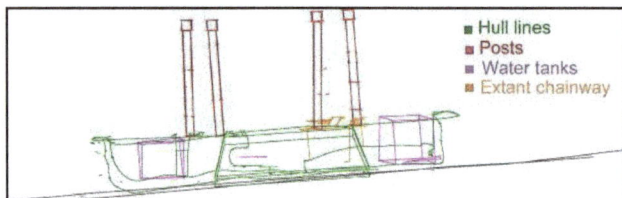

Plate 4.2   3D plan of FL11, seen from the bow (drawing: Ioanna Damanaki)

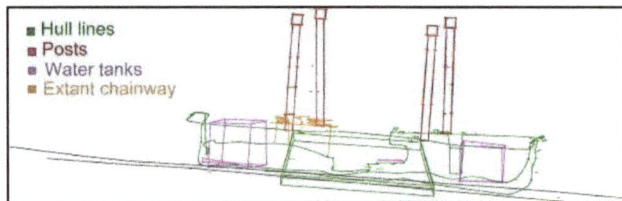

Plate 4.3   3D plan of FL11, seen from the stern (drawing: Ioanna Damanaki)

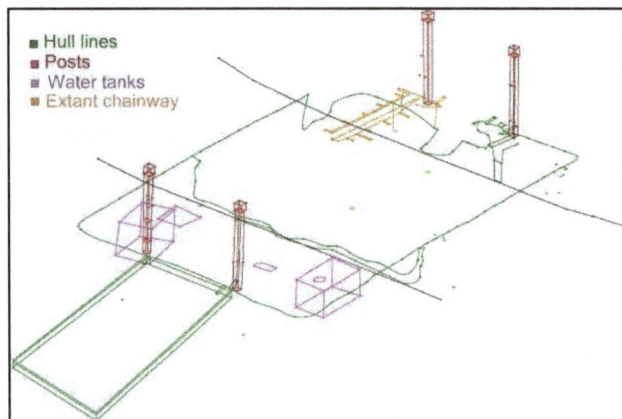

Plate 4.4   3D plan of FL11, seen from the port bow (drawing: Ioanna Damanaki)

Plate 4.5   General view of FL11. Note the wooden rubbing strake, chain-ways and mooring rings. Iron knees are visible inside the vessel on the left of the picture (photo: Alex Poudret-Barré)

Plate 4.6   Bulkhead remains inside FL11; the feature on the left is the inner end of a chain-way (photo: Alex Poudret-Barré)

Plate 4.7   Water tank located inside the hull of FL11. Also visible are the iron transverse beams to carry the decking, fragmentary remains of the decking and the remains of the iron bolts used to fasten the decking (photo: Alex Poudret-Barré)

Plate 4.8   View of the remaining boarding ramp of FL11 (photo: Alex Poudret-Barré)

Plate 4.9   One of the four hinges supporting FL11's remaining boarding ramp (photo: Alex Poudret-Barré)

Plate 4.10   Profile view of the chain-way on FL11, from starboard (photo: Alex Poudret-Barré)

Plate 4.11   Chain-way on FL11 in close up (photo: Alex Poudret-Barré)

Plate 4.12   L-shaped frames, knees and protruding knees at mid-height on FL11. Bolts and rivets are also visible (photo: Alex Poudret-Barré)

Plate 4.13   Iron bolts used to secure the rubbing strake on FL 11 (photo: Alex Poudret-Barré)

Colour Plates

Plate 4.14   A modern chain ferry continues the tradition of FL11. The King Harry Ferry, built in 2006, plies for custom across the River Fal, Cornwall (photo: Gerald Grainge)

Plate 4.15   FL1 with the floating pontoons that restricted access during the survey in 2007

Plate 4.16   The bow section of FL1 looking west with the stem post, false stem, ceiling planking and concrete ballast

Plate 4.17   The side-by-side composite frames of FL1 and the concrete ballast between the frames. The arrow shows a vertical cut on the port side illustrating salvage work undertaken on FL1

Plate 4.18   The sternpost (red) of FL1 with the rudder stock (blue), the inner post (green) and the knee (yellow). Looking west (scale=1 m)

Plate 4.19   Port side of FL2 looking south showing concrete covering over hatch

Plate 4.20   Repaired frames evident at the bow of FL2 (scale=1 m) (photo: Jane Maddocks)

Plate 4.21   External cover on FL2 closing access to seawater

Plate 4.22   General overview of the situation of FL9 in Forton Lake, looking north-east. Note the relative preservation of the bow area

Plate 4.23   Volunteers engaged in documenting the remains of FL9, looking south. The increased preservation in the bow area is again apparent

Plate 4.24   FL9: detail of the internal bow section (scale=1 m)

Plate 4.25   Internal view of FL9, looking north from the bow. The cross-beam is clearly visible along with the metal tanks on the port and starboard sides

Colour Plates

Plate 4.26   The wreckage of FL3 at Forton Lake

Plate 4.27   Photograph showing the composite frame structure of FL 3 and the evidence of burning

Plate 4.28   A photograph of the inside of the bow section of FL3, with the floor and ceiling planking (photo: Colin McKewan)

Plate 4.29   Remains of four collapsed tanks and laminated timber bulkhead of FL3 (photo: Colin McKewan)

Plate 4.30   FL3's sweep drum looking aft

Plate 4.31   The stern of FL3 looking north-west showing the inner post, transverse knee and outer propeller shaft bearing

Plate 4.32   MMS 293 in 1984 with the remains of the masts visible on the starboard side (courtesy of Philip Simons)

Plate 4.35   The boiler of FL7 (scale=1.8 m)

Plate 4.33   MMS 293 in the 1980s with '293' just visible on the port bow (courtesy of David Fricker)

Plate 4.36   FL7 in the 1980s (courtesy of Philip Simons)

Plate 4.34   FL7 taken from the south

Plate 4.37   The restored Pinnace 199 now known as Treleague at Portsmouth International Festival of the Sea in 2001 (courtesy of David Fricker)

75

Colour Plates

Plate 4.38   The wreck of FL10 in 2006 (taken from the north)

Plate 4.39   FL10 partially submerged at high tide

Plate 4.40   FL16 Landing Craft Assault (taken from the south)

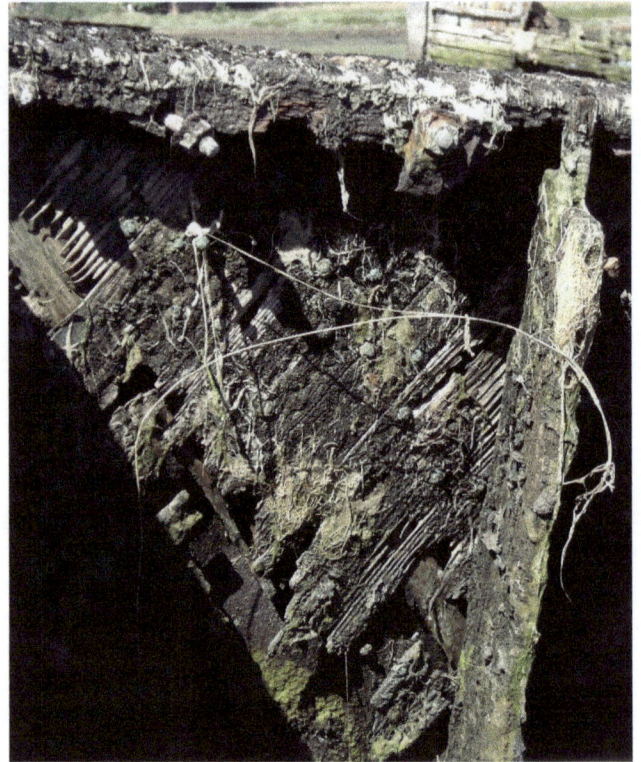

Plate 4.41   Diagonal planking on FL16

Plate 4.42   FL16 Landing Craft Assault (in the foreground) in 1987 (courtesy of David Fricker)

Plate 4.43   Recording the length of FL20 Landing Craft Assault from the south (courtesy of Roger Forster)

Plate 4.44   The remains of FL17 (photo: Tim Parker)

Plate 4.47   FL24 at high tide in 2006 (courtesy of Ken Pavitt)

Plate 4.45   Stern rail of FL17 (photo: Tim Parker)

Plate 4.48   FL24 from the south-east at low tide in 2006

Plate 4.46   FL23 at Forton Lake

Plate 4.49   Remains of FL4 (foreground), looking east. FL3 lies beyond. Taken in 1984 (courtesy of David Fricker)

Colour Plates

Plate 4.50   2006 aerial photograph of FL4. FL4 lies to the right of the other vessel (FL3). Colour detail from Fig. 1.2

Plate 4.51   FL18 (left foreground) and FL19 (right background) taken from the south

Plate 4.52   The ex-Admiral's barge Janet on the slipway at Forton in June 1992 showing the pulley system under the bow of the vessel, as well as the rail system running down the water (courtesy of Colin Baxter)

Plate 4.53   The excavated 2 m wide trench across the slipway revealing the track system. South is to the right

Plate 4.54   Close up of the track system showing the toothed rack rail that would have served as a brake during vessel movements in and out of the lake

Chapter 5: Project Review

Review of the archaeological methodology (Mark Beattie-Edwards)

As detailed in Chapter 3, the archaeological methodology employed during the project not only drew upon the previous work undertaken on the site by Ted Sutton, but also borrowed from the strategies employed by earlier projects with similar aims, such as that undertaken at Whitewall Creek (Milne *et al,* 1998), the River Hamble[1] and Itchen River.[2] With the fieldwork being spread over three years it was also possible to reflect on each season's work, learn lessons and make changes to the recording methodology for the following year.

It has been said that in developer-funded archaeology it is 'always a challenge to achieve a high quality of recording meeting the client's budgets and timescales, and allowing the story of the site to emerge' (Spanou, 2009: 49). The experience of the project has illustrated that grant-funded public archaeology is in many ways also subject to these limitations.

One methodological challenge that presents itself in a community archaeology project like the one at Forton Lake is how to train and supervise a group of volunteers to ensure that site recording is consistently illustrative and, importantly, representative of the actual archaeological material on the site. During the fieldwork phase the volunteer workforce on the project was varied in its previous experience, as well as diverse in its interests and abilities, with some people wishing to develop and improve their drawing skills and others simply happy to excavate. To compensate for the varied abilities of the team all project volunteers were briefed and supervised in the recording methodologies being employed by the project and team members with no previous experience were trained and supported during their time.

Another recording challenge that is always present during an intertidal archaeological project is the time constraints presented by the ever changing tide. To mitigate against this, the planning phase of each year's fieldwork utilized tidal prediction data to ensure that fieldwork sessions coincided with suitable tides that meant that access to the hulks could be undertaken during the day. This would ensure the most productive fieldwork session. The use of swift and repeatable recording methodologies employed during the project also allowed for this limited time on site. During the excavation phase the tide also posed a problem as it meant that twice a day the trenches would be filled with water and that vertical trench faces would be subjected to damage. Due to the limited time on site, and with the exception of FL29, all excavation during the course of the project was undertaken by the digging of trenches rather than by open area excavation.

The use of digital data recording in archaeology means that large amounts of information can be acquired using tools such as laser scanners, digital cameras, differential Global Positioning Systems (GPS) and electronic distance measuring devices such as total stations. The disadvantage of these data acquisition techniques is that they require both the availability of the equipment and the competence to use it. The recording strategy of the project was to try and utilize digital data capture, where appropriate, using GPS to determine location coordinates for each of the sites and digital photography in conjunction with 35-mm photography. Having said this, the majority of the project surveys were carried out using manual survey techniques such as 2D offset and 1 m square planning frames, sketching and ultimately the production of hand drawn scale drawings. This strategy meant that all members of the team each year were able to contribute and take responsibility for the recording of different sites.

The time spent on fieldwork during the project was affected by the amount of grant money specifically allocated to undertaking the fieldwork compared to other areas, such as equipment purchases, time spent preparing for fieldwork, outreach activities or to the writing up of the project results. Thanks in part to the work of Ted Sutton and to the visits to Forton Lake undertaken prior to grant submission, the NAS and the HWTMA project management team were able to allocate 23 days to fieldwork over the three years. At an early stage it was known that three weeks in the field would not be enough time to record every hulk at Forton with detailed plan drawings and that only a selected number would be recorded in detail. The choice of vessel was based on its significance combined with an assessment of its ease of safe access. When planning an archaeological project in a wider landscape that contains a variety of material remains, this decision process has to be followed as few, if any, projects or organizations will have adequate funds to record every heritage asset in detail. The archaeological remains have to be prioritized with resources allocated to each one as appropriate.

The NAS and HWTMA project management team worked to allocate resources to ensure that the work in the field was balanced with the requirements for outreach and post-excavation work. It was considered important to provide time for professional archaeologists to compile the records, photographs and illustrations and to undertake the publication and archiving. All too often in archaeology projects the time commitment and the cost of these elements are under-emphasized and under-budgeted. From the outset the project tried not to fall foul of this trap and hopefully the speed at which this monograph has been published is testament to this approach.

---

1   http://www.hwtma.org.uk/index.php?page=reports-2

2   http://www.geog.port.ac.uk/webmap/itchen/frameset.html

Project Review

Review of the outreach activities

(Alison James)

The wider public outreach programme was an important part of the project. The delivery of outreach events focused on two methods – 'on-site' open days and presenting the project at other local events. On-site events were held in 2006 and 2007 with combined attendance figures of around 300 people. Hosting these events on site meant that visitors could gain direct interaction with the heritage; however, the organization required (advertising, media, coordination with other organizations etc) was very time consuming. In the final year of the project the decision was made to focus on attending other local events which resulted in reaching a larger number of people.

Attendance at other events proved successful from the start of the project. The benefit of attending other large-scale local events, such as the Southsea Show, was clear. Attendance at events planned by others meant that key issues such as press and publicity, health and safety and other planning issues were dealt with by others. Large scale events meant that the potential audience was increased from a few hundred into many thousands of local people.

The schools programme can be viewed as a real success of the project. It illustrated how the challenges of working on a foreshore environment can be overcome to enable the provision of high quality educational experiences. A key challenge was encouraging schools to take up the workshops on offer. Despite fourteen schools being contacted up to a year in advance of the sessions only three local schools (two primary and one secondary) participated. However all available sessions were booked up. The sessions were designed to be as flexible as possible for the schools who took part. It became clear straight away that there was a major conflict between the normal school timetable and the tidal cycle of Forton Lake. The best tides for access were often early in the morning or late in the afternoon and thus outside a normal school day. Sessions were scheduled within the school timetable and the HWTMA Education Officers running the programme learnt to adapt workshops based on how many of the hulks were visible above water at the time of the session. Adaptation was important to the success of the programme; time was at a premium and often sessions had to be adapted in order to take advantage of a group's questions or make them more suitable for a particular group.

A lot of time went into the required risk assessments and health and safety planning associated with having up to thirty school pupils on the site at any one time. All pupils wore high visibility vests throughout the visit. Access to the site involved a route through a working boatyard and along the side of a road and under a fence; there were potentially many risks on route, but these were dealt with through adequate supervision and risk assessment. One trip was observed by PhD candidate (University College,

London), Trudie Cole, for her PhD thesis entitled *Archaeological Education and its Alignment to Child Centred Learning.* Cole felt that the 'pupils were excited by this aspect of the trip and enjoyed it, which opened the visit in a very positive way' (Trudie Cole, pers. comm.). Indeed this introduction to the daily working environment of an archaeologist quickly got pupils into character and can be viewed as a benefit, rather than an obstacle.

The workshops benefited from Cole's research in which she analysed the pupils from one school taking part before and after their sessions. Her research has shown that after a session there was a statistically significant change in the creativity of the pupils. She suggests this may be because, 'None of the pupils had visited hulks before and although they were using familiar skills, such as measuring and sketching, they had never before used them in that context. Perhaps this creative approach to using familiar skills was responsible for the impact on pupils' creativity' (Trudie Cole, pers. comm.).

Cole concluded that the full range of generic learning outcomes was present and suggests that the results 'indicated that the physical environment of the hulks and the unfamiliarity of the immediate landscape in a geographical area which was otherwise familiar to the pupils was of particular interest to them ... . The pupils were given the opportunity to explore their local area in more depth than they had previously and appreciated this. In terms of local identity and developing local pride the workshops were very successful' (Trudie Cole, pers. comm.).

This research is extremely positive as it appears the key aim of raising local awareness of the site was met with the school visits. An additional effect was that pupils would return home from school buoyed up with enthusiasm for the site. The lessons learned from this project would suggest that the involvement of local schools and their pupils has a high value when working within the local community. It is hoped that this engagement will be a lasting legacy from the project. The challenge now is to utilize the project results within a range of local heritage, community and education initiatives and facilities to continue and develop the local community's new relationship with the maritime heritage of Forton Lake.

Working on hulk collections

(Julie Satchell)

Nautical Archaeology on the Foreshore (Milne *et al*) was published in 1998 based on the experience of surveying a group of hulks in Whitewall Creek off the River Medway, Kent, in 1991 and 1992. There had once been over 80 abandoned vessels within the creek, but, when they were threatened with removal or burial to allow for development, a rescue survey was initiated. The introduction to this volume states:

> What is clear is that the remains of our vernacular nautical heritage have been neglected for too long.

More nautical surveys are urgently needed ... . That the hulks abandoned on the foreshore merit recording and study is unarguable, if for no other reason than that their numbers are fast diminishing (Milne *et al.*, 1998: 3).

The Forton Lake Archaeological Project was undertaken ten years after this publication and around fifteen years after the fieldwork on which it was based. However, the statement above remains as true now as it is did then. A brief review of published projects over the past ten years provides few substantial works on the archaeological recording of collections of abandoned vessels, although scratching below the surface into the grey literature and web publications reveals a slightly more positive situation. A review of the work at Forton Lake in the context of the recording of intertidal vessel remains in the UK over the past fifteen years provides the opportunity to put the work into context and, it is hoped, demonstrates the potential of these sites to add significantly to the understanding of nautical development, in addition to the study of the maritime cultural landscape.

The marginal nature of the intertidal zone appears to have affected long term research on these craft and the available funding to progress the required detailed survey and analysis work to unlock their full potential. Although there have been larger numbers of abandoned vessels recorded through initiatives such as English Heritage's Rapid Coastal Zone Assessments, this only provides evidence of their presence and basic details. Flagging up the existence of abandoned vessels is the important first stage of work; the challenge is to follow this with in-depth analysis.

There have been some obvious exceptions to this, the two largest projects recording hulks being at Purton in Gloucestershire (Parker, 1998; Barnett, 2007)[3] and on the River Hamble, Hampshire.[4] Other projects have included work on the River Exe,[5] the River Itchen,[6] the Salcombe Estuary (David Parham, pers. comm.), the Taw and Torridge in Devon (Preece, 2008)[7] and Maldon in Essex (English Heritage HER UID 802130/802124).[8] At Aberlady Bay in Scotland vernacular fishing craft also feature heavily amongst the 18 craft recorded in the RCAHMS Canmore database (Groom and Oxley, 2002).[9] The importance of these craft has been recognized by

Historic Scotland by scheduling them as monuments. In other examples the collections are more varied, for instance within the 14 abandoned craft in Bowling Harbour, on the Clyde to the west of Glasgow, there are fishing boats, leisure craft and Admiralty tenders all represented (RCAHMS Canmore, ID 43393).[10] Added to these studies of groups of hulks are surveys of single vessels and a trawl of the archaeological grey literature provides more evidence of this type of work. The growth in these surveys is also reflected in the number of NAS Part II projects (undertaken as part of the training scheme putting basic survey techniques into practice) featuring intertidal remains which have increased over time to represent approximately 60% of those submitted (Mark Beattie-Edwards pers. comm.).

It is clear that each collection is the result of unique forces which have played a part in the deposition of vessels in a particular area. Influences can be local, such as a backwater being suitable for 'storing' vessels at the end of their useful life or an area of the estuary bank needs reinforcing due to erosion, national, such as the decline in a particular trade or industry making a type of vessel redundant, or international as seen at the end of large scale naval conflicts when surplus vessels are abandoned. While each individual hulk has its own history, they also have a collective value having been deposited together in a particular geographic area to form part of the marine historic landscape.

Many of these survey projects have been undertaken within the last few years or are currently in progress. It is hoped this indicates a higher profile for these important heritage assets that will lead to increased work in this area and greater amounts of published data. Much work on collections of abandoned vessels has either relied on funding sources, which are focused on volunteer involvement (such as the Heritage Lottery Fund), or has been done in voluntary time. This has meant that the publication and the deposition of project records in a public archive have rarely been achieved. The work at Forton Lake demonstrates the potential for the development of research projects on this type of collection, which not only have considerable community involvement, but also provide fully published results.

It should also be noted that further relevant historical and research links exist between abandoned vessels and those represented on the National Historic Ships Register. There are over 1000 vessels on the register, within which there is a sub-set that forms the National Historic Fleet. The register has been particularly useful, when trying to identify individual hulks within Forton Lake and also in the assessment of their significance. The links between maritime archaeological research and those working on and with historic vessels have, to date, not been strong. However, it is clear that these two areas of study are intrinsically linked as part of the same historical

---

3   http://www.nauticalarchaeologysociety.org/projects/Purton/purton_report_2008.pdf

4   http://www.hwtma.org.uk/uploads/documents/Archaeological%20Projects/HambleHLFProjectReport1.pdf and http://www.hwtma.org.uk/uploads/documents/Archaeological%20Projects/HambleHLFProjectReport2.pdf

5   http://www.exe-estuary.org/exe_press_summer_05.pdf

6   http://www.geog.port.ac.uk/webmap/itchen/frameset.html

7   http://www.ndas.org.uk/hulks.html

8   http://www.univie.ac.at/aarg/worldwide/essex/essex.html

9   http://www.aberladyheritage.com/web/a-maritime-graveyard.html and http://canmore.rcahms.gov.uk/en/details/926694/

10   http://canmore.rcahms.gov.uk/en/site/43393/details/forth+and+clyde+canal+bowling+harbour

continuum. Further integration can only help enhance knowledge and understanding of nautical development and its remaining physical evidence, whether still floating or now a stationary part of the landscape.

Interpreting the archaeology of Forton Lake

The collection of hulks in and around Forton Lake represents an interesting aspect of the maritime history of the local area and also of wider aspects of British trade, transport and warfare over the past two hundred years. These hulks are not frequently appreciated for their potential to illuminate maritime heritage and are often seen as modern detritus. The project results have demonstrated that a number of the hulks have significant local, regional and national connections and have also highlighted the need to consider the Forton collection as a whole. There is a need to interpret its archaeological and historic significance within the social and economic development of the local area, in addition to comparing it with other collections of hulks to assess their ability to provide unique evidence on maritime and nautical development. Detailed assessment and analysis of these aspects was beyond the scope of this project and would merit further research. In this monograph an initial review of the hulks against key historical developments around Forton Lake has been presented to demonstrate links between the remains and economic, social and political developments and to highlight areas for future research.

Influential in terms of the deposition of vessels is the decline in use of Forton Lake for a range of military and civilian purposes. The shallow nature of the Lake does not make it conducive to regular use by larger vessels and requires maintenance dredging to keep it viable. The move to more regularly accessible berths available elsewhere in Portsmouth Harbour meant the use of Forton Lake declined, making it an attractive place to store vessels, which over time degraded, became unseaworthy and were subsequently abandoned.

The groupings of the hulks within themes in the catalogue indicate the key functions of the craft, which include transportation (FL5, FL15, FL29), fishing (FL1, FL2, FL9), ferries and lifeboats (FL11, FL21, FL22, FL30) and military vessels (FL3, FL7, FL10, FL16, FL17, FL20, FL23, FL24, FL31) with four vessels unclassified (FL4, FL18, FL19, FL26). The types of craft represented at Forton provide evidence of the maritime use of the Lake and the broader Portsmouth area. However it should not be forgotten that the variety of craft present at Forton has been artificially created or at least influenced by the individual purchase choices of the boatyards in the area and especially the F.J. Watts yard on Ferrol Road which was in business from 1938 until 1959. The disposal of obsolete or unprofitable vessels was an important work for boatyards, and many of those abandoned may have only ended up here because of the proximity of the boatyards.

With the role being played by the boatyards' purchases the high proportion of military vessels is not surprising considering the military importance of Portsmouth Harbour. The influence of the Royal Navy on Forton Lake in particular was expanded with the establishment of the Royal Clarence victualling yard on the south side of the Lake in the late 18th and 19th centuries. Buildings within the complex included a fleet watering point, a bakery, a flourmill, a granary, cattle pens and a slaughter-house, not to mention the nearby brewery and cooperage. The establishment of St Vincent barracks and training facilities in the 1920s added to the military presence in the area. These facilities made Forton Lake a busy waterway.

With the increased threat of invasion during the two world wars there was a national programme of defensive construction and the role of Forton Lake in naval activities was to be important because of the munitions and victualling establishments. However, after the Second World War there was a rapid decline in the requirement for naval vessels or those used for naval activity, with many being sold off or decommissioned in the late 1940s and the 1950s. The evidence from the survey of the hulks indicates that a number of these decommissioned vessels ended their days within Forton Lake.

The links of the war-related vessels to the historic naval area of Portsmouth Harbour should be stressed as they form an important body of evidence which should not be divorced from the broader maritime cultural landscape. Additionally the diversity of the types of craft within Forton Lake is important as they provide the opportunity to illuminate a range of social and economic developments and should not be overlooked. The collection as a whole spans from the 19th century to the 1960s. In terms of nautical development and seafaring this period saw huge changes with the move from sail to steam power and from wooden to metal ship construction.

Future work and research

With many archaeological projects focused on research there is always further work that can be undertaken and Forton Lake is no exception. From the outset the project had a range of aims and objectives, which included academic objectives to increase knowledge and understanding of the hulks and their environment, as well as objectives which were more focused on outreach and education. The project has managed to deliver on all of these aspects. However, there is potential to expand this in the future.

It is clear that the hulks in Forton Lake are subjected to harsh environmental conditions. The exceptions to this are the substantially buried vessels which, once sealed within anaerobic deposits, have much higher preservation potential. The erosive and degrading forces of the tidal cycle are demonstrated by the changes that have occurred to hulks between Ted Sutton's original survey in 1997, monitoring photographs taken by the HWTMA in 2001 and the work of the Forton Lake project. While it is not possible to prevent the ongoing deterioration of the hulks, there is potential to monitor these changes over time and to record any significant features or fixtures which become visible, particularly those related to more significant vessels. The development of an archive of data on the degradation process would provide interesting research material that could be applicable to other collections.

For a number of individual hulks there is scope to expand the field survey and excavation work, while others would benefit from more in-depth research into comparative examples. Important areas for future research include the need to answer questions such as: whether the unusual construction of FL29 has parallels in building traditions from either inland waterways or maritime examples; whether the admiralty type MFVs FL1, FL2 and FL9 can be identified; how rare a survival FL3, a motor minesweeper, is; whether FL17, the RAF Ferry Boat, is a unique survival and whether the grouping of Landing Craft Assault in Forton Lake forms the highest concentration of such craft nationally and internationally. This is not an exhaustive list as each section has highlighted areas where further work would benefit, but these questions help underline the significance of a number of the hulks within the collection and the need to understand their importance as individual craft, as a collection and in relation to the development of Forton Lake.

Threats and future protection

Archaeological sites in the intertidal zone present unique problems in terms of management and responsibilities. Many of the hulks have been, or are, privately owned, although they may have been abandoned with no intention of returning to them. There are also questions over responsibility between local councils and harbour authorities where the boundaries can become blurred. This lack of clarity extends to heritage protection, where in theory either the terrestrially based Ancient Monuments and Archaeological Areas Act 1979 could be used to schedule a site or the Protection of Wrecks Act 1973 could be used to designate it. Further confusion can set in with the National Historic Ships Register which includes some vessels in a considerable state of disrepair.

Some hulks within Forton Lake are clearly suffering from corrosion, most notably the metal ones. Others face human impacts from vandalism, especially those closest to shore. Despite attempts to highlight the historic nature of abandoned vessels there are still examples of the inappropriate clearance of these sites, often prompted by environmental concerns which do not consider the cultural heritage. A local example of this has been seen on the River Hamble, where the removal of metal hulks without any assessment was allowed.[11] The vulnerability of the Forton collection to such misguided environmental initiatives has perhaps been reduced with the installation of the Millennium Bridge towards the mouth of the Lake.

Although this bridge can be opened, it is likely to reduce maritime traffic and hence the need for dredging or works to keep the channel clear, which has the potential to impact the hulks. However, there are still issues related to the long term protection of these sites. This is especially pertinent for a number of the individual hulks, such as FL3, FL17, FL23 and the group of LCAs, which survey and research undertaken to date has indicated may be very rare or unique survivals of vessel types.

The hulks at Forton Lake are clearly degrading, some of them relatively quickly, and this increases the urgency for undertaking the surveys to ensure an archive demonstrating the extent of the remains. A record of the existence of each hulk is held within the Hampshire Historic Environment Record database, which provides them with some protection as they will be considered in the event of planning applications that have the potential to impact on them. However, this does not provide any formal heritage protection either individually or as a collection. The management and protection of abandoned vessels is an area which has not received much attention in the past. However, at the time of writing this monograph issues related to such collections are being reviewed through an English Heritage funded thematic survey of hulk assemblages (Mark Dunkley, pers. comm.; Hansard, 2009).[12] This work may lead to the application of protection for individual hulks and collections of hulks in the future.

The value of the project

The project has demonstrated that the remains of abandoned vessels are a part of our local and national heritage that deserves greater recognition, alongside wrecks in the marine zone and historic vessels whether still floating or in dry dock. There is a large public appetite for maritime heritage, which is witnessed through the numbers of those volunteering to be involved in practical fieldwork and of those who visit historic vessels and by the response to discoveries such as the Newport Ship in 2002 (Hunter, 2003). By highlighting how these vessels are part of the maritime heritage continuum, their status is increased and public understanding and appreciation enhanced. Only with broad support will the degrading remains of a vast array of vernacular craft be appreciated for their historic legacy and a record of them developed for present and future generations. The work at Forton Lake has developed such a record for 25 vessels; it is not claimed this work is exhaustive; instead it is hoped this will inspire further research on the collection in the future.

11   http://www.hants.gov.uk/decisions/decisions-docs/080711-rvhhbd-R0704170225.html

12   http://www.publications.parliament.uk/pa/cm200910/cmhansrd/cm091208/halltext/91208h0011.htm#09120858000259 and
http://www.museumoflondonarchaeology.org.uk/English/News/Current/HulkAssemblages.htm

Appendix A: Craft 'For Tender' lying at F.J. Watts Boatyard,
Parham Road, Gosport (August 1951 - February 1959)
Taken from the Admiralty Small Craft Disposal Lists
(List researched and compiled by Philip Simons July 2009)

This disposal list was generated following a meeting of individuals with an interest in the craft at Forton Lake on 28 June 2009, attended by Philip Simons, David Fricker, Danny Lovell, Mark Beattie-Edwards and Colin Baxter.

This tender list runs from August 1951 until February 1959. Before August 1951 the sales were not advertised in *Motor Boats and Yachting* magazine in a consolidated advertisement listing all the craft for disposal at various boatyards around the country; so there are no advertisements listing boats before this. There were no advertisements for any companies in May 1953 or in July 1953 and any other gaps in the list means that, although there were advertisements that month, no vessels were listed as for sale by F.J. Watts. Thanks to the RAF aerial photographs of the 1940s and 1950s as well as the photographic archive of Jack Smale, now held by Philip Simons, it is possible to see some of these craft moored at the yard (Fig A.1). The final listing for the F.J. Watts yard was in February 1959 and marked the end of an era for Forton Lake.

It is worth mentioning that some vessels appeared in more than one advertisement, but are only shown once in this list. The prices listed were the 'Provisional Reserve

Fig A.1 Jack Smale's 1951 photograph annotated 'HS Launch on sale list'. (The Jack Smale collection, courtesy of Philip Simons)

Prices'. 'Dumb' means not engined, 'No engine' means that the engine had been removed. Some additional information in brackets has been added to the list by Philip Simons, including details of former pennant numbers.

Date	Vessel	Number	Engined	Price
August 1951	36 ft Harbour Launch	43608	No engine	£120
September 1951	42½ ft Storing Tender	No 1	Chrysler petrol	£40
September 1951	16 ft Slow Motor Boat	44801	No engine	£10
October 1951	20 ft Dumb Boat	3418/44	Dumb	£40
October 1951	14 ft Lifeboat	1221	Dumb	£10
October 1951	16 ft Trawler Boat	1132	Dumb	£30
October 1951	13½ ft Dinghy	7979/18	Dumb	£14
October 1951	10 ft CB Sailing Dinghy	1400	Dumb	£18
October 1951	10 ft CB Sailing Dinghy	294/40	Dumb	£18
October 1951	10 ft CB Sailing Dinghy	813/44	Dumb	£18
October 1951	10 ft Pulling Dinghy	No Number	Dumb	£4
November 1951	40 ft Landing Craft (LCA)	1841	No engine	£10
December 1951	25 ft Fast Motor Boat	41551	No engine	£75
December 1951	25 ft Fast Motor Boat	42693	No engine	£75
December 1951	25 ft Fast Motor Boat	42350	No engine	£75
December 1951	25 ft Fast Motor Boat	42330	No engine	£75
December 1951	10 ft CB Sailing Dinghy	379/45	Dumb	£18
December 1951	10 ft Pulling Dinghy	No Number	Dumb	£8
February 1952	25 ft Fast Motor Boat	45656	No engine	£75
February 1952	25 ft Fast Motor Boat	41520	No engine	£75
February 1952	10 ft Pulling Dinghy	1624/44	Dumb	£6
February 1952	16 ft Pulling Dinghy	1339	Dumb	£8
March 1952	36½ ft Pulling Barge	No Number	(14 oared)	£100
March 1952	14½ ft Drifter Boat	No 9	Dumb	£15

Date	Vessel	Number	Engined	Price
March 1952	17½ ft Boom Boat	159 (or 158)	Dumb	£8
March 1952	13½ ft Dinghy	5759	Dumb	£8
February 1952	10 ft Dinghy	591	Dumb	£9
February 1952	10 ft Dinghy	No Number	Dumb	£8
February 1952	45 ft Motor Launch	No Number	No engine	£205
June 1952	10 ft Sailing Dinghy	1781/44	Dumb	£9
June 1952	16 ft Sailing Dinghy	5848	Dumb	£16
June 1952	10 ft Sailing Dinghy	1350	Dumb	£14
June 1952	10 ft Sailing Dinghy	3599/43	Dumb	£12
June 1952	10 ft Sailing Dinghy	43/43	Dumb	£10
August 1952	52½ ft Steam Launch	HL(S) 169 *Musket*	Steam	£250
August 1952	42 ft Motor Launch	1204	Vosper petrol	£150
August 1952	16 ft Fast Motor Boat	41311	No engine	£60
August 1952	16 ft Fast Motor Boat	41177	No engine	£16
August 1952	16 ft Slow Motor Boat	41471	No engine	£18
August 1952	16 ft Slow Motor Boat	43264	No engine	£18
August 1952	16 ft Slow Motor Boat	44808	No engine	£14
August 1952	14 ft Sailing Dinghy	2700/14	Dumb	£24
September 1952	10 ft Sailing Dinghy	582/43	Dumb	£18
September 1952	32 ft Motor Cutter	43718	No engine	£65
December 1952	48 ft RN Air Lighter	18B	Vosper V8 petrol	£200
December 1952	48 ft RN Air Lighter	19B	Vosper V8 petrol	£200
December 1952	48 ft RN Air Lighter	26B	Vosper V8 petrol	£200
December 1952	14 ft Dinghy (ASD)	1311/40	Dumb	£18
January 1953	50 ft Refueller Mk 1	2099	No engine	£300
March 1953	23 ft Motor Cutter	4483	Stuart petrol	£85
March 1953	10 ft Sailing Dinghy	1972	Dumb	£7
March 1953	10 ft Sailing Dinghy	1784/44	Dumb	£16
March 1953	14 ft Dinghy	191	Dumb	£24
March 1953	12 ft Dinghy	627/42	Dumb	£7
March 1953	17½ ft Boom Boat	No Number	Dumb	£22
June 1953	18 ft Airborne Lifeboat	A10	Sailing	£45
June 1953	18 ft Airborne Lifeboat	A11	Sailing	£45
June 1953	18 ft Airborne Lifeboat	A12	Sailing	£45
June 1953	18 ft Airborne Lifeboat	A13	Sailing	£45
June 1953	36 ft Pulling Pinnace	6798	Dumb	£40
September 1953	10 ft Dinghy	1960	Dumb	£6
October 1953	42 ft Sailing Pinnace	7413	Dumb	£75
October 1953	36 ft Rowing Pinnace	3068	Dumb	Offers
December 1953	16 ft Fast Motor Boat	43203	No engine	Offers
December 1953	14 ft Surf Boat Dinghy	275/49	Dumb	Offers
January 1954	117 ft MTB (C&N Type)	5517 (ex 517)	No engines	£120
January 1954	10 ft Dinghy	2087	Dumb	£18
June 1954	16 ft Fast Motor Boat	41712	Scammel petrol	£80
June 1954	110 ft MTB (Fairmile D)	796	No engines	£200
June 1954	25 ft Lifeboat	81142	Dumb	£60
June 1954	45 ft Motor Passenger Launch	421214	Atlantic diesel	£200
July 1954	10 ft Sailing Dinghy	1716/42	Dumb	£12
August 1954	42 ft Launch	151/46	Dumb	£70
August 1954	25 ft Motor Cutter	441069	Engine unmentioned	£45
August 1954	10 ft Pulling Dinghy	369/43	Dumb	£8
August 1954	10 ft Dinghy	2343/44	Dumb	£8

Craft 'For Tender' at F.J. Watts Boatyard

Date	Vessel	Number	Engined	Price
August 1954	61½ ft MFV	180	Engine unmentioned	£200
August 1954	61½ ft MFV	29	Kelvin K4 88 hp diesel	£800
October 1954	10 ft Sailing Dinghy	610/40	Dumb	£14
October 1954	10 ft Sailing Dinghy	1027/43	Dumb	£12
October 1954	120 ft German E Boat	ML6115	With diesel engines	£2,500
October 1954	110 ft (117) MTB (C&N)	5511 (ex 511)	No engine	£200
November 1954	110 ft MTB (Fairmile D)	5003	No engine	£200
November 1954	10 ft Dinghy	No Number	Dumb	£8
May 1955	10 ft Dinghy	1185	Dumb	
May 1955	13½ ft Dinghy	3611S	Dumb	£14
May 1955	14 ft Dinghy	618	Dumb	
May 1955	15½ ft Split Dinghy (2 halves)	No Number	Dumb	£18
May 1955	27 ft Whaler	321	Dumb	
May 1955	27 ft Whaler	108/Alex/42	Dumb	
August 1955	45 ft MFV	995	Engine poor	£350
August 1955	63 ft TRSV (60 ft TRSB)	43763	No engines	£300
August 1955	120 ft MMS	1600	No engine	Offers
August 1955	14 ft Dinghy	4066/45	Dumb	£18
August 1955	14 ft Sailing Dinghy	444/51	Dumb	£40
August 1955	10 ft Plywood Dinghy	1944	Dumb	£7
August 1955	16 ft Trawler Boat	No Number	Dumb	£18
September 1955	18 ft Mk IX Powered Canoe	1	No Engine	£10
September 1955	18 ft Mk IX Powered Canoe	2	Engine Seized	£20
September 1955	18 ft Mk IX Powered Canoe	3	Engine Seized	£20
September 1955	18 ft Mk IX Powered Canoe	4	Engine Seized	£20
September 1955	18 ft Mk IX Powered Canoe	5	Engine	£25
September 1955	18 ft Mk IX Powered Canoe	6	Engine Seized	£20
September 1955	18 ft Mk IX Powered Canoe	7	No Engine	£10
September 1955	18 ft Mk IX Powered Canoe	8	Part Engine	£10
September 1955	120 ft MMS	1763	No Engine	£500
September 1955	13½ ft Standard Balsa Raft	213/42	Dumb	£15
September 1955	36 ft Diving Boat	No Number	Not mentioned	£110
October 1955	45 ft MFV[1]	955	Engine Poor	£350
October 1955	110 ft MTB (Fairmile D)	MTB 5033 (785)	No Engines	£400
November 1955	75 ft MFV	1132	Lister diesel 160 hp	£1,200
November 1955	75 ft MFV	1019	Lister diesel 160 hp	£1,200
December 1955	112 ft ML (Fairmile B)	2866 (866)	No engines	£300
December 1955	112 ft ML (Fairmile B)	2338 (338)	No Engines	£300
December 1955	120 ft MMS	1606	Fairbanks diesel	£2,000
December 1955	110 ft MTB (Fairmile D)	MTB 5032 (779)	No Engines	£200
December 1955	14 ft Sailing Dinghy (ASD)	4065	Dumb	£8
January 1956	112 ft ML (Fairmile B)	2295 (295)	No engines	£350
January 1956	112 ft ML (Fairmile B)	2576 (576)	No engines	£400
January 1956	112 ft ML (Fairmile B)	2561 (561)	No engines	£350
January 1956	112 ft ML (Fairmile B)	2569 (569)	No engines	£350
January 1956	61½ ft MFV	41	Kelvin diesel seized	£700
January 1956	10 ft Sailing Dinghy	1126/42	Dumb	£8
March 1956	10 ft Dinghy	3703/43	Dumb	£12
March 1956	16 ft Dory Dinghy	2234/44	Dumb	£16

---

1   This is the same boat and had the same contract/folio number as MFV 995 in the August 1955 advert, but it is unclear which is the correct number, 955 or 995.

Date	Vessel	Number	Engined	Price
March 1956	30 ft Cutter (Built 1913)	6530	Dumb	£30
March 1956	25 ft Motor Cutter	41252	No engine	£35
March 1956	120 ft ML (112 ft Fairmile B)	2565 (565)	No engines	£600
April 1956	110 ft MTB (Fairmile D)	769	No engines	£400
May 1956	10 ft Dinghy	1938	Dumb	Offers
June 1956	25 ft Motor Cutter	43880	No engine	Offers
June 1956	117 ft MTB (C&N type)	5515 (515)	No engines	Offers
July 1956	115 ft MTB (Fairmile D)	5008	No engines	Offers
July 1956	120 ft ML (112 ft Fairmile B)	2577(577)	No engines	Offers
July 1956	120 ft ML (112 ft Fairmile B)	2575(575)	No engines	Offers
July 1956	120 ft ML (112 ft Fairmile B)	2493(493)	No engines	Offers
July 1956	120 ft ML (112 ft Fairmile B)	2461(461)	No engines	Offers
August 1956	120 ft ML (112 ft Fairmile B)	2220(220)	No engines	Offers
August 1956	120 ft ML (112 ft Fairmile B)	2901(901)	No engines	Offers
August 1956	32 ft Cutter	18/37	Dumb	Offers
September 1956	ML (112 ft Fairmile B)	2554(554)	No engines	Offers
September 1956	ML (112 ft Fairmile B)	2568(568)	No engines	Offers
September 1956	ML (112 ft Fairmile B)	2337(337)	No engines	Offers
September 1956	36 ft Motor Boat	45997/W126	Vosper V8 petrol	Offers
September 1956	14 ft Sailing Dinghy	HQ50	Dumb	Offers
October 1956	25 ft Motor Cutter	45914	No engine	Offers
October 1956	25 ft Motor Cutter	45915	No engine	Offers
November 1956	32 ft Sailing Cutter	72/39	Dumb	Offers
November 1956	120 ft ML (112 ft Fairmile B)	2886 (886)	No engines	Offers
November 1956	120 ft ML (112 ft Fairmile B)	2889 (889)	No engines	Offers
November 1956	75 ft MFV	1106	Lister dismantled	Offers
November 1956	112 ft ML (Fairmile B)	2564 (564)	No engines	Offers
November 1956	112 ft ML (Fairmile B)	2882 (882)	No engines	Offers
January 1957	25 ft Motor Cutter	45915	No engine	Offers
January 1957	13½ ft Motor Dinghy	39374	No engine	Offers
January 1957	13½ ft Motor Dinghy	44943	No engine	Offers
January 1957	32 ft Sailing Cutter	9302	Dumb	Offers
January 1957	120 ft MTB ex E Boat	5212	No engines	Offers
January 1957	36 ft Harbour Launch	441194	Vosper V8 petrol	Offers
January 1957	45 ft Motor Passenger Launch	421191	Atlantic diesel	Offers
February 1957	40 ft Naval Storing Tender	5	No engine	Offers
February 1957	32 ft Sailing Cutter	632/44	Dumb	Offers
February 1957	32 ft Sailing Cutter	135/41	Dumb	Offers
April 1957	60 ft TRSB	43774	No engines	Offers
April 1957	61½ ft MFV	49	Kelvin K4 diesel	Offers
April 1957	61½ ft MFV	302	Lister diesel	Offers
May 1957	61½ ft MFV	270	Waddop Engine	Offers
May 1957	45 ft Motor Passenger Launch	45635	Atlantic diesel	Offers
May 1957	90 ft MFV	1564 (*Sybella*)	Crossley diesel 240 hp	Offers
May 1957	40 ft NSB (ex LCA)	335	No engines	Offers
May 1957	25 ft Cutter	43865	No engines	Offers
May 1957	75 ft MFV	1204	Lister diesel 160 hp	Offers
May 1957	35 ft Motor Pinnace	41590	Dorman diesel	Offers
July 1957	61½ ft MFV	201	Lister diesel	Offers
July 1957	75 ft FC 27/MTB[2]	1032	No engines	Offers

2   This was the craft advertised; the actual boat was a 73 ft Vosper numbered 532, later renumbered MTB 1032 the FC 27.

Craft 'For Tender' at F.J. Watts Boatyard

Date	Vessel	Number	Engined	Price
August 1957	32 ft Motor Cutter	4033	No engine	Offers
August 1957	48 ft Air Lighter	33B	2 x Vosper V8 petrol	Offers
August 1957	14 ft Sailing Dinghy (ASD)		Dumb	Offers
August 1957	25 ft Motor Cutter	431098	Austin engine	Offers
August 1957	18 ft Dory	441271	Austin engine	Offers
August 1957	18 ft Dory	431310	Austin engine	Offers
August 1957	10 ft Dinghy	235	Dumb	Offers
August 1957	103 ft Store Lighter	C710	Dumb	Offers
September 1957	36 ft Motor & Pulling Pinnace	41818	No engine	Offers
October 1957	16 ft Trawler Boat	No Number	Dumb	Offers
October 1957	61½ ft MFV	106	Lister diesel 120 hp	Offers
October 1957	120 ft MTB (110 ft Fairmile D)	5001 (780)	No engines	Offers
October 1957	120 ft MTB (110 ft Fairmile D)	5015	No engines	Offers
October 1957	120 ft MTB (110 ft Fairmile D)	5020	No engines	Offers
November 1957	45 ft Fuelling Tender (LCI type)	41438	No engine	Offers
November 1957	45 ft Motor Launch	41117	Gardener 4 cyl diesel	Offers
November 1957	120 ft Steam Gun Boat (SGB 9)	*Grey Goose*	No engines	Offers
November 1957	37 ft Dumb Barge	165/49	Dumb	Offers
November 1957	40 ft Naval Servicing Boat (LCA)	338	No engine	Offers
November 1957	40 ft Naval Servicing Boat (LCA)	340	Ford V8	Offers
November 1957	60 ft Naval Servicing Boat (LCM)	347	2 x Hudson Invaders	Offers
November 1957	60 ft Mining & Diving Tender	HMS *Clearwater*	6-cyl German diesel	Offers
November 1957	120 ft (117 ft) MTB (C&N type)	5514 (514)	3 x Packard Engines	Offers
January 1958	10 ft Pulling Dinghy	351/52	Dumb	Offers
January 1958	25 ft Fast Motor Boat	441396	No engine	Offers
January 1958	30 ft Fast Motor Boat	44430	No engine	Offers
January 1958	30¼ ft Sailing Cutter	3333/16	Dumb	Offers
January 1958	32 ft Sailing Cutter	628/41	Dumb	Offers
January 1958	32 ft Sailing Cutter	1250/41	Dumb	Offers
January 1958	32 ft Sailing Cutter	40/38	Dumb	Offers
January 1958	35 ft Fast Motor Boat	4382	No engine	Offers
January 1958	35 ft Fast Motor Boat	44469	No engine	Offers
January 1958	42 ft Dumb Launch	159/49	Dumb	Offers
January 1958	40 ft NSB (ex LCA)	337 (ex 1781)	No engines	Offers
January 1958	75 ft FC 26/MTB[3]	1027	No engines	Offers
January 1958	120 ft MTB (110 ft Fairmile D)	5002	4 x Packard engines	Offers
February 1958	61½ ft MFV	179	Widdop diesel	Offers
February 1958	36 ft Motor Boat	42183	No engine	Offers
February 1958	24 ft Marine Tender (Ex RAF)	4408	No engine	Offers
February 1958	16 ft Dory Dinghy	2229/44	Dumb	Offers
March 1958	75 ft MFV	1030	Lister diesel	Offers
March 1958	75 ft MFV	1080	Lister diesel	Offers
March 1958	75 ft MFV	1203	Lister diesel	Offers
April 1958	60 ft TRSB (TRV)	421134	3 x Dorman diesels	Offers
April 1958	30 ft MB NAV *Culverin*	3594	No engine	Offers
April 1958	52½ ft Harbour Launch Diesel	39450	No engine	Offers
April 1958	45 ft Motor Passenger Launch	421201	No engine	Offers
April 1958	45 ft Motor Launch	43321	No engine	Offers
April 1958	16 ft Fast Motor Boat	44704	No engine	Offers
April 1958	16 ft Fast Motor Boat	44577	No engine	Offers

---

3   This was the craft advertised; the actual boat was a 73 ft Vosper numbered 527, later renumbered MTB 1027.

Date	Vessel	Number	Engined	Price
April 1958	110 ft MTB (Fairmile D)	5035 (793)	No engines	Offers
April 1958	110 ft MTB (Fairmile D)	5036 (794)	No engines	Offers
July 1958	45 ft Medium Speed Picket Boat	41768	2 x 6-cyl Gardner diesels	Offers
July 1958	52½ ft Harbour Launch Diesel	3546	6-cyl diesel	Offers
July 1958	40 ft Dumb lighter	61	Dumb	Offers
July 1958	45 ft Fast Motor Boat	3658	3 x Perkins P6M	Offers
July 1958	45 ft MFV	669	Atlantic diesel	Offers
July 1958	68 ft Dumb Craft (HSTTL)	*Struma* (RCT)	No engine	Offers
August 1958	75 ft MFV	1029	Lister 4-cyl diesel	Offers
September 1958	16 ft Fast Motor Boat	44606	No engine	Offers
September 1958	16 ft Fast Motor Boat	44609	No engine	Offers
September 1958	16 ft Slow Motor Boat	43289	No engine	Offers
September 1958	25 ft Motor Cutter	431185	No engine	Offers
September 1958	25 ft Motor Cutter	40110	No engine	Offers
September 1958	25 ft Fast Motor Boat	38211	No engine	Offers
October 1958	120 ft FPB	*Bold Pioneer* (P5701)	No engines	Offers
October 1958	32 ft Motor Cutter	451042	Dorman diesel	Offers
October 1958	10 ft Dinghy	756	Dumb	Offers
October 1958	16 ft Trawler Boat	ex *Moorfield*	Dumb	Offers
October 1958	16 ft Dory Dinghy	2592/44	Dumb	Offers
October 1958	16 ft Dory Dinghy	No Number	Dumb	Offers
October 1958	14½ ft Pulling Boat	No Number	Dumb	Offers
October 1958	16 ft Trawler Boat	501	Dumb	Offers
October 1958	14½ Drifter Boat	105	Dumb	Offers
November 1958	25 ft Fast Motor Boat	42319	No engine	Offers
February 1959	52½ ft Harbour Launch Steam	295	Steam engine	Offers

Forton Lake Maritime Archaeology Project: Maritime Archaeologist for a day!

Forton Lake is bursting with maritime archaeology that comes from time periods covering 100s of 1000s of years. The archaeologists that are working here this week are mainly investigating the ships that are dotted along the foreshore. When a ship is left to decay on the foreshore it is known as a 'Hulk', not a shipwreck. By investigating these hulks we can learn a lot about the history of this local area. Archaeologists investigate by measuring, photographing, drawing, researching and then they try to make an interpretation of what the hulk would have been used for and how it can be fitted into our understanding of the local history of the Gosport area.

Activity 1. Sketch Plan

When an archaeologist is excavating or drawing a site, they will make a quick, labelled sketch of it. This is very helpful for referring to once more detailed plans are made.

- Use the box below to sketch the hulk and label any parts that you can identify. Try to do two sketches: One of a birds eye view - this is called a plan. One of the vertical side of the hulk — this is called section.
- Measure the length and width, and height of the hulk and show this on your sketches
- Use your compass to show which way North is on the plan. Show which direction your section is laying by labelling the right and left points of the sketch
- Show which hulk you are looking at on the map below.

Plan Sketch	Section Sketch

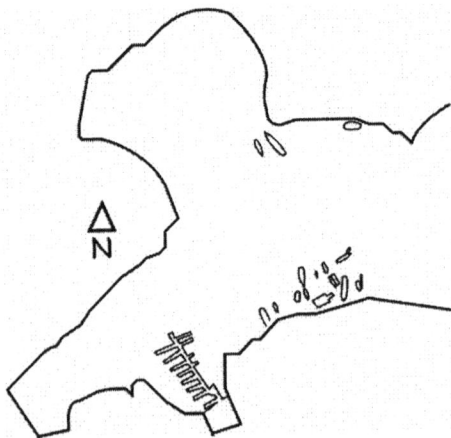

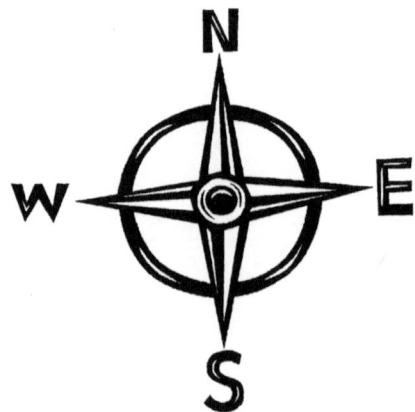

Activity 2. Planning Frame

To draw things found on site, archaeologists use planning frames. Look through the planning frame on site and use these squares to help you draw what is below the squares in the frame. You will end up with a drawing of a much smaller version of the archaeology on site.

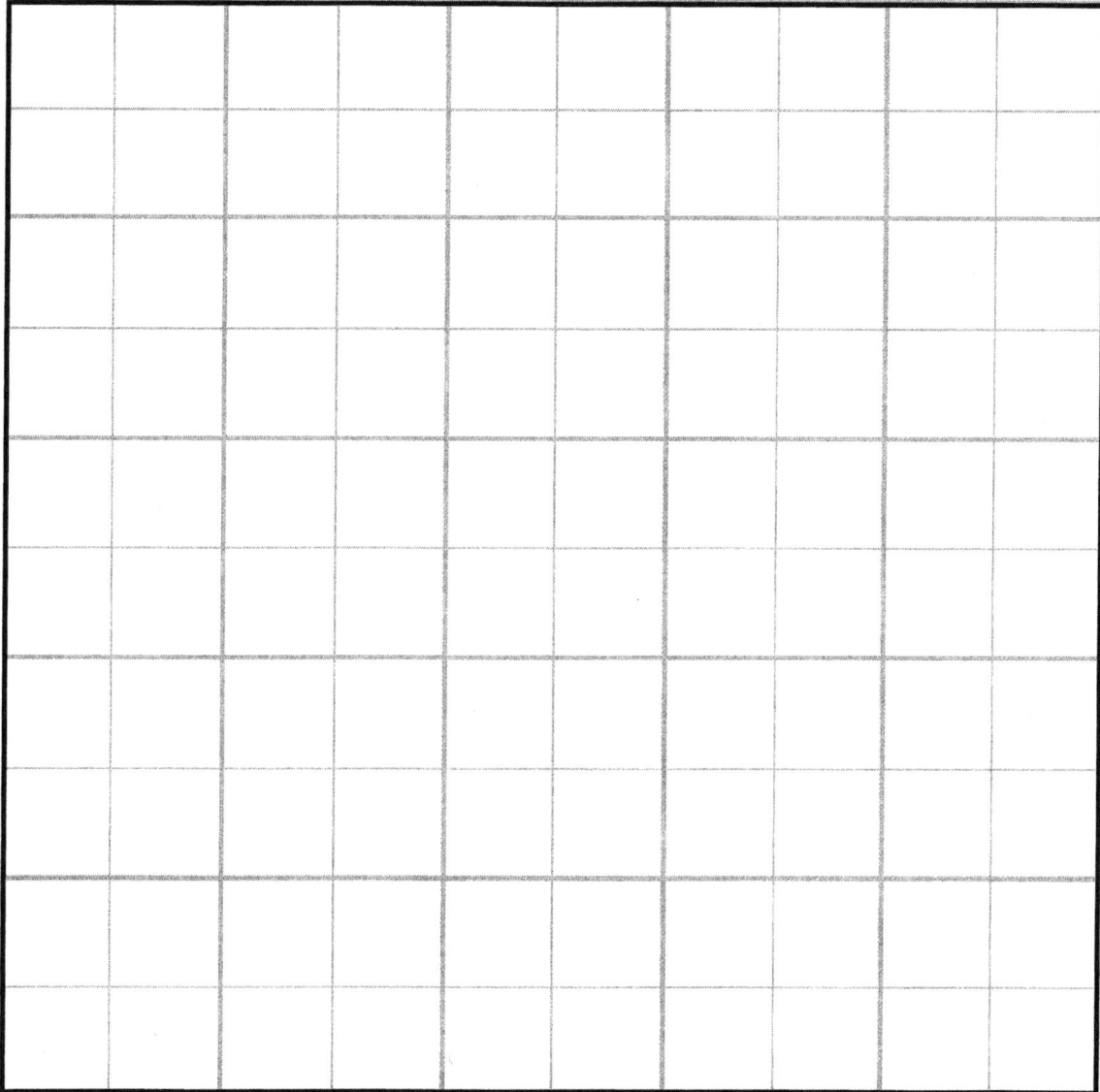

Activity 3. Observation and interpretation

Whilst Archaeologists are drawing and measuring, they must also be trying to form some interpretations of what they are looking at. The interpretation of a site or artefact will be based on careful observation and research. Unusual parts can often give clues, as can careful descriptions. Archaeologists use recording sheets that prompt them into looking carefully at the archaeology. These sheets also make sure that the record will be useful to somebody who may want to study the information on the future. It is essential that record sheets are carefully filled out as this is sometimes the only remaining record of a site.

SITE RECORD SHEET

Site Name:	Date:	Record Number:
Recorder:	Position:	

CONDITIONS:

Weather: Rain   Cold   Windy   Low Light   Other

Access: Mud   Tide   Slippery   Submerged   Other

ARTEFACT/SITE INFORMATION:

Size	Length:	Breadth:
Width:		Height:

Material:
Condition:
Estimate of age:
Details of construction:
Estimate of amount buried:
Description of lakebed:

INTERPRETATION:

Activity 4: Clues from Research

Archaeologists often look for clues in old archives to try to make sense of what a site could be. Old photos like the ones below have been used at Forton Lake to work out which ships the hulks used to be.

The Vadne (Gosport Ferry)

The Medina Chain Ferry

Look around the site at Forton Lake. Can you spot the remaining hulks of the two ships above?

Activity 5: Maritime Archaeology Foreshore Tools

The tools that foreshore maritime archaeologists use are very similar to the tools that normal archaeologists use.

Draw an arrow to match the tool name to the tools that Professor Archie O'Logy is carrying for a day at work. Tick any tools that you have used or seen in use today.

Trowel (small tool for carefully excavating mud)

Shovel (tool for digging mud)

Pencil

Scale (pole divided into sections to show the size of something)

Tape measure (for measuring lengths)

Camera (for making a photo record)

Plumb bob (weight on a string used to tell if something is directly below something else)

Planning Frame (frame divided into squares to help with drawing)

Nails (these are hammered in to fix strings at certain levels)

Line Level (tool with a bubble that shows if a surface or string is level)

Using a Planning Frame

A planning frame is a tool used by archaeologists to help them draw the things on an archaeological site. It is very useful for producing a quick, accurate drawing of a small collection of artefacts.

The archaeologists must look directly down onto the frame or there will be errors in their drawing. The frame helps the archaeologist draw accurately on land and underwater.

The archaeologists who are working at Forton Lake are using these. See if you can use one to draw like them!

Maritime Archaeologist Challenge

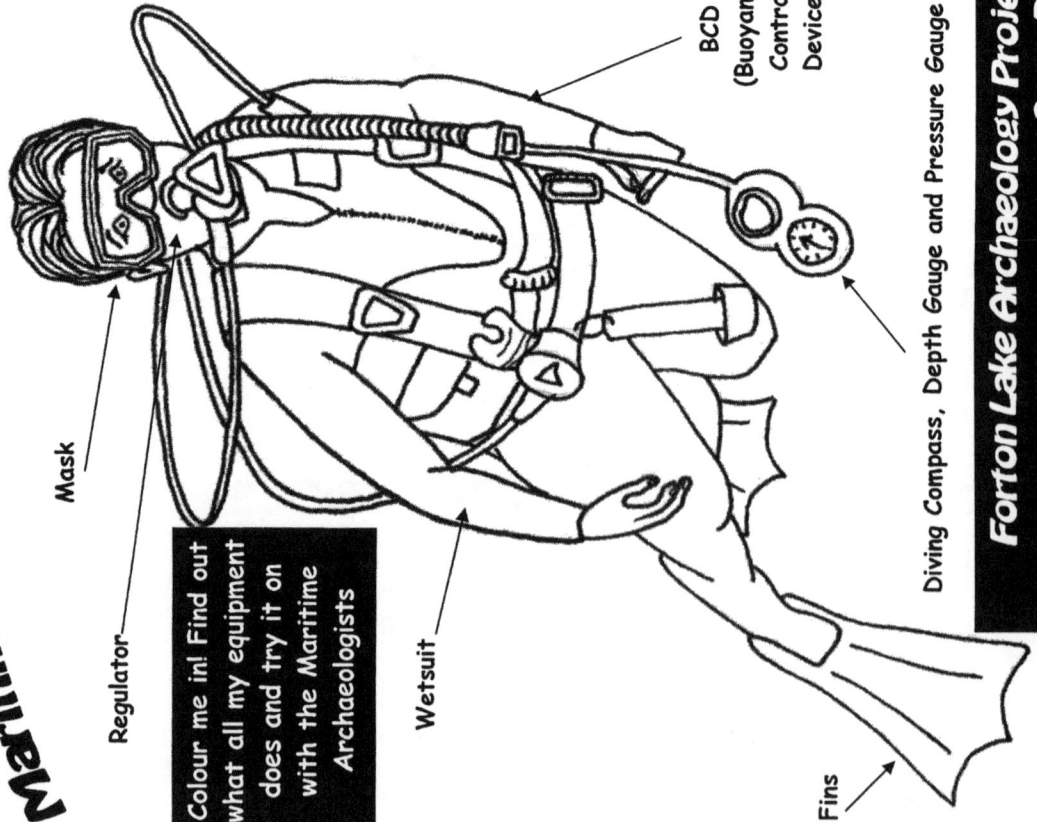

Nautical Archaeology Society

Colour me in! Find out what all my equipment does and try it on with the Maritime Archaeologists

Mask

Regulator

Wetsuit

Fins

BCD (Buoyancy Control Device)

Diving Compass, Depth Gauge and Pressure Gauge

Forton Lake Archaeology Project Open Day

Underwater Challenge

Maritime Archaeologists often have to work where they can see very little. In Forton Lake and in the Solent it is murky and dark. It is not always possible to bring all artefacts found to the surface for a closer look. This can be because of lack of money to raise the artefacts or to look after them properly, or even because the law says the artefact has to be left where it is. This means that archaeologists grow to rely on their senses more, for example touch. They try to record as much information about an artefact as possible while they are underwater

The Challenge

Imagine you are a Maritime Archaeologist working below the water of Forton Lake. There are a number of objects that need recording but you are working in an area where you can see very little, you will have to rely on touch alone. Feel the objects to get as much information as you can. Use the boxes provided to draw a sketch of what they might look like. Write down everything you can tell about the object.

Object 1 —
I think the object is a
Description:

Sketch

Object 2 —
I think the object is a
Description:

Sketch

So was it harder than you thought?

Even though you probably found the challenge hard, Maritime Archaeologists have even more problems than being able to see an object when they are trying to record it! They also have to deal with being underwater and using their diving equipment, the cold and the time limits of being underwater. Did you guess what the objects were correctly? As for the descriptions there are no set right and wrong answers. What is important is that another archaeologist could read your description and have an idea what the object you are trying to describe is.
We hope you enjoyed the challenge and maybe some day you will get to try working underwater!

Archaeological Excavation

Archaeologists use a trowel to carefully excavate the artefacts that they find.

Use the trowel to excavate the box. You will need to be careful as you might find old and delicate artefacts! Use this sheet to record what you find—like the archaeologists at Forton Lake!

Finds Record Sheet

Size (mm)		Colour
Material		Condition
Texture		Use?

Picture	Description

This is to certify that

has completed the Maritime Archaeologist Challenge

_____ (signed)   _____ (date)

Forton Lake Archaeology Project

Appendix C: Completing the Hulk Recording Proforma

(The text of this Appendix is reproduced with permission from Milne, G., McKewan, C. and Goodburn, G. 1998. Nautical Archaeology on the Foreshore: Hulk recording on the Medway.)

The form illustrated in Fig. 3.2 (page 11) is an example of the general type of proforma recommended for the recording of vessel remains. It indicates the range of data to be collected and is set out in two parts: the upper section is designed to be filled in during a Stage 2 survey, which does not involve any excavation of the silts within the vessel. The lower section should be completed during or after excavation, when more of the hull has been revealed as part of a Stage 3 survey. Depending on site conditions and the state of the hulk itself, it may even be possible to record data for some of the entries in the lower half of the form during the Stage 2 survey before any disturbance or excavation. This is to be encouraged, since the more information is collected at this early phase, the more valuable the evaluation of the vessel will be. The division of the form into two sections is therefore for general guidance only.

Locational data

The top four lines when completed provide the basic information required to locate and identify a particular vessel. The 1:10 000 sheet refers to the Ordnance Survey quarter sheet base map upon which the vessel's position will be plotted within the local Historic Environment Record (HER) (but note that some HERs use the 1:2 500 or 1:1 250 series). Once the information on the record form has been accepted by the appropriate Sites and Monuments Record (SMR) office[1], the vessel will be given a reference number, which will be added to the National Monuments Record and the HER boxes at a later date.

The *Vessel No* will be one of a series generated solely for that part of the foreshore currently being surveyed: for example, vessel number V15 in survey zone Whitewall Creek, site code WWC92, would refer to just one particular hulk investigated during the NAS project in 1992. The County, District and Parish details should then be entered as on other standard record forms. The Status box will be filled in at a later date, probably by the HER officer, and concerns any Scheduled Ancient Monument status of the vessel.

The National Grid Reference (NGR) should locate the centre of the remains of the vessel: under 100 km sq, enter the letter code of the main OS National Grid square in which the vessel lies, such as ST or TQ. Under NGRE (easting) and NGRN (northing), the grid references should be relative to the appropriate 100 km square (two,

three or four digits). Sometimes constraints on time may initially preclude provision of an NGR for each individual vessel within a group of vessels. In this situation, a single NGRE and NGRN should be provided, and under *Qualifier* enter the code in upper case which best indicates the reliability of the grid references: FCE (feature centred), GCE (group centred) and LO (locality only, a four-figure NGR).

Visible remains and dimensions

Under *Visible remains,* an outline of the remains should be drawn to demonstrate what proportion of the vessel survives, with the north point added to the compass rose to show the alignment of the remains. The measurements under visible dimensions simply record the size of the fragment of the vessel which survives, not the estimated length, beam (width) or depth of the vessel. Measurements are recorded in metres, not centimetres, in the following order: length x breadth x depth (eg 23.65 m x 2.65 m x 0.4 m).

If it seems clear that the vessel had once been longer (perhaps the stern of the hulk was obscured beneath a dune, or perhaps the bow had been destroyed), then that is indicated by the convention of adding a plus sign (+) after the measurement. If the length, breadth and width are recorded as 18.50+ m x 2.65 m x 0.4+ m, then this implies that the vessel was longer and deeper than the measurements quoted, but that it survived to its full width.

For the Size class box, a simple four-fold classification has been devised, upon which more detailed interpretations can be subsequently built when more information becomes available. The size class of the vessel is determined by the estimation of the original size and form of the vessel when complete, rather than solely on the extent of the visible remains. To take an obvious example, if a 5 m long fragment of what was once a large sailing barge is encountered, it would be recorded as a barge (BA) and not as a small boat (SB). Enter the most appropriate of these size-related guidance terms using one of these abbreviations:

> SB Small boat, usually less than 12 m
>
> BO Boat, usually in excess of 12 m
>
> BA Barge, a flat-bottomed vessel usually in excess of 10 m
>
> SH Ship, a sea-going vessel usually in excess of 25 m.

In many situations it may not prove possible to determine the function of a particular vessel until more detailed research has been undertaken. On occasions, the type of vessel may be known by a local name which does not

---

1   Now termed Historic Environment Record (HER).

appear in the English Heritage list: in this situation, the new term should be entered under *Type*, supported by a free-text entry under *Comments*, which might extend on to a continuation sheet.

Hull construction

The classification used to characterise the method of hull construction is indicated by a tick in the appropriate box:

Clinker – hull planking overlapping and fastened together, with transverse framing elements added later.

Carvel – hull planking lies edge to edge and is only fastened to the internal transverse framing.

Dugout – hull hollowed from a trunk (logboat)

Other – enter a brief description, eg sewn, double-diagonal planking etc.

Under *Material* state whether the hull is made of wood, metal, concrete etc. If more than one material is used, note which is the major component.

Propulsion

The main system of propulsion should be noted, if it can be reasonably deduced from the exposed remains:

Engine – propeller shaft holes (not commonly used before the late 19th century) or engine mounts.

Sail – a mast, a maststep, tabernacle or fittings such as chain plates. If details of the rig employed are available, enter them here, eg spritsail, lug, square sail.

Manpower – surviving rowing pivots (oar ports, thole pins) would suggest rowing. In the case of small boats such as logboats with no obvious fittings associated with propulsion, then poling and/or paddling may be surmised.

Towed – medium-sized craft that were not obviously powered may have been towed by men or horses on a towpath or by a powered vessel. The attachments for the tow-line may be identifiable.

Conditions, comments and dating

Under *Site conditions*, those conditions which relate to the vessel should be recorded, bearing in mind that the team which may be sent out to make the more detailed record of the vessel may not include the original recorder. For example, what is the approximate length of time for which the vessel is exposed between tides? Is it filled with silt, and if so, to what depth? Is access dangerous?

Under *Comments/Identification marks*, an opportunity is provided to enter any additional information (including bibliographic references or local tradition) which would facilitate an evaluation of the vessel's significance or archaeological value. Identification marks indicating the vessel's name, and number or port of registration may be visible and should obviously be recorded. Comments might also be qualitative; for example, the vessel may be the best preserved or stratigraphically the earliest in the group; it may be substantially dismantled; it may be significantly different from the others in its group or be similar to a better preserved example. Use a continuation sheet if necessary.

Under *Period*, an assessment of the structural attributes may allow the establishment of a date range for the construction of the vessel. If possible, enter the date range in years (eg 1900–1945). Summarise the reasons for assigning these dates under *Comments/Identification marks* or on a continuation sheet. If the craft can only be associated with a broad cultural period, an appropriate entry should be made. For early/later 18th-, 19th- and 20th-century vessels, the following codes are used: E18, L18, E19, L19 and E20 (pre-1945).

Signing off

Once the upper part of the form and the Stage 2 survey have been completed, the form should be signed with the date and initials of the field-worker under *Date & name*. These observations may require validation by an appropriate specialist, who should check the result and sign the *Checked* box, before more intensive work is conducted.

Structural details

The completion of the lower half of the record form will almost certainly be part of a Stage 3 survey, although some information may be obtained during a Stage 2 survey. The survival or absence of features listed below should be recorded under *Surviving elements*.

Timber species

If someone on site is able to make field identifications of common wood species, such as oak, tropical hardwood, softwood and elm, note this information in the box for a particular feature. For example, write oak under *Keel*. The species used for boat building and shipbuilding varied through time and with the type of vessel and origin of vessel. This class of information can be important in understanding the significance and possible dating of a vessel or its parts: timber of the elm group has not been found in English vessel remains before about AD 1500, for example. However, there are many problems associated with attempting secure species identification actually on the foreshore; the process is best undertaken from samples examined in the laboratory.

End visible

Tick this box if it is not possible to determine whether the visible end is the bow or the stern.

Completing the Hulk Recording Proforma

Bow

If it is possible to determine which end of the vessel is the bow, then tick this box. The bow is the front end of the vessel, sometimes known as the prow or head.

Stern

If it is possible to determine which end of the vessel is the stern (rear end of a vessel), then tick this box. It is usually marked by the presence of the rudder (although certain craft were provided with rudders at both ends!).

Scantling

This is the maximum cross-sectional dimensions of timber, equivalent to width and thickness. It is important to record such information where possible as it may give an idea as to the size and function of a fragmentary or largely buried vessel. Put at its simplest, large ships tend to have heavier timbers than small boats, and cargo vessels tend to have heavier and more closely spaced frame timbers than fishing craft. When noting dimensions, use metres (m) and millimetres (mm). During field survey, it will not usually be possible to measure timbers to an accuracy greater than *c.* 5 mm. If the average measurements vary greatly, note an overall average.

The depth and thickness of a floor timber, futtock, rib, stempost, sternpost, keel or deck beam are often expressed in terms of a moulded and a sided dimension. These terms derive from the practice of cutting the curved edges of timbers to a pattern called a mould: the sided dimension of frames is in the fore-and-aft direction (width), whilst the moulded dimension is from inboard to outboard (depth). The scantlings should be recorded for various features, such as keel, keelson, flat bottom planking and futtocks.

Keel

This main central strength member runs along the centreline of the bottom of a vessel. It is joined to the stempost (at the bow) and sternpost (at the stern). Some flat-bottomed craft may only have a shallow plank-like keel or none at all. Record the visible length, timber species and scantling.

Keelson

This longitudinal strength member lies along the inside centreline of a vessel on top of the transverse floor timbers. Record the visible length, timber species and scantling.

Flat bottom planking

The bottom of the vessel is formed by flat bottom planking, extending as far as the sides at the turn of the bilge. In some flat-bottomed vessels, thick, straight, outer bottom planks may have a structural function in place of a keel.

Floors

Floor timbers are the lowest transverse frame elements in the bottom of a vessel. In some vessels the type of floors will help to identify the nature of the craft. For example, many 20th-century yachts have metal floors attached to bent frame timbers, a practice which was virtually unknown in contemporary working and unknown in any vessel before about 1800. Record visible length, any timber species, average scantling and other relevant details, such as whether the floors are of iron plate or they rise steeply.

Futtocks

These are frame timbers extending up from the floor timbers to form part of a composite frame, the uppermost elements of which will rarely survive in vessels within the foreshore zone. Record the visible length, timber species and scantling. Note if the futtocks are clearly joined to the floor timbers, or simply lie between them.

Ordinary external planking

Such timbers form the outer hull planking of the vessel. Record the visible length, timber species and scantling.

Internal planking

Fitted inside a hull on the frame elements, this is also known as ceiling planking. In small and medium-sized craft, its presence may indicate that the vessel was designed to carry cargoes. Record the visible length, timber species and scantling.

Wales and stringers

Both are longitudinal strength members or thick planks. Stringers are usually found in flat-bottomed or composite craft, and wales in round-hulled craft and on the upper parts of flat-bottomed vessels. Record the nature of the fastenings, timber species, length and average scantling, and tick if they are fixed internally or externally. If none are present, write none.

Metal knees

These angled brackets were used to strengthen joints between structural elements in vessels, such as deck beams and inwales, beam shelves, stemposts and keels. In some small flat-bottomed craft, the sides may be braced with knee-like frames. Note if the knees are made of iron, steel or non-ferrous metal, and if the arms taper or are webbed with a metal plate. Record the maximum scantling dimensions, taking any pronounced taper into account.

Timber knees

These bracket timbers were set vertically (hanging knees) or horizontally (lodging knees). The most ancient types were grown to shape – that is, each one was cut from a naturally curved piece of timber. Knees in later vessels can also be cut from slabs of straight timber, jointed out of two pieces or, in the last forty years, laminated in strips. Very small craft might even have bent timber knees. Record if they are grown knees or cut knees with a tick in the appropriate box; note the timber species (if known) and scantling, together with other relevant observations.

Other

In the *Other* box, comments should be entered on any significant structural features not obviously covered in the categories above, such as the presence of single-piece grown or bent timber frames, the presence of fuel tanks, water tanks, bunkers or wet wells (water-filled fish storage tanks).

Bulkheads

These wall-like divisions were normally across the long axis of a vessel. They may be planked and framed in a variety of ways in wooden vessels, or made of plywood or metal plates. Their presence and construction provide evidence of the date and function of the vessel. Tick if present and state their number and method of construction. If none are present, write none.

Frame spacing centre to centre

The average spacing of the frames of a vessel from mid-point to mid-point is the frame spacing. This value relates directly to the intended use of a vessel, since cargo vessels and post-medieval warships generally have more closely spaced frame elements than personnel transport, fishing craft or early medieval warships. Record the average value and state whether this refers to the floors only or to the upper framing.

Deck

A permanent platform in a vessel above the level of the ceiling or internal planking is a deck. Such a platform may be full (ie continuous), partial (as in most 19th-century small craft in which only the bow end was decked over), or perhaps just around the side of the vessel parallel to the large central hold or holds. Although the decking may not have survived in many vessels abandoned on the foreshore, some deck beams or the associated knees which supported them may be present. From a study of their positions, it may be possible to say how many deck openings are represented: tick if any such evidence for decking survives and note whether it was a full, partial (bow only?) or side deck. If no evidence is present, write none. It is worth remembering that most

large ancient craft were not fitted with watertight decks nor were many relatively small vessels of recent date.

Deck structures

Hatches, hatch coamings, entranceways, wheelhouses and rails are structures which would have stood above the level of the deck. They will only survive in more recent craft. Although items such as winches will most probably have been removed, the positions once occupied by such equipment may still be discernible, together with evidence of other items which were set at deck level, such as towing posts. Tick if any deck structures are present and state which type. If none, write none.

Engine remains

Most engines were made largely of metal and were normally salvaged before a vessel was abandoned, leaving no more than the tell-tale engine mounts. Note the extent of the survival of the engine and its type (eg internal combustion, steam, other). If none, write none. A maker's name and other information may be visible on the engine or boiler plates, and this should be recorded under *Comments/Identification marks*.

Mast and spars

Vessels abandoned on the foreshore may retain some of their spars, the pole-like large fittings (booms, yards, derricks) used for sailing and for handling gear or cargoes. Masts may be represented by stumps or by the tabernacle, the device for hinging a mast. The presence of a mast may also be indicated by metal chain plates on the hull of the vessel. Record any such survivals; if none are present, write none.

Rudder

The presence of the rudder or remains of related fastenings will usually indicate the stern of the vessel, although in some early craft, rudders were fastened to the starboard side. A vessel which was towed – a dumb barge or lighter – may not have had a rudder at all. Many small and some medium-sized craft were never fitted with rudders, but were steered by other means. Tick if the rudder is present or else write none.

Mooring gear

The equipment used to hold a vessel in position often takes the form of ropes and iron chains and anchors; the latter may also be made of stone, or of lead with timber elements. Record the presence of such survivals with a brief description. If none are present, write none.

Fastenings

The range of fastenings used to join floors and futtocks to planks, or planks to planks, will provide important information concerning the dating of the vessel. Wooden fastenings are known as treenails. Fastenings could also be of copper (nonferrous) or of iron. Alternatively, they could be of fibre, as in the case of the Bronze Age vessels from the Humber, Severn and Dour estuaries. Tick the appropriate box (or boxes). If, for example, most fastenings are of iron with only a few wooden treenails, then indicate the function of the treenails – treenails joining the futtocks to the external hull planking would be recorded as 'treenails: futtock/ external planking'. On a continuation sheet, also record the method used in the case of nonferrous and other categories, with expanded descriptions and annotated drawings where appropriate.

Seam waterproofing

Over the centuries, different methods have been employed to ensure that the joins between planks were watertight: hair, moss, textiles and tar have all been used. Caulking is material driven between planks, usually in carvel-built vessels, and luting is material laid between planks during construction in clinker- built craft. Record whether caulking or luting is used, and note the materials.

Toolmarks

The identification of the tool kit used to build a particular vessel can be a useful method of dating its construction. For example, timbers were cleft in the period between *c.* AD 600 and 1300 and hand sawn by various methods after that date. They were not commonly machine sawn with circular saws until the end of the 19th century. However, the recognition of tool marks on degraded timber can be very difficult. Record the general presence of marks left by tools such as the axe, adze, trestle saw, pit saw and circular saw. This can be done by annotating the field drawings, although it may be necessary to obtain expert assistance with some of the identifications.

In very ancient finds, the presence of holes which are clearly drilled may indicate an Iron Age or later date range for a planked or dugout boat, since prior to that period gouges were used for such work.

Perhaps the easiest and most important tool marks to identify are saw marks, which can be a guide to the method of conversion of a timber and can be useful for dating: circular saw marks, for example, cannot date before *c.* 1790 and the use of such tools was comparatively rare until the late 19th century. Hand sawing was dominant in Europe until the 19th century, although powered saws were used from the 16th century, and other styles of sawing are known from the Roman and medieval periods. Hand-saw marks can be distinguished from those cut by a machine saw by the changes of angle along the length of a sawn surface. No sawn planking has yet been found used in British clinker boat finds prior to about 1300. The use of slightly irregular radially cleft oak planking is unlikely after *c.* 1800.

Before sawing was widely used on timbers, cleaving and hewing processes were used to produce planks. Prehistoric boat timbers were all hewn or split, while Roman planks were sawn and hewn. By contrast, sawing was not used in the earlier medieval period up to *c.* 1300. In the 18th and 19th centuries, the practice of planing timbers in many boats and ships became increasingly common; the surfaces left in many of the vessels built during the last 100 years are largely smooth and featureless.

Surface treatment

The evidence that a vessel may have been tarred or painted can survive several hundred years, although it will often be fragile and easily brushed off. Record the colour and thickness of any such deposits, which may be very small. Annotate the relevant field drawings.

Contents

The study of the contents of vessels may provide clues as to the date, function and possible origin of the craft. Finds in the hull of an abandoned vessel might represent the cargo, ballast, the crew's personal belongings or part of the ship's gear, such as the rigging blocks or pump (which may be represented by cast-iron pump valves or bored-out tree trunks). Alternatively, it may be material which found its way into the vessel after it was hulked. The finds should be numbered, either individually or in groups, and their positions plotted on the vessel plan. List the range of material discovered and record the find numbers in the relevant section on the form (under *Contents*). Finds from most foreshore vessels will require wet storage in the first instance and the help of staff trained in archaeological conservation should be sought. It is therefore essential to have discussed what will happen to the finds with appropriate museums before the project begins.

Cross-references

The written record compiled on this form will be supported by a measured plan of the vessel, together with other drawings as required. Enter the reference numbers of the drawn records in the boxes provided under *Drawing nos*. If a very detailed drawn record was made and there is insufficient room to enter all the numbers in the space provided, then enter them on a continuation sheet. A full record of a vessel should also incorporate both black-and-white and colour photographs: the relevant reference numbers should also be entered on the form under *Photo nos*. Tick in pencil when the photographs have been taken. Once they have been developed, their archive reference numbers can be added.

Timber samples

A separately numbered timber record form should be filled in for each timber sampled for dendrochronology or for any other individual timber which merits more detailed recording and study. These numbered timbers should also be indicated on the main vessel plan and the relevant sample numbers should be added to the hulk record form in the box provided (*Timber sample nos*).

Finds and environmental samples

A separately numbered finds record form or environmental sample form should be filled in for each group of finds discovered in association with the vessel or each sample of material taken from within or around the hull. The position of these samples or finds groups should be indicated on the main vessel plan. Enter the relevant numbers in the box provided on the hulk record form (*Finds/Sample nos*). The information on the finds is in addition to that recorded under *Contents*.

Continuation sheets

Use a continuation sheet with the same number and locational data as on the primary form for additional

entries and additional information, such as for bibliographic material. Remember to circle the appropriate initial on the primary form to show whether or not a continuation sheet has been used.

Checking

When as much of the record form as possible has been filled in, add the date and your initials under *Date & name* (both may differ from that recorded in the upper part of the form). The record form should then be checked by an appropriate person who will initial the *Checked* box. The data can then be entered into the local record.

Bibliography

Published works[1]

Adams, R.B., 1986, *Red Funnel and Before: Ships of the Southampton, Isle of Wight & South of England Royal Mail Steam Packet Company*, Southampton.

Admiralty, 1912, *1912 Stokers' Manual*, HMSO, London.

Bates, M.R., 2001, 'The meeting of the waters: raised beaches and river gravels of the Sussex Coastal plain/Hampshire Basin', in Wenban-Smith, F.F. and Hosfield, R.T., eds, *Palaeolithic Archaeology of the Solent River: proceedings of the Lithic Studies Society day meeting held at the Department of Archaeology, University of Southampton on Saturday 15 January 2000*, London, 27–45.

Blue, L., 2004, 'Theoretical Construction of the Bude Canal Tub Boat', *The Tub Boat: Bude Canal and Harbour Society Newsletter*, **29**, 9–12.

Borthwick, A., 1965, *Yarrow and Company Limited: the first hundred years, 1865–1965*, Glasgow.

Carr, F.G.G., 1989, *Sailing Barges*, Lavenham.

Childs, B., 1993, *Rochester Sailing Barges of the Victorian era*, Rochester.

Cocker, M.P., 2006, *Coastal Forces Vessels of the Royal Navy from 1865*, Stroud.

Dawkes, G., Goodburn, D. and Rogers, P.W., 2009, 'Lightening the Load: Five 19th-century River Lighters at Erith on the River Thames, UK', *International Journal of Nautical Archaeology*, **38(1)**, 71–89.

Dix, J.K., 2001, *The Geology of the Solent River System*, in Wenban-Smith, F.F. and Hosfield, R.T., eds, *Palaeolithic Archaeology of the Solent River: proceedings of the Lithic Studies Society day meeting held at the Department of Archaeology, University of Southampton on Saturday 15 January 2000*, London, 6–14.

Engvig, O.T., 2006, *Viking to Victorian: Exploring the Use of Iron in Ship Building*, Los Angeles.

Fox, U., 1966, *Joys of Life*, London.

Godwin, H., 1945, 'A submerged peat bed in Portsmouth Harbour. Data for the study of Post-Glacial History. IX', *New Phytologist*, **44(2)**, 152–5.

Holt. W.J., 1946 'Admiralty Type Motor Fishing Vessels', *Transactions of the Institute of Naval Architects*, **88**, 295–307.

Hunter, K., 2003, 'The Discovery and Lifting of the Newport Ship', *Conservation News*, **82**, 16–18.

Kelly's Directory of Gosport, Alverstoke, Fareham and District, 1894, London.

Kelly's Directory of Gosport, Alverstoke and Fareham, 1938–39, London.

Lambert, J. and Ross, A., 1990, *Allied Coastal Forces of World War II, Volume I: Fairmile Designs and US Submarine Chasers*, London.

Lavery, B., 2009, *Assault Landing Craft, Design, Construction and Operations*, Barnsley.

Leather, J., 1984, *Barges*, London.

McKee, E., 1983, *Working Boats of Britain*, London.

Melvin, M.J., 1992, *Minesweeper: The Role of the Motor Minesweeper in World War II*, Worcester.

Merritt, J., 1977, 'Ferrol Road in 1859', *Gosport Records*, **14**, 7–9.

Milne, G., McKewan, C. and Goodburn, G. 1998, *Nautical Archaeology on the Foreshore: hulk recording on the Medway*, Swindon.

Palmer, A. and Palmer, V., 1996, *The Pimlico Chronology of British History: from 250,000 BC to the present day*, London.

Parker T, 1998, 'Survey of the Purton Hulks', *Archaeology of the Severn Estuary*, **9**, 91–3.

Preece, C., 2008, *A Field Guide to the Archaeology of the Taw and Torridge Estuaries*, Bideford.

Renfrew, C., and Bahn, P., 1991, *Archaeology: Theories, Methods and Practice*, London.

Simper, R., 1997, 'The South Coast', in Greenhill B., and Mannering J. (eds), *The Chatham directory of inshore craft: traditional working vessels of the British Isles*, London, 101–27.

Smyth, W.H., 1867, *The sailor's word-book: an alphabetical digest of nautical terms*, London.[2]

Spanou, S., 2009, 'Archaeology on the (Edinburgh Tram) line: reflections on a recording methodology', *The Archaeologist*. **74**, 49.

Sparks, B., Momber, G. and Satchell, J., 2001, *A Decade of Diving, Delving and Disseminating: the HWTMA 1991–2001*, Southampton.

Waller, M.P and Long, A.J. 2003 'Holocene coastal evolution and sea-level change on the southern coast of England: a review', *Journal of Quaternary Science*, **18 (3–4)**, 35–9.

---

1 As well as works publicly available in academic and other libraries, contributors have also referenced internet sources, private publications and unpublished material. These are listed separately. Private publications may be available from their publishers, but some are known to be out of print; others are available in collections such as those of the National Archives or the Royal Air Force Museum.

2 A revised edition was published by Conway Maritime Press in 2005.

White, L., 1989, *The Story of Gosport,* (second, revised edition, Burton, L., and Musselwhite, B. eds), Southampton.

Williams, G.H., 1974, *The Earlier Fortifications of Gosport*, Gosport.

Williams, J.F., 1994, *They Led the way: The Fleet Minesweepers at Normandy, June 1944*, Blackpool.

Internet sources

Aberlady Heritage:
A Maritime Graveyard:
http://www.aberladyheritage.com/web/a-maritime-graveyard.html

British Ports Association:
http://www.britishports.org.uk/public/uk_ports_industry

Exe-press:
Incredible Hulks (2005)
http://www.exe-estuary.org/exe_press_summer_05.pdf

Hamble Local History Society:
Underdown, I, *Hamble: A brief history* (1999):
http://www.hamblelocalhistory.hampshire.org.uk/bhistory.htm

Hampshire County Council:
River Hamble Harbour Board, 11 July 2008:
Harbour Master's report, Item 9:
'Recovery and Reinstatement of eastern Bank Habitat':
http://www.hants.gov.uk/decisions/decisions-docs/080711-rvhhbd-R0704170225.html

Hansard:
Adjournment Debate, 8 December 2009:
http://www.publications.parliament.uk/pa/cm200910/cmhansrd/cm091208/halltext/91208h0011.htm#09120858000259

HWTMA:
Recording Archaeological Remains on the River Hamble: Final report, (2008)
http://www.hwtma.org.uk/uploads/documents/Archaeological%20Projects/HambleHLFProjectReport1.pdf and
http://www.hwtma.org.uk/uploads/documents/Archaeological%20Projects/HambleHLFProjectReport2.pdf

HWTMA/NAS:
Forton Lake Archaeology Project Year 1 report (2006):
http://www.nauticalarchaeologysociety.org/projects/forton%20lake/Forton%20Lake%20Project%20YR1%20Final%20Report.pdf

Forton Lake Archaeology Project Year 2 report (2007):
http://www.nauticalarchaeologysociety.org/projects/forton%20lake/Forton_Lake_Project_YR2_Report_Final.pdf

Forton Lake Archaeology Project Year 3 report (2008):
http://www.nauticalarchaeologysociety.org/projects/forton%20lake/Forton_Lake_Project_YR3_Report_Final.pdf

Intellectual Property Office:
http://www.ipo.gov.uk/about/contact.htm

Ministry of Defence:
Defence Standard 02-706 (NES 706) Welding and Fabrication of Ship's Structure (2000)
ftp://217.17.192.66/mitarb/lutz/standards/dstan/02/706/00000100.pdf

Museum of London: Archaeology:
Heritage protection: Thematic survey of Hulk Assemblages:
http://www.museumoflondonarchaeology.org.uk/English/News/Current/HulkAssemblages.htm

NAS/Friends of Purton:
Barefoot, I., Barnett, P., and McNeil, E., *Purton Hulks Recording Project 2008: Project Report* (2009):
http://www.nauticalarchaeologysociety.org/projects/Purton/purton_report_2008.pdf

National Archives, Kew:
Air Ministry, Ferry Boat, 40ft., Mk.3 Ferry Boat, 40 ft, Mk.3 (1949):
Air Publications and Reports:
http://www.nationalarchives.gov.uk/catalogue/displaycataloguedetails.asp?CATLN=6&CATID=4136880
Catalogue reference: AIR 10/4986.

Natural England:
http://www.naturalengland.org.uk/ourwork/conservation/designatedareas/spa/default.aspx

National Register of Historic ships:
MFV 1502:
http://www.nationalhistoricships.org.uk/ships_register.php?action=ship&id=1384

North Devon Archaeological Society:
Preece, C., *Taw and Torridge Hulk Survey* (2010):
http://www.ndas.org.uk/hulks.html

Oxford Dictionary of National Biography:
Prosser, R.B. (Ritchie, L.A. rev.), 'Thomas Morton (1781–1832)' (2004):
http://www.oxforddnb.com/view/article/19374 – subscription website.

Portsmouth Harbour Project:
http://www.envf.port.ac.uk/geo/research/portsmouth/background.htm

historic maps:
http://www.envf.port.ac.uk/geo/research/portsmouth/port4.htm

Portsmouth Harbour, Spithead and Isle of Wight Word Heritage Bid:
http://www.rad.clara.net/heritage/index.html

Bibliography

RCAHMS:
Forth and Clyde Canal, Bowling Harbour:
http://canmore.rcahms.gov.uk/en/site/43393/details/f
orth+and+clyde+canal+bowling+harbour/

Groom, D. and Oxley, I., *Scotland's ship graveyard survey: interim report 1. Aberlady Bay, East Lothian,* .illustrated and bound typescript report (MS 2083), Connect Archaeology, University of St Andrews. (2002):
http://canmore.rcahms.gov.uk/en/details/926694/

Royal Air Force Museum, Hendon:
Marine Craft Records:
http://www.rafmuseum.org.uk/london/collections/arc
hive/marine_craft_records.cfm

Royal Naval Museum:
History of the Museum's Pinnace:
http://www.royalnavalmuseum.org/collections_boats
_pinnace.htm

Pinnace Machinery:
http://www.royalnavalmuseum.org/collections_boats
_pinnacemach.htm

Royal Naval Patrol Service Association:
http://www.rnps.lowestoft.org.uk/rnpsbooks.htm

Southampton City Archaeological Unit/ HWTMA:
The River Itchen Archaeology Project, Hulk survey (1999):
http://www.geog.port.ac.uk/webmap/itchen/frameset.
html

Thames Valley Archaeological Services:
Ford, S., *Fort Ramparts, Priddy's Hard, Gosport, Hampshire, An Archaeological Watching Brief for Crest Nicholson (South) Ltd* (2004):
http://www.tvas.co.uk/reports/pdf/PHG04-20wb.pdf

Uffa Fox On-Line:
http://www.uffafox.com/uffabiog.htm

Worldwide Aerial Archaeology:
Aerial Archaeology in Essex:
http://www.univie.ac.at/aarg/worldwide/essex/essex.
html

Private publications

Air Ministry, 1952, *33 ft Bomb Scow, Mk 1, General and Technical Information and Repair and Reconditioning Instructions.* RAF Museum Archives, Hendon.

Barnett, L.P., 2007, *Fore & Aft: The Story of the Purton Ships Graveyard*, Friends of Purton Publishing. Gloucester.

Burton, L., and Musselwhite, B., 2004, *The Book of Gosport: Celebrating a Distinctive Coastal Town*, Halsgrove Publishing, Tiverton.

Holtham, T. 2003, *RAF Marine Craft Directory Series, Vol. 3 – CRAFT 41.5 ft – 27 ft (includes all Seaplane Tenders, Firefloats & Ferry boats)*, World Ship Society Small Craft Group.

Holtham, T., 2009, *Royal Navy Landing Craft Directory Series vol. 1 – L.C.A. Landing Craft* Assault, World Ship Society Small Craft Group.

HWTMA 2006, *SCOPAC Research Project – Archaeology & Coastal Change*, Report prepared on behalf of SCOPAC.

Unpublished Material

Parker, T, 2009, *Survey and Research of FL17 at Forton Lake, Gosport*, unpublished NAS Part 2 report (copy obtainable from the NAS office).

Index

Index

www.ingramcontent.com/pod-product-compliance
Lightning Source LLC
Chambersburg PA
CBHW061002030426
42334CB00033B/3337